FINDING SOLID GROUND

In Politics, The Economy, and Jesus' Teaching

Rev. Robert Emerick

outskirts
press

Finding Solid Ground
In Politics, The Economy, and Jesus' Teaching
All Rights Reserved.
Copyright © 2018 Rev. Robert Emerick
v2.0

The opinions expressed in this manuscript are solely the opinions of the author and do not represent the opinions or thoughts of the publisher. The author has represented and warranted full ownership and/or legal right to publish all the materials in this book.

This book may not be reproduced, transmitted, or stored in whole or in part by any means, including graphic, electronic, or mechanical without the express written consent of the publisher except in the case of brief quotations embodied in critical articles and reviews.

Outskirts Press, Inc.
http://www.outskirtspress.com

ISBN: 978-1-4787-9362-5

Outskirts Press and the "OP" logo are trademarks belonging to Outskirts Press, Inc.

PRINTED IN THE UNITED STATES OF AMERICA

Ralph —
I don't expect anyone to agree this with me, but I hope this does some good. Thanks for your friendship!
Bob

DEDICATION

This book is dedicated to:

My grandchild on the way

The children of Bay Ridge United Methodist Church
Kira and Isobel Cianci
Calum and Matteo Hines
Gianna Schlagel

"The Academy"
Provie, Donny, and Bridget Duggan
Sean McCauley
Matt and Josh Perloff

And to all the young people growing up today

Here are some good things you can believe in.

With respect and affection,
Robert Emerick

Table of Contents

WELCOME i

PART ONE
   Finding Solid Ground In Politics And The Economy 1

PART TWO
   Finding Solid Ground In Jesus' Teaching 97

THE JESUS QUOTES IN THE FOUR GOSPELS
   Compiled by Eleanor Ruth Geryk.................................... 123

RESOURCES 245

WELCOME

The year 2019 will mark 230 years since we established our Constitution. But in the U.S. today, we seem to be deeply divided over some basic questions:

-How can we make our economy and our government work better for us and the next generations?

-Should we engage in politics, or just disengage?

-Should we be "players" in a commercial society, or should we be citizens in a civil and humane society? Is it possible to be both?

-Should we strive to create equal opportunity for everyone?

-Should health care be mainly a commercial enterprise?

-Should we continue to pool our resources to make it easier for older people to live?

-Should every person have equal civil rights, and the equal right to receive justice, or should some people have "more" rights and justice than others?

-Should a person's gender, ethnicity, skin color, language, or gender-orientation affect the way they are treated?

-Should we make sure that everyone who is eligible to vote can easily do so, or should we make it harder for some people to vote?

-Should the members of any religion, and those who follow no religion, feel *equally at home* in the U.S., or should some form of Christianity be our official, or preferred, national religion?

-Should the U.S. be mainly for the benefit of the people who look like the first immigrants from the other side of the Atlantic?

-How should the people who were here first be treated?

-Should we live in a healthy environment that isn't over-heating?

-Should we care about how animals are treated?

I'm sure you can think of other questions that are dividing us today. What are your answers to these questions? Do you know anyone whose answers are different from yours?

As I get older, I find that I worry more about the quality of life, and the way of life, that the younger people and their children will receive as their inheritance. We are so divided over the questions listed above that we have come to a **dead-end.** I don't want the next generations to be trapped in the divisions we live with now. We need to find solid ground to build a better way of life. If we can't achieve that, our conflicts are going to get much worse.

We are all affected by the turmoil and distress caused by our deep divisions. Whether we know it or not, regardless of our age, where we grew up, what language(s) we speak, whether or not we are religious, where we live in the U.S. today, or what identity groups we belong to, *our daily lives and future prospects are directly tied to how we deal with the dead-end.*

Our answers to the questions listed above will determine how we deal with the dead-end.

Since early in 2011, I have engaged in intensive study to find a way out of the dead-end that *my own mind and heart can fully accept, and be proud to pass along to the next generations.*

The effort succeeded for me. Part One is offered to everyone who feels the time has come for our nation to consider a different way forward.

In the course of my study, I found that our dead-end can be traced to the ideas and ideologies that emerged in Europe over 500 years ago, and were powerful forces in the establishment of our nation.

Our dead-end is caused by a **mistake** in our understanding of these *inherited* ideologies. Our mistake is thinking that the differences between and among the ideologies that divide us—such as liberalism, conservatism, capitalism, socialism, and libertarianism—cannot be resolved in a wholesome way because *they prescribe completely different ways of life.*

These conflicts were necessary and productive in the past. They have shown us different ideas about what we can believe and value about ourselves, our society, and how we should govern ourselves. Some ideologies emphasize individuals' liberty, and others emphasize the common good.

But these ideologies are all bankrupt now—they can't help us anymore. Our divisions have become *unnecessary* and *unproductive* because we have not recognized that each of these differing views is important—even the ones we *despise*—because each one emphasizes a different aspect of human well-being.

And it has become harder for us to see how we can resolve our differences because fanning the flames of conflict for money and power has become a big business.

The way out of the dead-end is to use our founding American philosophy to make a better way of life for ourselves and for those who are forced to inherit what we leave behind.

Some specific background: In 1781, the Congress and the states established a confederacy in our first constitution, *The Articles of Confederation and Perpetual Union*. *The Articles* declared that we are The United States, and that each of the states is sovereign and independent. The Perpetual Union was "a firm league of friendship" of the sovereign states. (Maybe this was due to the fact that the states started out as colonies directly under British rule. Their "legal" connection was with England, NOT with each other. This is the root of our ongoing conflicts over states' rights vs. federal responsibilities.)

By 1787, it was obvious that the confederate form of government had failed, and our new nation was in grave danger of failing. In response to this crisis, *a new constitution* was established *by the people of The United States* in 1789, to form a *Federal* government, to correct the confederacy's inherent weaknesses.

It's important to know that the new constitution, <u>including</u> The Preamble, was *the first and only national founding document established directly by the people of The United States* in local meetings. It was NOT established by the authority of the Congress or the state governments.

The Preamble to our *Federal* constitution established the purpose—the set of six goals—of our new constitution, government, and nation. This book proposes that The Preamble is solid ground for a better way of life because it declares the national will of the people of The United States *as* the purpose of our constitution. Here is The Preamble (it is one long sentence): **"We the People of the United States, in Order to form a more perfect Union, establish Justice, insure domestic Tranquility, provide for the common defence, promote the general Welfare, and secure the Blessings of Liberty to ourselves and our Posterity, do ordain and establish this Constitution for the United States of America."**

The genius of the Preamble is that it reconciled the apparently irreconcilable divisions we inherited from our European roots. By calling for a more perfect union, and by giving equal importance to the general welfare and the blessings of liberty, the Preamble acknowledged that **human beings are individuals who live in groups, and our self-governance must be based on that fact**. In 1789, *we the people* declared that democratic governing authority, effective national union, justice, tranquility, defense, our general welfare, and individual liberty are *mutually dependent*—none of the goals can be achieved unless all of them are achieved.

The values and beliefs that *the people* of The United States established in 1789 reconciled the conflicting ideological views that we inherited. But *we* have not understood and fulfilled that reconciliation in *our* politics and economic policies.

I see no evidence that high schools and colleges teach this aspect of our history. Ignorance of this part of our past makes it much harder to resolve our differences today. (Am I the only person who didn't learn about the *importance* of The Preamble in school? I don't know about you, but for me history class was mostly about memorizing the dates of important events.)

So, Part One will *briefly* summarize the history and substance of our ideologies. When we know this part of our history, it will be easier for us to *bring together the best features of our apparently irreconcilable views into a democratic way forward that is based on our own tradition.*

Our politics, and our civil and economic policies, should uphold the national goals which were formally and democratically established by the people of The United States in 1789. Our politics and policies must be judged on how well they serve our national goals established in The Preamble—NOT on how well they serve our beloved but bankrupt and divisive inherited ideologies.

This book does not favor any political party or current ideology. Firm believers in any of these ideologies, or staunch members of any political party, will find much to object to in Part One of this book. **But I do have a bias.** I grew up in the 1950s and '60s in a town called Ellerslie (population about 250), near the City of Cumberland, in the mountains in the narrow strip of western Maryland that is in walking distance of West Virginia and Pennsylvania. I'm sure that many people who grew up there had a different experience than I did. But in that small town I developed a strong feeling and belief that *we should care about the well-being of every person equally.*

I am an ordained minister in The United Methodist Church, and a licensed clinical social worker. Like many people, I see that our anger and anxiety over politics and the economy negatively affect everyone's well-being.

I feel bad for children who have to live with their parents' anger and distress. Our conflicts are dividing families, couples, friends, and communities. Anger and distress are bad for everyone.

And I have often wondered why Christianity isn't a better advocate for our nation's well-being.

Something that the Bay Ridge United Methodist congregation in Brooklyn, N.Y. and I went through together (more on this in Part Two), and the findings of my study referred to above, made me take a deeper look at what Christianity is, and its role in our thinking and way of life today. This deeper look led me to a different understanding of what Christianity *should* be about. I will share that understanding with you in Part Two, because I believe Jesus' teaching can help us find solid ground for a better life.

Even if you have no interest in Christianity, I invite you to read Part Two. It isn't very long, and you might be surprised by what you read. Part Two focuses on Jesus' teaching. I do NOT try to convert anyone to Christianity, or tell anyone what to believe about any religion, or even religion in general.

Many people want Christianity to be of more help to our nation. But they feel frustrated because the Christianity they have experienced, or have heard about, can't help very much because, to some extent, it is part of the problem. And it also seems to be coming to a dead-end.

According to the Pew Research Center, about 70% of U.S. residents identify themselves as Christians. But the *percentage* of almost all segments of the U.S. population who identify with traditional Christianity is *dropping*. And the percentage of The Millennials (born between 1981 and 1996) who say that churches have a *positive* impact on the U.S. has *dropped* from 73% in 2010 to just 55% in 2015.

Why the drop in Christian identification and church reputation?

More people than ever before, and, according to Pew Research, most Millennials, don't believe in *any* form of discrimination, but they do believe in using our government to promote the common good, "the general welfare."

Traditional Christianity is in decline because many (most?) traditional churches are continuing their long history of preaching and practicing various forms of discrimination, and many (most?) churches do not promote the common good strongly enough.

How can this be?

The main reason is that traditional Christianity has NOT focused primarily on Jesus' teaching, *as he said we should* (John 7:16 and 14:15).

Jesus taught that life should be lived "...on earth as it is in heaven" (Matthew 6:10). **This means living the kind of love Jesus embodied** (John 13:34 and 15:12), **which means treating others the way we want to be treated** (Matthew 7:12 and Luke 6:31).
But instead of focusing on Jesus' teaching, traditional Christianity has focused mainly on its own doctrines, rituals, and institutional interests as the core of Christian faith and practice. The Church's Creeds (the "official" statements of belief) do not include Jesus' teaching. This means that ***believing*** **in Jesus' teaching, or at least *wanting to believe* in his teaching, has not been a requirement for membership in The Church**.

As Christianity begins its third millennium, our solid ground is to focus on the moral and spiritual principles of Jesus' teaching as the *authentic core* of Christianity. Christianity should ground itself in the humane truth, power, and beauty of Jesus' teaching because his principles are solid moral and spiritual ground for *all* aspects of life—including human relations and democratic government.
Jesus' teaching gives moral and spiritual validation to our highest hopes for all of creation—for humankind, for our fellow creatures on the earth, and for the earth itself, which supplies our food, air, and water.

The principles of Jesus' teaching should be Christianity's message to ourselves, and to the world, as we begin our third millennium.

Jesus' principles and The Preamble are realistic idealism. The information in Part One shows that The Preamble is intended to be applied, and actually works, in the real world. Part Two shows how The Preamble resonates with Jesus' teaching.

We <u>all</u> do better when <u>everyone</u> does better.

I hope this book will be useful to everyone who wants to make life better for ourselves and for those who come after us.

Rev. Robert Emerick Brooklyn, New York June 1, 2016
I welcome your comments: findingsolidground@aol.com

PART ONE
FINDING SOLID GROUND IN POLITICS AND THE ECONOMY

THE WORK THAT became Part One of this book began in 2011, during the campaign for the presidential election of 2012, in the powerful undertow of The Great Recession.

In that campaign, I heard conflicting claims about what we should do to create jobs and strengthen the economy. For example, I heard that taxing the high income "Job Creators" is bad for job creation. And I heard that we need to cut government spending, and *especially* we need to cut, or at least privatize, government benefits to "The Takers" because things like Social Security, Medicare, Medicaid, food stamps, and other government "handouts," create dependency on the government, and will eventually bankrupt our nation.

But I also heard that we should maintain or increase government benefits because it's the right thing to do. And I heard that we need to increase government spending on infrastructure.

A lot of what I heard sounded like common sense, but I was disturbed by the realization that I didn't actually know enough to be able to judge for myself if any of the claims were true. And I didn't want to have to trust anyone's word on such important matters—even if it sounded like common sense—because our current and future material well-being was (and still is) at stake.

So, early in 2011, I decided to see if a non-expert like me could find facts that would help me know if *anyone* was telling "the truth, the whole truth, and nothing but the truth" about how to strengthen the economy and create living wage jobs. I thought that if no facts *could* be found, then at least I would know *for myself* that the economic policy claims were based on *something other than facts.*

Doing research in my spare time over the course of eight months, using government and non-government websites for comparison, I compiled information on eleven economic indicators (including unemployment rates, tax rates, growth rates, government spending and revenue, and federal debt) going back to the year 1900. I then used this database to look for patterns among the indicators, to see if I could answer my own questions. For example, my first study was a comparison of unemployment rates, growth rates, and tax rates on the *high income* Job Creators, to see if higher taxes on them go along with higher unemployment and a weaker economy (see the answer below***).

The most important thing I discovered is that a non-expert *can* find out enough to be able to fact-check economic policy claims. **My general finding was that the U.S. economy was stronger from 1946 to 1971 than it has been since 1972.** Based on this finding, in October of 2014 the Bay Ridge United Methodist Church in Brooklyn, N.Y., placed an ad in *The New York Times* offering an award of $33,000 to economists and policy experts who can identify the *policy factors* that historically go along with the stronger economy. The award focuses on policies because, *while we can't control everything that happens in the world, we can determine our course of action.* (See "The Economic Well-Being Award" at bayridgeumc.org, or google Church Economics Prize.)

Further, I discovered that much of what I was hearing that sounded like common sense was actually nonsense. For example, when I compared unemployment rates, growth rates, and higher taxes on the high income Job Creators, I discovered that ***higher taxes on the high income Job Creators generally go along with a stronger economy and lower unemployment!

This startling discovery of the actual correlation of taxes on the high income Job Creators, unemployment, and economic strength led me to wonder, *who are* The Job Creators and The Takers, and what, exactly, is a handout?

I found that, as they were used in the campaign, the terms *Job Creators, Takers,* and *handout* are misleading. But what's worse is that these terms get in the way of learning how the economy really works, and what policies would *probably* make the economy stronger.

For example, one might not think of a state as a Taker receiving a handout. But according to an article in *The Wall Street Journal* ("Which States Take the Most from the U.S. Government?" March 27, 2014), the states that have lower taxes—in order to attract business and create jobs—also receive more federal aid than the states that have higher taxes. And my own follow-up research found that, ironically, those *lower* tax rate states generally have *higher* unemployment! In other words, the lower tax states are able to function to the extent that they do because they receive more federal aid, but this policy may NOT produce the advertised benefit of lower unemployment—unless, of course, the unemployment rate would be worse without the federal aid. Maybe the states' race to the bottom of the tax scale is not the best way to reduce unemployment. I wonder, who benefits from this policy?

And one might not think of big corporations and wealthy individuals as Takers. But what about corporate subsidies, the tax breaks given to corporations to locate, or remain, in certain areas, and special individual and corporate tax loopholes, deductions, and exemptions? Are these handouts to Takers? (By the way, in the 2016 presidential campaign, I heard some people say that both major parties are controlled by big business, but we should vote for a businessman because a businessman would do a better job of "running the country like a business" because *"businesses don't take handouts!"*)

Why should big business failure be covered by other tax payers for years and years? Wouldn't it be better if businesses had to take responsibility for themselves, and buy "business failure insurance" from a company like Lloyds of London if they want to be shielded from their failure?

And what about corporations and high net worth individuals who engage in legal tax evasion? A 2006 U.S. Senate report stated that $1.6*trillion* is "offshored" by wealthy *individuals!* Is that a form of taking—taking advantage of their financial power to "persuade" elected officials to write tax law according to their wishes? This is a serious issue for all of us. My research shows that the national debt soars when we don't collect enough tax revenue to pay for the things we want our government to do.

And we might not think of government entitlement and benefit recipients as Job Creators. But think what would happen to local businesses, jobs, housing, and the tax base if the money spent and the services used by the Social Security, Medicare, Medicaid, and food stamp recipients are lost to a *community* because those entitlements and benefits were cut, or "phased out?" I know that some stores and restaurants in Brooklyn would have a little less business if I didn't have Social Security. Multiply my example by tens of millions around the country.

The so-called Takers who receive entitlements and benefits are actually *Job Creators* because we create local demand for local products and services—and that creates local jobs. Maybe it's best for the *local* economy if the middle and lower income Job Creators are taxed at a much lower Federal rate than the high income Job Creators, because local demand strengthens the local economy. It's worth considering.

And, contrary to what I was hearing, I found that cutting government spending does *not* strengthen the economy.

I learned that the terms "big government" and "small government" are misleading. For example, between 1946 and 1971, when the economy was stronger, the Federal government had over a <u>million</u> more people on the payroll than we have today.

Everyone knows that we face some serious problems in our economy. And I think we really do not yet understand the economy as well as we need to—the economy seems to be infinitely complex. But the problems we face cannot be addressed intelligently, and we can't develop effective economic policies, if we continue to rely on ideological assumptions and distracting slogans rather than facts. Part One includes what I have learned about the economy and economic policy, and the economic model that guides my thinking about how the economy really works.

When I saw how easily economic nonsense is disguised as common sense, I began to wonder why anyone would ignore facts, and make false claims about the economy. Are we *purposely* being misled? Maybe we just don't know enough to know that we really don't know what we are talking about. But why would anyone who *claims* to know what they are talking about ignore the facts, and bet our lives on the information spin? Shouldn't policies be based on facts?

These questions led me to wonder about the *slogans and assumptions that drive our thinking:* Where did they come from, and why are they so powerful in our minds and feelings?

My study showed that the beliefs that dominate our thinking and attitudes today were born in Europe centuries ago, and they have a history. The powerful ideas about individual liberty, social union, and governing authority that we have inherited spawned the slogans and assumptions that have led us to a dead-end.

For example, as a *reaction against* the smothering, restrictive power of governing authority in medieval Europe, it's easy to see why many would think that government should not interfere with individuals' liberty. According to this view, individual liberty will produce the best of all possible worlds. This idea came to be called **classical liberalism**.

Another example: as a *reaction against* classical liberalism, it's understandable that some believed that too much liberty leads to the anarchy, chaos, and violence of the French Revolution. They believed that a strong social union, built on *something like* the medieval nobility, along with social customs, traditions, and prejudices—"the social fabric"—are needed to maintain social order. According to this view, strong central governance and a stable social order will produce the best of all possible worlds. This idea came to be called **classical conservatism**.

These two *apparently* contradictory ideas—classical liberalism and classical conservatism—were the first big ideas on the subject of what life can, or should, be like without the restrictive power that people had to live with under the medieval system. They are the roots of our current political and economic conflicts.

But neither one of these ideas, nor any of their branches that currently *prevail* in our politics and economic policy-making—liberalism, conservatism, capitalism, socialism, and libertarianism—is sufficient to guide us in a way that saves us from falling short of our hopes and potential. It's clear to me that when one of these ideologies dominates our thinking and attitudes, we sabotage our own aspirations and potential. (To see how prevalent these ideologies are, try to have a conversation about current events without using the ideological words.)

We cannot have a good understanding of the present if we don't have a good understanding of the past. If we only believe what we hear and see in media, or if we just accept the opinions of people who say things that sound like common sense, we cannot build a better world for ourselves, the children, grandchildren, and great-grandchildren. *If we don't have the information we need to think for ourselves, we are only following one herd or another.*

None of the prevalent ideologies we *live with* today is good enough to *live by* today. The good news is that we don't have to be stuck in the conflicts we inherited from our European background. We *can* integrate the best aspects of each branch of our social, political, and economic family tree. I think our Preamble *requires* us to do so.

The ideologies that are causing so much distress and anger today have a history. *Knowledge of their history helps us understand their intent and limitations.*

For example, it's important to see that **the Free Market idea** was a *reaction against* the economic system of The Middle Ages. When we know this, we can see that the Free Market idea was a *revolt* against the smothering power, and *inequality of opportunity*, that characterized the medieval economic system. The lesson here is that **too much centralized economic power (like the medieval economy) can hurt a lot of people**. The lesson is NOT that the unregulated free market is always the best economic system even if it hurts people, our fellow creatures, and the earth.

And it's important to know that **19th century socialism** was seen as *medicine for the misery* that most people suffered under the *brutality* of the unregulated Free Market capitalism which had hijacked Adam Smith's Invisible Hand theory. The lesson here is that **an unregulated pure market economy can hurt a lot of people**. The lesson is NOT that a centralized economy is always the best economic system even if it hurts people, our fellow creatures, and the earth.

Below, I present what I have learned about where our current ideologies came from, why the Preamble is important, and why we need a democratic and pragmatic "Preamble Way" in our politics and economic policy-making.

FINDING SOLID GROUND IN POLITICS AND THE ECONOMY

<u>Outline of Part One</u>

THE ROOTS OF OUR INHERITED IDEOLOGIES 13
    The Characteristics of Medieval Europe's Way of Life 14
    Enforced Conformity to Religious Authority 14
    The Divine Right of Kings 15
    Fixed Social Classes 15
    The Feudal/Mercantile Economy 16
    Reactions Against The Medieval Way Of Life 18

SUMMARY OF OUR CURRENT IDEOLOGIES 33

WHAT'S GOOD ABOUT OUR INHERITED IDEOLOGIES 49

WHY THE PREAMBLE MATTERS 54

THE U.S. ECONOMY
FACTS, FICTIONS, AND THE WAY FORWARD 57
    Facts 58
    Fictions 66
    The Way Forward 69
    The Principles of a Preamble Economy 75

THOUGHTS ON SOME CURRENT CHALLENGES 76
    The Commercial Society 76
    Citizens United 82
    Corporate Taxation 82
    Global Trade 84
    The Power of Individuals in the Economy 86
    The Economy and The Environment 89

THE PREAMBLE WAY FORWARD 89

THE ROOTS OF OUR INHERITED IDEOLOGIES

LET'S TAKE A brief look at our past. I will quote and paraphrase what some real scholars have said because I certainly don't know this subject as well as they do, and I can't say it as well as they have. My cited resources are listed by the author's name and a code of the letters in their title, and are listed with the codes in the Resources at the end of the book, in case you want to learn more.

I have selected the quotes carefully. Each one presents information we need to know in order to understand our current conflicts. I have tried to make the quotes as brief as possible without sacrificing essential content.

The quotes are self-explanatory, but I will add some comments, too. I'll tell you when I am stating my own opinion.

The information below is taken from a Church & Community public presentation I made in Brooklyn, N.Y., on April 19, 2012, titled "*The Roots of Conflict in U.S. Politics and Economics.*"

That presentation began with these words: "The conflicting beliefs and values in U.S. politics and economics can be considered on their merits. That is, we can discuss (and argue about) these beliefs and values as being 'good' or 'bad,' 'true or false,' 'right' or 'wrong.' In the way that beliefs and values are usually discussed and argued about, we generally rely on common assumptions and personal feelings about what these beliefs 'say,' and what the values 'mean.'

"We can gain a better understanding of our conflicts when we know where they came from. The beliefs and values which drive our politics and economic policy today have roots in medieval Europe's way of life, and the *reactions against* that way of life."

The Characteristics of Medieval Europe's Way of Life

The Medieval period of European history, also known as The Middle Ages, may be said to begin around the year 900. (McNeill, pp.243-244, pp.248ff)

Enforced Conformity to Religious Authority

The Christian Church "saw its mission as saving souls..." This mission was "...something that could best be done by teaching and upholding orthodoxy, or 'correct belief.'" (Ball and Dagger, PIDI, p.52)

"...church and state were supposed to be partners in the defense of Christendom." There was no clear separation between church and state. (Ball and Dagger, PIDI, p.52)

Those who did not support the church's views were seen as threats to its mission. In response to such threats, the church used its powers and "...called upon the kings and other secular powers to use theirs, to enforce conformity to church doctrine." (Ball and Dagger, PIDI, p.52)

"The last execution of The Inquisition [the enforcement of Church doctrine] was in Spain in 1826. This was the execution by strangulation of the school teacher Cayetano Ripoll for purportedly teaching Deism." (Wikipedia, "Inquisition")

(NOTE: Deism is a school of religious and philosophical thought. Thomas Jefferson, Benjamin Franklin, James Madison, Alexander Hamilton, Ethan Allen, and Thomas Paine were associated with Deism.)

The Divine Right of Kings

Connecting *God, gods,* and *divinity,* with *authority* and *power* is common in human experience. (McNeill, pp.7-8,10, and Britannica Online Encyclopedia, see "tianming"-mandate of heaven)

An example of this from the Christian *Bible:* "Every person is to be in *subjection to the governing authorities. For there is no authority except from God...* Therefore, whoever resists authority has opposed the ordinance of God; and they who have opposed *will receive condemnation* upon themselves." (*Romans,* Chapter 13, verses 1 and 2, emphasis added)

Another example: "Submit yourselves for the Lord's sake to a king...or to governors...for such is the will of God..." (*First Peter,* Chapter 2, excerpts from verses 13-15)

These and other passages from *The Bible* were used to establish the "**Divine Right of Kings doctrine**... which asserted that **kings derived their authority from God and therefore could not be held accountable by any earthly authority**... By the 16th and 17th centuries...the new national monarchs were asserting their authority in matters of both church and state... The bishop Jacques-Benigne Bossuet (1627-1704)... asserted that the king's person and authority were sacred. The English Royalist Sir Robert Filmer...held that the state is a family and that the king is a father..." (Britannica Online Encyclopedia, "divine right of kings", emphasis added)

"The divine-right theory of kingship... asserts that **no monarch is subject to...the will of his people**..." (Wikipedia, "Divine right of kings", emphasis added)

Fixed Social Classes

"...**one's prospects were fixed by one's social rank**. This was especially true under **feudalism**, which became the main form of social and economic organization in [medieval] Europe." (Ball and Dagger, PIDI, p.53, emphasis added)

Medieval feudalism divided "...society into two broad classes of people: nobles and commoners. As feudal relationships were passed down the generations, a distinct class of land-owning nobles or aristocrats took shape. **These nobles thought themselves naturally superior to the commoners**... They also believed that their nobility entitled them to **exercise authority over the commoners** and to enjoy privileges and *liberties* unavailable to common men and women." (Ball and Dagger, PIDI, p.53, emphasis added)

In France, "One of those privileges was **exemption from most taxes**." (Ball and Dagger, PIDI, p.65, emphasis added)

"...the children of free commoners and serfs were locked into the social position of their parents, and *no amount of effort or ability could improve their stations in life*." (Ball and Dagger, PIDI, p.54, emphasis added) {Question: Did Medieval Europe have a caste system?}

The Feudal/Mercantile Economy
The Feudal Economy:
"Lands were generally not for sale, labor was not for sale, and capital was not for investment." (Heilbroner, WP, pp.27-28)

"**Work was not yet seen as a means to an end—money and the things money buys... Work was an end in itself**... part of a tradition... a way of life." (Heilbroner, WP, p.26, emphasis added)

"A few people were aristocrats or nobles, some were free, and **a great many were serfs—peasants who lived and worked in bondage to an aristocrat** in exchange for protection." (Heilbroner, WP, p.30, emphasis added)

"**Serfs farmed plots of land owned by the lord of the manor, and from their plots they had to provide for their families and _pay rent_ to the lord**... What was most distinctive about serfdom was the lack of freedom to choose where to live and what work to do. Serfs were legally attached to the land or the person of the lord." (Heilbroner, WP, p.53, emphasis added)

The Mercantile Economy:

"**Mercantilism:** The economic policy of promoting a country's wealth at the expense of others by establishing _monopolies_ and regulating foreign trade to favor domestic industry." (Ball and Dagger, PIDI, p.255, emphasis added)

"To the mercantilists... **national power was the natural object of economic endeavor**, and the most important ingredient in national power was **gold**." (Heilbroner, WP, p.39, emphasis added)

"...the European nation-states engaged in an economic warfare that frequently led to real combat. **One tactic was to establish colonies**, exploit their resources, and forbid the colonists to buy from or sell to anyone but the so-called mother country. **Another [tactic] was to set high tariffs, or taxes on imported goods**, to discourage the sale of foreign goods and encourage the growth of domestic industries. **A third tactic was the monopoly**, the practice of granting exclusive control over a market to a single firm... **[some monopolies] received the exclusive right to govern as well as trade** with vast colonial territories... These attempts worked to **the advantage of some**...those who were able to secure the privileges—and **the disadvantage of others**. _The middle class generally fell into this second camp._" (Ball and Dagger, PIDI, p.68, emphasis added)

Reflection - Imagine what life was like in the medieval system:

Enforced Conformity to Religious Authority:
You actually believe that you *must accept* what the religious authorities say as THE TRUTH about everything—partly because you only know what they tell you, but also because you fear torture, death, and the damnation of your soul in Hell.

The Divine Right of Kings:
You actually believe that the monarch is appointed by God, and therefore has the DIVINE RIGHT to do whatever he wants with your life. The monarch's will is supreme, and you have NO right to question or oppose him. You have NO legal rights.

Fixed Social Classes:
You have NO chance to improve your circumstances, or to choose your own path in life. The commoners had no chance to become nobles.

Feudal/Mercantile Economy:
Your material well-being is determined by your family's social status.

Can you imagine living like that? Would you want that way of life for yourself or the children you know?

Some people may have a psychological preference for living within the boundaries of custom and tradition, in a society in which independent thought and self-expression are considered unnecessary or wrong.

But here's what happened...

Reactions Against The Medieval Way Of Life
"Some scholars in the Renaissance (late 1300s and 1400s) said that '...life on earth is not just a wearisome journey that

the Christian must take on his or her way to heaven. On the contrary... *life is worth living fully... human beings are <u>capable</u> of wondrous things...*'" (Ball and Dagger, PIDI, pp.30-31, emphasis added)

<u>Reactions Against Enforced Conformity to Religious Authority</u>
"**Martin Luther** (1483-1546) [a Roman Catholic Doctor of Theology] posted his famous 95 theses [statements against what he saw as corruption in the Church] on the door of the church at Wittenberg in 1517. By themselves, the 95 theses were not a direct threat to the *authority* of the Church." (Ball and Dagger, PIDI, p.54, emphasis added)

"Luther's theses circulated quickly through the German principalities and found a receptive audience among Christians disturbed by the corruption of the Church. They also caught the attention of the German nobles, many of whom regarded the Church as their main rival for earthly power." (Ball and Dagger, PIDI, p.55)

"Luther was commanded by his superiors in the Church to admit that he was mistaken. He refused." (Ball and Dagger, PIDI, p.56) "Luther was excommunicated [his membership in the Church was revoked] in 1521." (Ball and Dagger, PIDI, p.54)

"Luther called for strict attention to scripture... And in place of the Church's emphasis on the authority of priests, bishops, and the Pope, Luther called for the 'priesthood of all believers.'" (Ball and Dagger, PIDI, p.55)

"Despite some early remarks defending *freedom of conscience...* he expected that everyone who read the scriptures could not help but understand them as he did. But... Luther's proclamation opened the floodgates for a variety of interpretations of the Bible and a profusion of [politically sponsored] Protestant sects." (Ball and Dagger, PIDI, p.55, emphasis added)

The "arguments for *freedom of conscience* planted the seeds of religious toleration... **John Locke** (1632-1704) said it was better to tolerate some differences of religion than to try to win converts at the point of a sword." (Ball and Dagger, PIDI, p.56, emphasis added) "... Locke said that **religious belief is normally a private concern and not a proper subject for government**..." (Ball and Dagger, PIDI, p.59, emphasis added)

Reactions Against the Divine Right of Kings

Magna Carta: "...in the Magna Carta, the Great Charter of rights that the feudal barons of England forced King John to accept in 1215, the king agreed that 'No free man shall be taken, or imprisoned or outlawed, or exiled, or in any way destroyed except by lawful judgment of his peers or by the laws of the land.' But in this case, 'free man' referred only to the barons and other nobles. *Those of lesser rank could be taken, imprisoned, or killed without the lawful judgment of their peers*—without, that is, a trial by jury." (Ball and Dagger, PIDI, p.54, emphasis added)

Niccolo Machiavelli (1469-1527): In his most famous work, *The Prince*, completed in 1513, Machiavelli argued that, since human nature is "dominated by self-interest and insatiable desires," *a strong ruler who does whatever is necessary to stay in power* is needed to maintain order and satisfy his subjects. But in a lesser known work, *Discourses on Livy* (completed shortly after *The Prince*), Machiavelli argued that self-government in a republic—*a free government ruled by impersonal law—is the best way to avoid tyranny, corruption and complacency... all classes should share power and keep each other in check*... citizens must be free to assemble, to argue among themselves, to expose corruption and criticize their leaders and one another." (Ball and Dagger, PIDI, pp.31-33; see also Reese, "Machiavelli, Niccolo", emphasis added)

{An observation: It is remarkable that *The Prince* prescribes the form of medieval governance, while *Livy* prescribes a republic. Both books were written almost simultaneously. Either Machiavelli's mind was divided, or he was demonstrating the "Machiavellian" approach to politics. But from what I have read, he had nothing to gain by writing a book favoring a republic. Maybe a Machiavelli scholar could clear this up.

My opinion: In these two books, Machiavelli is presenting an emerging political dilemma. **In *The Prince*, he says that a strong central government is <u>best able</u> to** *maximize social stability,* **and in *Livy* he says that a republic (in which power is de-centralized) is <u>best able</u> to** *minimize tyranny and corruption.* Below, we will see how this dilemma is resolved in The Declaration of Independence and The Preamble.}

Thomas Hobbes (1588-1679): Hobbes published his book *Leviathan* in 1651: "...Hobbes maintained that the people of a country should obey those who have power over them. But he refused to base his conclusion on the simple claim that this was God's will. Even though Hobbes cited scripture, his argument was fundamentally secular... as it was based on self-interest rather than divine commands." Hobbes asserted that in the state of nature, everyone is free and equal, and "...no one is born to hold a higher rank or status than anyone else—and have a natural right to do as they wish. The problem is human nature: 'I put for a general inclination of all mankind, a perpetual and restless desire of power after power that ceases only in death.' This leads individuals into conflict with one another, and *turns the state of nature into a 'war of every man against every man'*" (Ball and Dagger, PIDI, pp.57-58, emphasis added) "...in such condition [there is] continual fear and danger of violent death;

and *the life of man [is] solitary, poor, nasty, brutish, and short."* (Ball and Dagger, IIR, p.70, emphasis added)

"Nothing, in Hobbes's view, could be worse than this. So the individuals in the state of nature enter into **a <u>social contract</u> to establish political authority**. To provide for their security, they surrender all but one of their rights***to those to whom they grant authority... government is founded in the consent of the people. But by their consent, they authorize the sovereign to do *anything* to maintain order and peace. This includes the power to force everyone to worship as the sovereign requires, for Hobbes saw religious differences as one of the leading sources of conflict." (Ball and Dagger, PIDI, pp.58-59, emphasis added)

***The right to defend themselves against the sovereign, if the sovereign directly threatens their survival.

{My opinion: Thomas Hobbes is the most important "bridge" thinker between medieval authoritarian governance and democratic governance. He upheld one of the main ideas of the medieval way of life by maintaining the absolute sovereignty of a central authority. But he shifted the *foundation* of that sovereign authority from God to *the general will of the people*. Thus, sovereign authority remained, but now was legally constituted and established by a secular authority—the will of the people—NOT divine authority. "The People" became the sovereign authority. I think Hobbes is the most important bridge thinker because this profound shift gave new life to an ancient form of egalitarian secular governance. (see Erdal and Whiten in the Resources) The Preamble and Constitution established our social contract—*the general will of the people*—in the U.S.}

John Locke (1632-1704): Locke published his *Two Treatises of Government* in 1689/90. "Locke said that in the state of nature, everyone is free and equal, with no ascribed social status. There are natural rights—'life, liberty, and property'—which a person can choose to forfeit, but no one can simply take them away. Unlike Hobbes, Locke said that the state of nature is not a state of war. But the state of nature is 'inconvenient' because many people are unwilling to respect the rights of others... [therefore] the residents of the state of nature enter into **a social contract to make a set of laws and a government** to make, interpret, and enforce laws... Government derives its authority from the governed... To give anyone total and *absolute power* over our lives would be irrational and *contrary* to the will of God.* Locke believed that non-Anglican Protestants should have freedom of worship. He also believed that Catholics should not be tolerated because they would try to deliver England to the power of Rome,** and that atheists should not be tolerated because anyone who denied the existence of God, salvation, and damnation could not be trusted at all."*** (Ball and Dagger, PIDI, pp.59-61, emphasis added)

*Notice that Locke overtly contradicts the Divine Right of Kings doctrine, and Hobbes, on absolute power.

**In the presidential election of 1960, I heard people say that John F. Kennedy, who was Roman Catholic, would take orders from the Vatican.

***Hence the courtroom oath with the hand on *The Bible*, "... so help me God"?

The Declaration of Independence, 1776: Excerpt from the second paragraph: "We hold these truths to be self-evident, that all men are created equal, that they are endowed by their Creator with certain unalienable Rights, that among these are Life, Liberty, and the pursuit of Happiness. That to secure these rights, Governments are instituted... deriving their just powers from the consent of the governed. That whenever any Form of Government becomes destructive of these ends, it is the Right of the People... to institute new Government, *laying its foundation on such **principles** and organizing its powers in such **form***, as to them shall seem most likely to effect their Safety and Happiness." (Ball and Dagger, IRR, p.96, emphasis added)

{My opinion: **The Preamble establishes the principles** of the Federal government that was instituted after the failure of the confederacy, and **the structure of the Constitution establishes the form** of the Federal government.}

Reactions Against Fixed Social Classes

Thomas Hobbes wrote that in the state of nature, "...no one is born to hold a higher rank or status than anyone else..." (Ball and Dagger, PIDI, p.57)

John Locke wrote that in the state of nature, everyone is free and equal, with no ascribed status. People are "... equal one amongst another without Subordination or Subjection..." (From the *Second Treatise Of Government*, paragraph 4) (Ball and Dagger, PIDI, pp.60-61)

Reactions Against the Feudal/Mercantile Economy

Economic Liberalism: "In both the Old World and the New... liberalism was a vigorous revolutionary force in the [1600s and 1700s]. In the name of *natural rights and the rights of man, liberals struggled for individual liberty* against *the social, political, and religious* arrangements that lingered from the Middle Ages... the early liberals sought wider opportunities for more people, not just the privileged few born into nobility. One form of opportunity, economic opportunity, was particularly important to the merchants, bankers, and lawyers who came to make up the middle class... *For them, acquiring wealth was the main avenue of social advancement.*" (Ball and Dagger, PIDI, p.67, emphasis added)

{My Opinion: If we view economic liberalism through the lens of the medieval system, the notion of social advancement through the acquisition of wealth means that *the emerging middle class wanted to live like the nobles.* Recall the quote above which states that the middle class were generally not included among the advantaged in the mercantile system. Perhaps the thought, "Maybe I, or my children, can live like a noble" is one of the motives behind *economic* liberalism. This thought has been around for hundreds of years. I think it is the root of The American Dream—the idea that everyone has (or should have) the *opportunity* to acquire some financial surplus, some leisure, and own their home *(their own "manor house")*.

It is impossible to over-estimate the power of this idea. *From the medieval perspective*, "social advancement through the acquisition of wealth" should be understood as an expression of individuals' sense of dignity and liberty (self-determination). But in its extreme form, it has also produced a lot of harm. (see *Social Darwinism*, below)

How do we think of, and measure, "success"? Do we think of success in financial terms? }

Capitalism: "...*economic exchanges are a private matter* between persons pursuing profits... The idea that *the best way to promote the good of society as a whole is to let people pursue their private interests* became the cornerstone of liberal economic thought in the [1700s]... A group of French thinkers known as the Physiocrats developed this idea... *Arguing against mercantilism...* their advice to governments was '*Laissez faire, laissez passer*' (let it be, leave it alone)." (Ball and Dagger, PIDI, pp.68-69, emphasis added)

Bernard Mandeville: In "a poem published in 1705... Originally titled '*The Grumbling Hive*' [later titled '*The Fable of The Bees*'], Mandeville's message was that '*fraud, luxury, and waste* may be sources of sin but they *are also causes of prosperity*." (Heilbroner, TWP, p.19, emphasis added)

"Mandeville insists that the use of mild fraud, the encouragement of luxury, and *the appeal to pride* are necessary [in] what we might call a ***business civilization***." (Heilbroner, TWP, p.22, emphasis added)

{My opinion: From early in its history, Christianity has recognized Seven Cardinal Sins (also known as The Seven Deadly Sins), because they are powerful "forces" that take us away from God. Greed, pride, and gluttony are on the list. Paralleling Machiavelli's *The Prince*, in which even the *appearance* of "Christian virtue" is abandoned in politics, so that cardinal sin becomes *political* virtue, with Mandeville, sin becomes *economic* virtue. This is probably the beginning of the idea that a "business civilization" has a different set of vices and virtues than a "Christian society." The general idea is that "Christian" virtues don't work in the real world. To quote the famous line from the 1987 film *Wall Street*, "greed is good." Some say that Mandeville was writing sarcastically, but the idea stuck. See Rev. Thomas Malthus, below.}

Richard Cantillon (1680-1734): Cantillon's *Essay on the Nature of Commerce in General* was published in 1755, "...21 years after his untimely death—he was murdered by his cook." His *Essay* was "...the first attempt to depict the workings of a **market-driven society** as constituting a 'system' with a ***spontaneous mechanism of self-adjustment***." (Heilbroner, TWP, p.30, emphasis added)

Adam Smith (1723-1790) was a Scottish moral philosopher who published two major works: *Theory Of Moral Sentiments* in 1759; and, *An Inquiry Into The Nature And Causes Of The Wealth Of Nations* in 1776. He is generally regarded as the founder of Free Market theory, and economics as we know it. But as the following material will show, while he did promote the Invisible Hand concept, **Smith's work has been grossly misrepresented in our high schools and colleges. It is impossible to overestimate the damage done to our thinking by the distortion, which continues today. The material below will help to correct our distortion of Smith's work.**

FINDING SOLID GROUND IN POLITICS AND THE ECONOMY

"*Smith agreed with the Physiocrats' attack on mercantilism and monopoly*, and called for an economic policy that would allow individuals to compete freely in the marketplace." (Ball and Dagger, PIDI, p.69, emphasis added)

"*Smith did not approve of accumulation for accumulation's sake*... Rather, in the accumulation of capital Smith saw a vast benefit to society." (Heilbroner, WP, p.64, emphasis added)

"What [Smith] sought was **'the invisible hand'**... whereby the 'private interests and passions of men' are led in the direction 'which is most agreeable to the interest of the whole society.'" (Heilbroner, WP, p.54, emphasis added)

{My opinion: It seems to me that Smith's "Invisible Hand" is roughly the same idea as Cantillon's "spontaneous mechanism of self-adjustment." It should be noted that The Great Depression of the 1930s, and, more recently, The Great Recession, are evidence of the weakness of the Invisible Hand theory. I think economics today is mostly about understanding how the "Invisible Hand/spontaneous mechanism of self-adjustment" works, so that, ironically, *it can be managed better*.

The lasting residue of this concept is the assumption that the private sector is the real economy, and that government spending is just an adjunct to the private economy. This seems to be the bias of the Economics textbooks I have looked at. (If anyone can recommend a Mixed Economy textbook, I would appreciate it.) Keynesian economic theory prescribes a course of action when the private sector's Invisible Hand/self-adjusting mechanism doesn't work. See John L. Larson, *The Market Revolution in America*, listed in the Resources, for a summary of the history of major market panics in the U.S.}

"...it is not [Smith's] aim to espouse the interests of any class. He is concerned with promoting the wealth of the entire nation." (Heilbroner, WP, p.53)

FINDING SOLID GROUND

"It was not until 1800 that [*Wealth Of Nations*] achieved full recognition... Its protagonists...were the rising capitalist class—the very class Smith had excoriated for its 'mean rapacity,' whose members he said [should not] be the rulers of mankind.' All this was ignored... in Smith's [praise] of a free market, the rising industrialists found the theoretical justification they needed to *block* the first government attempts to *remedy the scandalous conditions* of the times." (Heilbroner, WP, pp.67-68, emphasis added)

[**Charles Dickens** (1812-1870) depicted the misery and "scandalous conditions" accompanying capitalism in England. (Ball and Dagger, PIDI, pp.74-75)] {My personal favorite of Dickens' work is *A Christmas Carol*.}

"Smith was neither anti-labor nor anti-capital; if he had any bias it was in favor of the consumer. 'Consumption is the sole end and purpose of all production', he wrote, and then proceeded to castigate those systems that placed the interest of the producer over that of the consuming public." (Heilbroner, WP, p.68)

Here are some quotes from Adam Smith's *Wealth of Nations* (re-published by Random House in 1994) that will correct the distortion of his work:

"The liberal reward of labor is the natural symptom of increasing wealth. The scanty maintenance of the laboring poor is the natural symptom that things are going fast backwards." (Book 1, Ch.8, p.84)

"High earnings of labor are an advantage to society." (Bk.1, Ch.8, p.90)

"It is but equity that those who feed, clothe, and lodge the whole body of the people should have a share of the produce of their own labor as to be themselves well fed, clothed and lodged." (Bk.1, Ch.8, p.90)

"...in reality high profits tend to raise prices more than high wages... Our merchants and master-manufacturers complain much of the bad effects of high wages in raising the price, and thereby lessening the sale of their goods both at home and abroad. They say nothing concerning the bad effects of high profits. They are silent with regard to the pernicious effects of their own gains. They complain only of those of other people." (Bk.1, Ch.9, pp.112-113)

"...the rate of profit is always highest in the countries which are going fastest to ruin." (Bk.1, Ch.11, Pt.3, p.287)

"The proposal of any new law or regulation of commerce which comes from this order [the dealers of trade or 'manufactures'] should always be listened to with the most suspicious attention. It comes from an order of men who have generally an interest to deceive and even to oppress the public, and who have, upon many occasions, both deceived and oppressed it." (Bk.1, Ch.11, Pt.3, p.288)

"...the natural [economic] liberty of a few individuals which might endanger the security of the whole society ought to be restrained by the laws of all governments." (Bk.2, Ch.2, p.353)

"Political economy proposes two distinct objects: first, to provide a plentiful revenue or subsistence for the people, or more properly to enable them to provide such a revenue for themselves; and secondly to supply the state or commonwealth with a revenue sufficient for the public services." (Bk.4, Intro., p.455)

"...the mean rapacity, the monopolizing spirit of merchants and manufacturers, who neither are, nor ought to be, the rulers of mankind...may be prevented from disturbing the tranquility of [others]." (Bk.4, Ch.3, Pt.1, p.527)

"Consumption is the sole end and purpose of all production; and the interest of the producer ought to be attended to only so far as it may be necessary for promoting that of the consumer... But *in the mercantile system, the interest of the consumer is almost constantly sacrificed to that of the producer;* and it seems to consider production, and not consumption, as the ultimate end and object of all industry and commerce." (Bk.4, Ch.8, p.715, emphasis added)

{QUESTION: Does this tell us anything about supply-side, or "trickle-down", economics?}

"The rich, in particular, are necessarily interested to support that order of things, which can alone secure them in the possession of their own advantages... Civil government, so far as it is instituted for the security of property, is in reality instituted for the defence of the rich against the poor, or of those who have some property against those who have none at all." (Bk.5, Ch.1, Pt.2, p.771)

"[The] scheme of making the administration of justice subservient to the purposes of revenue, [produces] very gross abuses." (Bk.5, Ch.1, Pt.2, p.772)

"The third duty of the sovereign or commonwealth is that of erecting and maintaining those public works and public institutions for the facilitating of commerce of the society, and those for promoting the instruction of the people. The institutions for instruction are of two kinds: those for the education of the youth, and those for the instruction of people of all ages." (Bk.5, Ch.1, Pt.3, p.779)

On education and training as a type of Capital: "...the acquired and useful abilities of all the inhabitants or members of society... the acquisition of his education, study, or apprenticeship, always costs a real expence, which is a capital fixed and realized, as it were, in his person. Those talents make part of his fortune, [and] likewise [the fortune] of the society to which he belongs." (Bk.2, Ch.1, p.306)

"The subjects of every state ought to contribute towards the support of the government in proportion to the revenue which they enjoy under the protection of the state." (Bk.5, Ch.2, Pt.2, p.888)

"It is not unreasonable that the rich should contribute to the public expense, not only in proportion to their revenue, but *more than that proportion*." (Bk.5, Ch.2, Pt.2, p.907, emphasis added)

Thank you, Adam Smith. I'm sorry your work has been misrepresented.

{My opinion: When Adam Smith prescribes government's role as providing public works and institutions, and that these works and institutions should be fully supported financially, he is prescribing what might be called the political economy's **Visible Hand**. If the **Invisible Hand** is the free market's tendency to increase the wealth of the entire nation, and thus make greater prosperity *possible* for all of the people, then the Visible Hand is the set of laws and policies by which the government provides for the financial support of the public works and institutions. The reader can speculate about which hand is the right or left. I think **Adam Smith is clearly saying that the economy is ambidextrous. The Invisible Hand and the Visible Hand are both essential.**}

In 1798, **Rev. Thomas Malthus** published "*An Essay on the Principle of Population, as It Affects the Future Improvement of Society...*" Malthus is included as a reaction against the medieval system because his idea that society should NOT help "the unworthy poor" fits well with Social Darwinism, discussed below. Addressing the perceived problem of unlimited population growth and limited food supply, Malthus said, "The tendency of the population to exceed food production is restrained by the 'positive' checks to population ...famine, misery, plague, and war. *Poverty [is] the natural punishment for the 'lower classes.' Relief... only makes matters worse, as more children would survive.*" (Canterbery, p.75, emphasis added. See also Ball and Dagger, PIDI, p.138)

{My opinion based on my own research: Putting aside the obvious objections to Rev. Malthus' ethics, he could not have known that greater shared prosperity is now the single best indicator of a lower rate of population growth. This means that the **best way to reduce the *rate* of population growth is to promote shared prosperity.**}

Socialism: Note: I believe in The Preamble. I don't believe in socialism, or *any* of our current ideologies. But in the U.S., we seem to be opposed to learning about socialism. We have a strong negative reaction to the word itself. But whether or not we dislike the word *socialism*, we should at least be aware of what socialism is so the word can't be used to deceive us.

Contrary to what some people in government and media say, the public institutions and services, and programs like Social Security, Medicare, Medicaid, and food and housing subsidies, which *promote the general welfare*, are NOT socialism. Such things are NOT "creeping socialism," either. People who say things like that either don't know what they are talking about, or they want to manipulate us with "alarming" words.

I include Socialism as a reaction against the medieval way of life because its fundamental belief is that *ordinary people* (in medieval terms, the commoners), *give themselves governing power through their common "ownership" of the economy and its benefits*—not through individual economic liberty.

"**Modern socialism, like classical conservatism, began in part as a response to the liberalism of the late 18th and early 19th centuries**... Like the conservatives, socialists objected to the liberal emphasis on competition and individual liberty... human beings are by nature social creatures... cooperation, not competition, [is] the foundation of a society in which everyone can enjoy a decent measure of liberty, justice, and prosperity... [Socialists] have generally argued for either centralized or decentralized control of [the economy]... Those who favor centralized control want the state or government to assume responsibility for managing property and resources in the name of the whole society... [those who favor decentralized control say that public property and resources are managed best by] groups at the local level... especially the workers and consumers..." (Ball and Dagger, PIDI, pp.118-119, emphasis added)

"The first name one associates with socialism, or at least with its communist variant, is probably that of **Karl Marx (1818-1883)... Yet socialism predated Marx by many centuries**: Plato's *Republic* (around 380 B.C.)... Christians of the first and second centuries... certain monastic orders... St. Thomas More (1478-1535)... Count Claude-Henri de Saint Simon (1760-1825)... Charles Fourier (1772-1837)... Robert Owen (1771-1858)... [and] many other thinkers..." (Ball and Dagger, PIDI, pp.120-121, emphasis added)

"Marx earned his doctorate in philosophy in 1841 {I read somewhere that his thesis topic was Epicurus} ...**he came to believe that the political and economic system of his day was so rotten that it could not be reformed from within**... a warrant was issued for his arrest." [by the Prussian police] (Ball and Dagger, PIDI, pp.125-126, emphasis added)

Marx "settled in England in 1849, and worked on *Capital* in the British Museum, the first volume of which was published in 1867... he also worked as a foreign correspondent for *The New York Tribune*... *The Communist Manifesto* (1848) calls on the workers of the world to unite, and throw off their chains... *The Manifesto* provides an analysis of mid-19th century social conditions... and urges that these conditions require revolution." (Reese, "Marx, Karl")

{Note: Adam Smith and Karl Marx both give labor the key position in the creation of wealth.} (Reese, "Smith, Adam" and "Marx, Karl")

SUMMARY OF OUR CURRENT IDEOLOGIES

Classical Liberalism: "From its beginning more than 300 years ago, the hallmark of liberalism has been the attempt to promote individual liberty... The words 'liberal' and 'liberty' both derive from the Latin 'liber,' meaning *free*. 'Liberal' did not enter the vocabulary of politics until early in the [1800s]... a faction of the Spanish legislature adopted the name 'Liberales.' From there the term traveled to France and Great Britain, where the party known as the Whigs evolved by the 1840s into the Liberal Party. *These early liberals shared a desire for a more open and tolerant society in which people would be free to pursue their own ideas and interests with as little interference as possible.*" (Ball and Dagger, PIDI, p.49, emphasis added)

"...liberals contend that the individual must be free to decide for himself and herself what goals to pursue in life. The individual is the best judge of what is in his or her interest... so each person ought to be free to live as he or she sees fit—so long as the person does not interfere with the freedom of others to live as they see fit... No person's liberty is more important or valuable than any other's... Liberalism seeks not equal success in life, but *an equal chance to succeed*... Liberalism, in short, promotes individual liberty by trying to *guarantee equality of opportunity within a tolerant society.*" (Ball and Dagger, PIDI, p.51, emphasis added)

John Stuart Mill (1806-1873): "Mill was probably the leading liberal philosopher of the 19th century. Whether he was supporting women's rights or arguing that the government should set minimum educational standards, Mill's great concern was to defend and extend individual liberty." (Ball and Dagger, PIDI, p.72) "Freedom is a good thing, he argued, because it promotes 'man as a progressive being' ... *freedom is vital to personal development.*" (Ball and Dagger, PIDI, p.74, emphasis added)

Classical Conservatism: "In one sense conservatism is easy to define, in another quite difficult. It is easy because all conservatives share a desire to *conserve* or preserve something—usually the traditional or customary way of life of their societies. But... different conservatives are likely to have different ideas about what elements of their way of life are worth preserving... that is what makes conservatism difficult to define... [for example,] As many communist countries move toward free market economies, the hard-line communists who resist this change are sometimes called conservatives." (Ball and Dagger, PIDI, p.91, emphasis added) [Note: These words were published in 1991, soon after the fall of the Berlin Wall.]

Edmund Burke (1729-1797): Burke published *Reflections on the Revolution in France* in 1790: "...there is widespread agreement that the founder of conservatism was Edmund Burke... From Burke's point of view, the atomistic [individualistic] conception of society is simply wrong. Burke argued for an organic conception of society—*individuals are related to society as parts are related in the human body... society is like a fabric*—'the social fabric'—its members are like the interwoven threads... government must be rooted in the *customs, traditions, and prejudices* of a people, who must acquire the habit of obeying, respecting, and even revering it... government makes ordered liberty possible..." (Ball and Dagger, PIDI, pp.93-98, emphasis added)

"Early classical conservatives were trying to preserve or restore an aristocratic society that was under attack from liberalism... They defended the traditional social hierarchy; they insisted on the need for a government strong enough to restrain the passions of the people; and they were often *skeptical of attempts to promote individual freedom and equality of opportunity*..." (Ball and Dagger, PIDI, p.92, emphasis added) "...[it is] much wiser to cherish a peaceful and stable society than to risk its loss in the futile quest for perfection..." (Ball and Dagger, PIDI, p.93)

Now, here's where the lines between liberalism and conservatism blur in our confusing current ideologies:

"Lacking a history of feudalism and hereditary aristocracy, having no monarch... and *no established national church*... **classical liberalism came to be called conservatism in the United States**." (Ball and Dagger, PIDI, pp.104-105, emphasis added)

{My opinion: Regarding classical liberalism in the U.S., it is important to know that most of the people who started the Independence Movement in the American colonies, including George Washington, were land-owners and merchants. *President George Washington called them "the Monied Gentry."* (Larson, p.20) They didn't want their business activity to be restricted or taxed by an "outside" power, the British government (The Empire). The colonies had no vote in Parliament—the slogan then was "no taxation without representation."

As it turned out, many of them didn't want to be restricted by, or pay taxes to, *their own government,* either (look up *Shays' Rebellion*). The Articles of Confederation did NOT give the national government the power to enforce taxation. That was one of its weaknesses—we had no way to force ourselves to pay back what we had borrowed from France to conduct our War of Independence from England! The struggle over the authority and power of the Federal government, in which Hamilton and Jefferson were involved, continued after 1789. (Larson, pp.17-23)

In Article I, Section 8 of our Constitution, we *unquestionably* gave ourselves the authority to *tax ourselves* to "provide for the common Defence and general Welfare of the United States." But in spite of that, *the struggle over the Federal government's mandate to promote the general welfare continues even today...* see below.}

"**Neo-classical liberals** [*individualist conservatives* in the U.S.]...would argue that government interferes with individuals' freedom to compete economically." (Ball and Dagger, PIDI, p.111) "...**Margaret Thatcher** and **Ronald Reagan** [were] individualist conservatives who advocate[d] reducing the size and scope of government to free individuals to compete for profits." (Ball and Dagger, PIDI, p.92, emphasis added)

Neo-conservatives would argue that strong public institutions (like public education) are necessary to help people become independent, but that these institutions should embody conservative (*classical* liberal) values and beliefs. (Ball and Dagger, PIDI, pp.112-113, emphasis added)

Welfare liberals would argue that strong, active government is necessary to promote "the general welfare," individual freedom, and equal rights and opportunity. Without government intervention, many people will be deprived of their civil rights and real opportunity. (Ball and Dagger, PIDI, pp.74-78)

{Comment: Neo-conservatism and welfare liberalism both say that government should be strong enough to provide social institutions that promote Liberalism's agenda.

But there is a fundamental difference of emphasis within Liberalism. "Civil" liberalism says nothing is more important than developing every individual's ability to be an informed and self-determining *person*, with equal civil rights and opportunities, in an "open and tolerant society." Economic liberalism says nothing is more important than individuals' right to acquire wealth.

Civil and welfare liberalism's point is that without government intervention, many individuals would be deprived of the blessings of liberty—and that is not good for the *general* welfare. Therefore, government must be strong enough to successfully <u>counteract</u> <u>the dominant group's prejudices and customs that interfere with</u> <u>equal rights, opportunity, and the pursuit of happiness for all.</u> We see how important this is in the ongoing equal rights, opportunity, and justice struggles in the U.S. today.}

Extreme ideologies have grown from Classical Liberalism and Classical Conservatism. From liberalism has come what I call **Anti-Government Individualism**. From conservatism has come **Socialism, Communism,** and what I call **Reactionary Neo-Noble Conservatism.**

Liberal Extremes

Anti-Government Individualism lives in ***Libertarianism*** (Robert Nozick 1938-2002), ***Libertarian Anarchism*** (Murray Rothbard 1926-1995), (Ball and Dagger, PIDI, pp.82-83) and ***Objectivism*** (Ayn Rand 1905-1982).

Libertarianism says that maximum individual liberty will create the best of all possible worlds, and that the *absolute minimum* of government is best. Government should protect us, then get out of our life. (Ball and Dagger, PIDI, p.82) {I believe their slogans are, "Government is a necessary evil," "The government that governs least governs best," and "The government should get its hand out of my pocket, and keep its nose out of my business!"}

Libertarian Anarchism says that <u>*all* government is an *unnecessary* evil</u> because it interferes with individual liberty. (Ball and Dagger, PIDI, p.83)

{My opinion: Ayn Rand called her ideas **Objectivism**. Rand's brand of extreme individualism is presented in her *fiction novels* that portray the exhilaration of "rugged individuals" acting solely on their desires, without much thought about the consequences of their actions on others.}

Conservative Extremes

Because **Socialism and Communism** emphasize the social fabric, they are rooted in conservatism. But they have never been serious forces in U.S. politics and economics. Those who claim they are (for example, Congress initially opposed the GI Bill because they thought it was socialism, and therefore "un-American") either don't know what they are talking about, or they are trying to manipulate us.

Reactionary Neo-Noble Conservatism: This is a *tribal* way of thinking about the social fabric that currently lives in notions of GROUP SUPERIORITY that are cherished by some people today.

This extreme ideology maintains conservatism's idea that government must conserve a society's customs, traditions, and prejudices. But for these conservatives, this means preserving *their* group's customs, traditions, and prejudices—which usually means maintaining various forms of discrimination against not-males, not-whites, not-English-speakers, not-"Christians," not-heterosexuals, not-"true Americans," etc.

Like the medieval nobles, <u>the neo-nobles believe they are naturally superior to others</u>, and therefore have the right to rule, and benefit the most from, the social order. This view believes that the U.S. should be ruled by a particular group of people, the "true Americans"—generally, the nominally Christian white men. (I say "nominally Christian" because they apparently believe that Jesus was a white "Christian" male supremacist. There is no evidence to support this view. There is more on this in Part Two.)

This form of conservatism is **reactionary** because it wants to turn back the social clock to a "Golden Age"—maybe the 1940s and '50s, when white males clearly ruled society with very little overt opposition, or maybe even to the medieval period, when *"truth" and power were completely controlled by the men who controlled religion and government.*

The believers in this tribal ideology are *outraged by the fact that soon they will lose their privileges.* They sense that they will not be able to control *"their"* country because the U.S. population is changing. Some politicians and segments of the media are making a lot of money, and gaining political power, by fanning the flames of *tribal rage*. The flame-fanners blame *the outsiders* for what's wrong with *their* country today. And some white men want white women to see themselves more as white than as women in the struggle against *the outsiders*, even though women are still second-class citizens in many of our social institutions and organizations.

Moderate forms of this superiority ideology are far more common than we may care to acknowledge. It is a thread in the social fabric in the U.S. Through social learning, we all "absorb" what we hear and see around us.

All forms of discrimination are continuations of the smothering and restrictive aspects of the medieval noble/ commoner system. Therefore, we shouldn't be surprised when "outsiders" *demand* their right to equal opportunity and civil rights, as happened in classical liberalism's reaction against the medieval system.

We still have the "lingering arrangements" of a medieval caste system of nobles and commoners in the U.S. today. But fortunately, as Pew research shows, this tribal mentality is NOT prevalent among The Millennials. Therefore, I have hope that this way of thinking will disappear over the next 50 years.

The extreme ideologies thrive on the ongoing *noble/ commoner split*, but in different ways:

Anti-Government Individualism's *immediate* goal is neither to maintain nor eliminate the split. But since the split still exists, their immediate goal is to become nobles in the social order, and they want no government "interference" with their effort.

Reactionary Neo-Noble Conservatism's goal is to maintain the split, with themselves as the nobles. They want to make sure that their nobility is not diluted or polluted by people who they *feel* are inferior to them.

Socialism's goal is to minimize the split by giving the commoners—"ordinary people"—ownership of the economy.

Communism's goal is to eliminate the split in a classless society.

The medieval and post-medieval dynamics, in the form of how we deal with the noble/commoner split, are still powerful influences on our beliefs and values. Such is the power of the past to influence the present and the future.

Between these extremes are the political and economic policy issues that are dividing us today—big government vs. small government, active government vs. passive government, the role of government in the economy, the collection and allocation of resources for government, and the regulation of business and private life. In other words, **if and how we should limit or promote "the general welfare," and if and how we should limit or promote "the blessings of liberty."**

And the differences in our ideas concerning the other goals stated in The Preamble—union, justice, domestic tranquility, and defense—are also are inextricably woven together with how we understand "the general welfare" and "the blessings of liberty." We can separate these issues in our minds, arguments, speeches, and think-tank papers, but they are like the segments of an orange—they are parts of the whole, living reality of daily life.

The wide range of our current political and economic ideologies can be traced to the medieval system. Some of our beliefs today echo the medieval way of life, some are *reactions against* those echoes, some are *reactions against those reactions, and so on.*

Extreme liberalism rejects The Preamble because it sees the general welfare as a danger to individuals' liberty. *Extreme conservatism* rejects the Preamble because it sees *some* individuals' liberty as a danger to *their* general welfare.

The Preamble is rooted in classical liberalism _and_ classical conservatism. We can consider what's good and bad about these two ideologies, to find the solid ground of The Preamble Way in both of them. The Preamble Way is our way forward.

But before we do that, there is something else we have to think about: If we can't *learn* from the Preamble, we will always be living in the ideological turmoil of the past five centuries.

Must we remain stuck in the past, or can we learn from the past and move forward?

This question points to three more ways of thinking that we need to be aware of because they have been powerful influences in our history, and they influence the way we will answer the above question. The three ways of thinking are *Social Darwinism, the idea of the state of nature,* and *the idea of progress.*

Social Darwinism

Social Darwinism has had a major influence on the *way* we think about society, the economy, and politics. (Hofstadter, pp.5-12) It lingers in our minds and culture, feeding false assumptions. It was born in England in the 1800s. When it migrated to the U.S., it gave a false "scientific" credibility to the *type* of ideas put forth by Mandeville, Cantillon, and Malthus. It has also served to support *Anti-Government Individualism* and *The Gospel of Wealth.*

Social Darwinism: "An application of Charles Darwin's principle of *natural selection*, first to the economic order, and <u>by extension to society at large</u>... human society [is] engaged in a competitive struggle whose ruthlessness should not be checked if the fit are to survive. The phrase, 'survival of the fittest' came from Darwin's rival, Alfred Wallace, in 1858 [Darwin wasn't the only one working on a theory of evolution]; it was promoted by the English philosopher Herbert Spencer in 1864. John D. Rockefeller and Andrew Carnegie cited the phrase with approval, Carnegie saying that *the law of competition 'may be sometimes hard on the individual' but it 'insures the survival of the fittest...'* From his professoriate at Yale, William Graham Sumner (1840-1910) urged *'liberty, inequality, survival of the fittest.'*

"Carnegie, Rockefeller agreeing, blunted the aggressiveness of the doctrine by requiring that those who win out in the economic struggle become philanthropists. In *The Gospel of Wealth*

(1901), Carnegie argued that it is the duty of the entrepreneur to amass as much wealth as possible and then to administer it wisely, acting as a trustee for his poorer brethren, 'doing for them better than they would or could do for themselves.'" (Reese, "Social Darwinism", emphasis added)

Let's take a quick look at the principle of **natural selection**. Darwin's (1809-1882) *first* book, *The Origin of Species*, was published in 1859. Here is a summary of natural selection:

"...living things are mutable [changeable]: they come into existence, change, and not infrequently perish... the increase of organic beings is checked by the competitive efforts of other beings to survive and reproduce, both within and beyond the species... *Such competition constitutes a struggle for existence on the part of every species... All organic beings tend to vary... They pass on these variations by inheritance...* The above conditions, taken together, provide a principle of natural selection... *favorable variations survive, while unfavorable variations are eliminated...*" (Reese, "Darwin, Charles", emphasis added)

Whether or not the term "survival of the fittest" is stated openly, this notion has been used to justify "us against them," and "me against you," in many forms of often deadly rivalry: nation against nation, person against person, tribe against tribe, race against race, religion against religion, religious faction against religious faction, ethnicity against ethnicity, rich against poor, gang against gang, specie against specie (for example, "the spotted owls have to go because we can sell these trees"), etc. This system says that *the "Winners" live at the expense of the "Losers."* The winners will live and dominate, and the losers will die out. Does this sound familiar?

But this is Social Darwinism's major error: natural selection is NOT about "kill or be killed." It's about *ADAPTATION*.

Charles Darwin's work has been grossly distorted, just as Adam Smith's work has been. It would be impossible to overestimate the harm this has done to our thinking. The material presented below will help to correct the distortion. Darwin wrote a *second* book, *The Descent of Man*, first published in 1871. **The Descent of Man specifically addresses *human* evolution.** I doubt that the main idea in *Descent* is taught in our schools.

In *Descent*, Darwin says that moral development and cooperation are the keys to *human* evolution and survival. Here are some quotes from *The Descent of Man* (re-published by Penguin Putnam in 2004). The quotes reveal Darwin's theory of *human* evolution:

"...any animal endowed with social instincts would inevitably acquire a **moral sense or conscience**... The social instincts lead an animal to feel a certain **sympathy** to [the other members of] its immediate association [its immediate group]." (p.121, emphasis added) {Note: Adam Smith also recognized the importance of sympathy.}

"...it can hardly be disputed that the social feelings are instinctive or innate in [other] animals; and why should they not be so in man?" (footnote, p.121)

"...after the power of language had been acquired... [the expression of] how each member ought to act for the public good would naturally become the guide to action..." (p.122)

"...these [social] sensations were first developed in order that animals which would profit by living in society should be induced to live together... *the social instinct seems to be developed by natural selection*..." (p.129, emphasis added)

"...sympathy is much strengthened by habit... In however complex a manner this feeling may have originated, as it is one of high importance to all those animals which aid and defend one another, it will have been increased through natural selection; for *those communities which included the greatest number of the most sympathetic members would flourish best*..." (p.130, emphasis added)

"Although man as he now exists has few special instincts... this is no reason why he should not have retained from an extremely remote period some degree of love and sympathy for his fellows..." (p.132)

"*To do good...to love your enemy*, is a height of morality..." (footnote, p.137, emphasis added)

"...**the standard of morality [is] the general good or welfare of the community**..." (p.145, emphasis added)

"As man advances in civilization, and small tribes are united into larger communities... reason would tell each individual that he ought to extend his social instincts and sympathies to all members of the same nation... This point being reached, there is only an artificial barrier to prevent his sympathies extending to all nations and races... *The idea of humanity* seems to arise from our sympathies becoming more tender and more widely diffused, until they are extended to *all sentient beings*." (p.147, emphasis added)

"**The moral sense...the social instincts...naturally lead to the golden rule, 'As you would that [others] should do to you, do to them likewise,' and this lies at the foundation of morality.**" (p.151, emphasis added)

"**...the moral qualities... love and the distinct emotion of sympathy... As they are highly beneficial to the species, have in all probability been acquired through natural selection.**" (p.680, emphasis added)

Thank you, Charles Darwin. I'm sorry your work has been misrepresented.

Darwin's theory of *human* evolution doesn't sound at all like Social Darwinism. But it is Preamble-friendly. **The Descent of Man provides a <u>natural foundation</u> for the general welfare**, and it says that natural selection prescribes a *humane and moral view* of life in society and human evolution—as opposed to the brutality mentality that is commonly attributed to *The Origin of Species*.

The moral qualities—love and sympathy, and treating others the way we want to be treated—are the keys to human evolution and survival. This is how we adapt to other human beings, "all sentient beings," and the earth itself, *which makes survival possible.* **Moral evolution is the form of *adaptation* that makes us "fit" to survive.** Did you learn this about Darwin in school? I didn't.

The Idea of the State of Nature

The idea of the state of nature shows how our minds work. This idea says that everything (for example, trees, rocks, and people) has its own *inherent* nature—things are what they *naturally* are, and they *always* "work" according to their inherent nature.

Our minds *automatically* use this way of thinking about the world, nature, people, society, and life in general. For the purpose of seeing how this very broad idea affects our thinking, we can say that it is the idea that things (for example, people and their way of life) *cannot* be other than what they *naturally* are.

We *depend* on our ideas of what things are and how they work. But our ideas are not necessarily true. For example, for centuries it was generally believed that the sun circles around the earth. **(One of the goals of science is to establish clear, reliable, valid, and *testable* ideas of what things are and how they work.)**

There are two types of ideas of the state of nature: pre-evolution, and evolutionary.

The *pre-evolution type* says that things are as they appear to be, and they won't change. Old sayings that illustrate this type of thinking are, "The leopard can't change its spots," and, "You can't fight city hall." Another example of the pre-evolution type is Thomas Hobbes' view of human nature, presented above:

Hobbes said that, in the state of nature, all people are born free and equal, but we have "a restless desire for power, that ceases only in death." In Hobbes' view of the state of *human* nature, freedom, equality, and the desire for power are human beings' natural characteristics—and *nothing* can change our human nature.

Other examples of the pre-evolutionary type are the idea that some people are born "bad" and others are born "good"; and, some "kinds" of people are "Makers" and others are "Takers." Another example: in the Middle Ages it was thought that "life is a wearisome journey on our way to heaven"—and that's just the way it is, and always will be. This way of thinking says, "There's nothing new under the sun."

Of course, Charles Darwin's work is a good illustration of the *evolutionary type* of the idea of the state of nature. He said that species survive by adapting to their environments, and species change over time due to these adaptations. **This view says that <u>adaptation</u> is our inherent nature that cannot change**.

One interpretation of Darwin's work is the notion of "survival of the fittest"—life is a constant, competitive struggle for survival. The Winners live at the expense of the Losers, and that's just the way nature is, and nothing can change that.

But as we saw from Darwin's theory of *human evolution*, humans and other sentient beings have sympathy. **Human survival depends on our moral and mental evolution—the development of our sympathy, our "social feelings."**

As noted above, in contrast to the medieval view of life, the Renaissance view was that human beings "are capable of wondrous things." The evolutionary perspective on the Renaissance view is that **we are *capable* of moral and intellectual *development, and other "wondrous things,"* because *this capability is built into our human nature*.**

We are capable of thinking, and cultivating our social feelings, to make life better, in order to survive. We can and *must* achieve the wondrous things we are capable of, so that we can survive and *thrive*. This idea of the state of human nature says that our survival depends on our moral and mental "thrival."

***Darwin's view of human evolution says that human beings can consciously direct our evolution. if we refuse to thrive mentally and morally*, Natural Selection *will work against our survival*.**

Darwin's concept of our *human state of nature* brings us to *the idea of progress*.

The Idea of Progress

Because it is grounded in a pessimistic view of human nature and human possibilities, classical conservatism is not optimistic about making the world a better place. (Ball and Dagger, PIDI, pp.92-93) This view says that we *probably* are already living as close as we can get to *the best of all possible worlds*, because, human nature being what it is, efforts to improve society are likely to "backfire" and make things worse, not better. In other words, classical conservatism believes that ***progress would probably tear the delicate social fabric.***

Further, the classical conservative *mentality* may be reluctant to embrace the idea of progress because that would mean changing current circumstances, to welcome the marginalized members of a society—and *that* would mean that society *cannot, and should not,* be controlled by <u>*any*</u> custom, authority, tradition, prejudice, or power *that does not value all members of society equally.*

But in contrast to the notion that progress is probably not possible—because life is just a series of ups and downs, good times and bad; and, in spite of our best intentions, anything we try to do to improve things will probably backfire in *unintended negative consequences*; and, therefore we shouldn't try to change things too much—**there is the notion that progress is possible.**

Life can get better. "Life is worth living fully." "Human beings are *capable* of wondrous things."

The idea of progress says that our best days *can* lie ahead of us because *we can* make the world a better place: "... the conception of progress is to be *contrasted* with the view that the Golden Age was in the past... The secular idea of progress began to gain prominence in the 1700s...and came to characterize Western societies. The shock of 20th century warfare has weakened the belief which, however, still continues." (Reese, "Progress", emphasis added)

Darwin's view of human evolution supports the idea of *moral progress*.

The *intent* expressed in The Preamble is *to make the nation better than it was in 1787*. That means making progress. The Preamble *does not say*, "We the people should just keep things as they are now so that we don't make things worse."

<u>Preamble</u> progress means that we *always* strive to make our democratic union "more perfect," achieve justice for all, achieve public safety and tranquility, find humane and effective ways to defend our nation (more on this in Part Two), promote the general well-being, and promote civil liberty for all.

WHAT'S GOOD ABOUT OUR INHERITED IDEOLOGIES
Classical Liberalism: John Stuart Mill said that freedom promotes Man as a progressive being, and that freedom is necessary for personal development. Liberalism says that each individual is born free and equal, with the potential to enjoy life, and that we have the right to pursue happiness. {I believe that, as individuals, each one of us is *naturally* sovereign. (Emerick, 2010, pp.36-38, 82-83)}

THE MINIMUM DIFFERENCE between liberalism and the medieval way of life is that liberalism frees us from the medieval system's *smothering* restraints and constraints on our individuality. It favors equal rights, and an equal opportunity to enjoy life (as the nobles do) with some surplus and leisure, and even own property. THE MAXIMUM DIFFERENCE is "...*to secure the blessings of liberty.*" No two individuals are exactly alike. Every person has something to offer. We *can* have a positive view of our individual potential and possibilities. *Being human has intrinsic value.* (Ullmann, p.109, pp.140-151; Painter, pp.1-15, p.259; Morris, pp.1-19; Barth, pp.14-15; Russell, p.95.)

Classical liberalism says that we *can* develop and express our individual *human* being: we *can* develop our self; we *can* learn about everything; we *can* believe in our worth and dignity; we *can* exercise our right to self-determination; and we *can* pursue our personal goals. Each person *can become* prepared and able to take responsibility for his or her own life. (By the way, it's interesting to see how the right to self-determination has become more important in professional codes of ethics over time.)

Classical liberalism carries an essential truth: we are sovereign individuals. Recognition of the *intrinsic* worth and dignity of the individual, and the right to self-determination, are essential to human well-being.

But classical liberalism's gift to us becomes a curse when it turns into Anti-Government Individualism in all of its forms—when we believe that we are *nothing but* individuals, and that even *democratic* government (including The Preamble) smothers individuals' liberty.

Anti-Government Individualism works against human well-being because it ignores the value of living in the social body. It fails to grasp Hobbes' and Locke's point about individuals *choosing* to use our democratic political authority—our social contract—to make life better.

FINDING SOLID GROUND IN POLITICS AND THE ECONOMY

The Preamble promotes the blessings of liberty, but rejects Anti-Government Individualism—it rejects Libertarianism, Libertarian Anarchism, Objectivism, and "pure" Capitalism.

Classical Conservatism says that we are NOT just individuals who just happen to live on the same planet. Society *is* a body. Individuals are connected to each other like parts of the physical body. The well-being of each part depends on the well-being of the other parts, and the well-being of the whole depends on the well-being of each part. The body may be healthy or unhealthy, thriving or dying, but it *is* a body. If you doubt this, do some research on the French Revolution. When France was going bankrupt in the late 1700s (partly because France financed our War of Independence from its rival, England), King Louis XVI was not able to persuade the nobles (who didn't want to pay taxes) to help in the crisis, and the commoners suffered. King Louis XVI and Queen Marie Antoinette, and many others, were publicly executed by the commoners in Paris, and many nobles fled the country. (McNeill, p.446 and pp.513-530; Roberts, pp.326-328).

The ways we affect one another within the social body can be either rational or irrational, moral or immoral (morality is about how we treat each other). We can democratically choose common goals and use facts to help us achieve our goals, or we can have a dog-eat-dog-kill-or-be-killed-free-for-all in which some parts of the body take too much of the "blood" that is necessary for the well-being of the whole body. This strategy may succeed for a while, but eventually the entire body becomes sick because the undernourished parts can't live and function as the whole body needs them to. (Roberts, p.326)

The Social Darwinist dog-eat-dog-kill-or-be-killed way of life, in which it is a virtue to be a social, political, and economic "killer," is cancer in the social body. The cancer feeds on the body until it eventually destroys itself by destroying its own food supply.

Darwin said that human survival is enhanced by living in groups. There is a great deal of evidence to support the idea that, regardless of its politics, *the social body is essential for human survival* (Erdal and Whiten, pp.139-150). {I think the evolutionary purpose of society is the survival and well-being of *all* of its members. (Emerick, 2010, pp. 61, 63)}

The idea that society is a body is inherent in The Preamble. Thinking *about* the social body as a *state* goes back to Plato (428-348 B.C.E). A state is a social body under one government. According to Plato, the virtue of the state is *justice expressed in law*. (Reese, "Plato")

Conservatism's MINIMUM DIFFERENCE from the medieval system is that, *if it chooses to*, the democratic social body *can stand up* to political, military, economic, and religious bullies, *and be self-governing*. THE MAXIMUM DIFFERENCE is that **the individual members of the social body can <u>choose</u> to be a sovereign, democratic state.** (*Sovereign state* means that there is no greater power within the social body. The democratic social body *controls itself* through its sovereign state. No other authority or power has the *legal right* to control it.) As a democratic sovereign state, the individuals in society *require themselves to pool their resources* to shape their common life, according to their democratically-established goals (in our case, The Preamble).

The Preamble-directed democratic political process can be our social body's development into healthy "adulthood." We can learn how to use our government to do "all the good we can, in every way we can." (John Wesley) In other words, by engaging in the Preamble-directed democratic political process, we can become rational, moral, self-directing and self-governing adults.

When we are able to recognize that we live in a social body, the value of SOVEREIGN CENTRAL DEMOCRATIC AUTHORITY becomes obvious: When we exercise our freedom to *choose* to be individuals living in democratic social union, we are able to develop the mind and heart of the whole social body, *and* of the individuals who are members of that body.

Classical conservatism carries an essential truth: it emphasizes our union in a social body. The democratic governance of the sovereign state for the well-being of our social body, and the individuals who live in it, is essential to human well-being.

But classical conservatism's gift to us becomes a curse when it turns into Reactionary Neo-Noble Conservatism—when we believe that our tribal group is the "true" social body, and that *some* people are really not equal members of "our" social body.

Reactionary Neo-Noble Conservatism works against human well-being because it ignores the value of Hobbes' and Locke's point about *all* individuals' *natural* freedom and equality, with the *natural right to choose* their own path in life, and live as equal members of the social body.

The Preamble promotes a "more perfect union" and "the general welfare," but rejects Reactionary Neo-Noble Conservatism, "pure" Socialism, and Communism.

THE PREAMBLE WAY OF LIFE is very different from the medieval way of life. THE MINIMUM DIFFERENCE from the medieval way is that The Preamble rejects *un-democratic* sovereign power and the negative view of human possibilities. THE MAXIMUM DIFFERENCE is that The Preamble *demands* the use of *democratic* sovereign power, through law and government (the Constitution is "the law of the land"), to enforce and develop our social contract in the U.S. by achieving our Preamble goals for ourselves and the next generations.

In contrast to the medieval way of life, the people of The United States declared and demanded that *our* government should protect and promote the social *and* individual pursuit of happiness.

The Oxford philosopher Thomas Hill Green (1836-1882) said that *poverty, illness, prejudice, and ignorance are obstacles to individuals' freedom.* He also said that *government authority and resources must establish institutions and policies to remove these obstacles*, so that everyone can live fully and freely. (Ball and Dagger, PIDI, p.77, emphasis added) Further, Green said that individuals are not subordinate to the state—rather, through their government, individuals "provide the conditions for individual development." This is the function of the state. (Reese, "Green, Thomas Hill")

Here we have the idea that social institutions, including government, should nurture individuals, and individuals should nurture the social institutions that nurture them. *"One for all, and all for one."*

HUMAN BEINGS ARE INDIVIDUALS WHO LIVE IN GROUPS. Our self-governance must be based on that fact. The Preamble says that *individuals' well-being is the key to social well-being, and that social well-being is the key to individuals' well-being.*

WHY THE PREAMBLE MATTERS

"Although the preamble is not a source of power for any *department* of the federal government, the Supreme Court has referred to it as *evidence of the origin, scope, and purpose of the Constitution.*" (emphasis added)

(caselaw.lp.findlaw.com/data/constitution/preamble/) {See Marbury v. Madison (1803), Justice Story's Commentaries (1833), Jacobson v. Massachusetts (1905), United States v. Butler (1936), Steward Machine Co. v. Davis (1937), and Helvering v. Davis (1937)}

FINDING SOLID GROUND IN POLITICS AND THE ECONOMY

The Preamble's connection to The Constitution is evident in Article I, Section 8, in which *we specifically give ourselves the right to tax ourselves* to provide for defense and the general welfare. The connection is also evident in the Bill of Rights and the other amendments which address liberty, justice, and the general welfare.

Consider these words by Mortimer Adler (1902-2001), who was Professor of the Philosophy of Law at the University of Chicago, and William Gorman, Fellow at the Center for the Study of Democratic Institutions in Santa Barbara:

"The Declaration of Independence states the ultimate objective to be achieved by a just government. The Preamble states objectives that serve as means to that ultimate objective; for without the elements of the shared common good specified in the Preamble, the individual persons who compose the community cannot effectively engage in the pursuit of happiness... The reason for their association in a political community is to secure for themselves these common goods, indispensable to their pursuit of happiness." (Adler and Gorman, p.81)

"The six objectives assigned to government by the Preamble ...are like parts of an organic whole, not a mere collection of items... [for example,] no unity without justice; no domestic tranquility without justice;...or no justice without liberty...and so on. Given the interrelations of the six objectives, grave errors of emphasis are conceivable and even likely to occur. For example, an inordinate devotion to tranquility...might be a threat to justice;...an inordinate devotion to the common defense... might subvert justice and liberty." (Adler and Gorman, pp.81-82)

"The political life of the nation should be assessed by the way in which we have implemented the six purposes in the Preamble... the history of the nation should be examined for mistakes of policy in trying to achieve one or another of these objectives at the expense of others." (Adler and Gorman, p.82)

The Preamble is the social, political, and economic philosophy of The United States. It is the <u>only</u> philosophy that should be used to interpret the Constitution, because it is the only philosophy that has been <u>formally and officially endorsed</u> *by the people* of The United States.

THE PREAMBLE PHILOSOPHY IS GOAL-ORIENTED. IT IS NOT PARTY OR BANKRUPT IDEOLOGY-ORIENTED. The Preamble's statement of a <u>set</u> of humane and civil goals of equal importance integrates the best insights of liberalism *and* conservatism. It is balanced, comprehensive, and unifying. We should be very proud of it.

Every generation inherits the task of *maintaining and promoting all of the goals set forth in The Preamble*—fully, equally, and simultaneously. The general Welfare cannot be sacrificed on the altar of the Blessings of Liberty, and the Blessings of Liberty cannot be sacrificed on the altar of the general Welfare. We are on solid ground when we fully accept *all* of the goals of our government.

And we must recognize that, whether we like it or not, *all* members of the social body *really are* members of the social body. **The Preamble does not exclude anyone.**

The fact that some people have to struggle for their rights, or an equal opportunity, to fully and freely enjoy the Blessings of Liberty, shows that *we have not understood and upheld our established American philosophy.*

In the United States, *we already have equal civil rights* (for example, the right to marry, the right to vote, and the right to equal justice). The *denial* of anyone's rights without due process of *constitutional* law violates our nation's purpose.

In a *truly* free society, what <u>legal right</u> does anyone have to deny to others the blessings of liberty that they want for themselves? The question is not whether some people

should be _given_ equal civil and human rights. *The real question is, what right does anyone have to <u>deny to others</u> the rights they already have?*

THE U.S. ECONOMY
FACTS, FICTIONS, AND THE WAY FORWARD

What I have learned about the economy confirms the genius of The Preamble.

The information below is based on a Church & Community presentation I made on June 15, 2013, in Brooklyn, N.Y., titled "The U.S. Economy: What Happened?"

Economics has been called "the dismal science." The economy seems to be infinitely complex (see Kuznets, and Deaton, in the Resources). Yet nothing is more important for determining the quality of life, and equality of opportunity, for all of us. The economy is directly related to the quality of our democracy, and ALL of our social institutions, including the family, education, law, justice, health care, government, public safety, not-for-profits, and religious institutions.

(I have often wondered why religious institutions are alarmed by decreasing income, yet we have not addressed our members' stagnant wages over the past 40 years.)

Economic policies affect our environment—for example, how we regulate food and energy production, and the environment.

Politics and economics are two sides of the same coin. They are both about real world power, potential, and opportunity—human well-being. Adam Smith used the term "political economy."

"A capsule history of the economy and economic policy during the twentieth century... breaks down into three parts. The first [third], from 1896 to 1932, was an unstable period in which economic policy leaned strongly toward laissez-faire. It ended with...the collapse of the economic and financial system in the winter of 1933... The second third began with the inauguration of Franklin Delano Roosevelt on March 3, 1933. It lasted until January 1969... [This] period was characterized by successful government efforts to control cyclical instability; support resource creation; and correct flaws in labor, product and finance markets... [During this period] the United States experienced not only a great growth in economic output but also a society in which income became more evenly distributed than...ever before. The final third...began with the 1969 inauguration of Richard Nixon—and is still ongoing. In terms of performance, it is somewhat like the first third... we observe both that the amplitude of the business cycle is increasing and that incomes are...more unequally distributed... Furthermore, financial 'crises,' which were [almost] absent during the second third, have returned with a vengeance." (see Minsky, in Whalen, p.xii, emphasis added)

Facts

THE GREAT DEPRESSION marked the U.S. economy in the 1930s. When President Franklin Delano Roosevelt (FDR) took office in 1933, the unemployment rate was 24.9%. Between 1929 and 1933, the entire economy shrank by 39% (measured as GDP- Gross Domestic Product).

THE NEW DEAL was the name given to the policies and legislation FDR employed to deal with The Great Depression. It included increasing the Federal debt to increase Federal spending, in order to increase employment and demand, to get the economy moving. Private enterprise was unable to make the economy work because the self-adjusting Invisible Hand didn't work. It seems that private capital doesn't like to take much risk, so government spending was necessary. I believe this is Keynesian economic theory. (See Dr. Tracy Mott's comments, below.)

FINDING SOLID GROUND IN POLITICS AND THE ECONOMY

THE NEW DEAL WORKED. Between 1933 and 1937, the GDP rose 60%, "...the most rapid peacetime growth in American history." (Lind, p.287) During this time, unemployment decreased by 42.5%—from 24.9% down to 14.3%. **(Note: the unemployment rate was actually lower than 14.3% because those who were employed in the public works programs were counted as being unemployed!)**

In 1938, under pressure from Congress, FDR chose to fulfill a campaign promise he had made: to balance the Federal budget. The 1938 reduction in Federal spending, and the requirement on banks to recapitalize, (which led to excessive recapitalization - private conversation with my friend Dr. Tracy Mott), coincided with a 32.6% increase in unemployment, and a 2.4% decrease in GDP. The reduction in Federal spending *reduced demand* in the economy.

The resumption of Federal spending in 1939 coincided with a *decrease* in unemployment of almost 2% in one year, and a 3.5% *increase* in the GDP.

During the NEW DEAL years, taxes on the wealthy were high in comparison to today's rates. In 1936, the capital gains rate was 39%, and the marginal tax rate on income over $2million was 78%. In 1938 the capital gains rate was reduced to 30%.

During WWII (World War Two, 1941-1945), the capital gains tax rate averaged 25%, and the marginal tax rate on income over $2million (about $14million in today's dollars) averaged 85.6%.

Federal debt grew from 45% of GDP at the beginning of WWII, to 120% of GDP at the end of WWII.

The average wartime unemployment rate was 3.9%, and the GDP rose almost 85%.

After WWII, Federal spending continued with the GI Bill **(the benefit program serving *eight million* veterans, which many**

in Congress opposed, charging that it was socialism!), the Marshall Plan (which rebuilt Europe and Asia), the first Federally-subsidized public housing (which created jobs, and decent housing for the working poor), and the Eisenhower Interstate Highway System (which increased commerce 700%).

My friend Dr. Hugh Kelly has pointed out the importance of "The 24 Hour City" as an urban economic form of creative critical mass, or what Acemoglu and Robinson call "centralization" (Acemoglu and Robinson, pp.241-244). Dr. Kelly notes that the GI Bill and the Federal Highway System were key factors in the development of the 24 Hour City, and the post-war U.S. economy in general. (Kelly, pp.40-43)

The GI Bill was part of the foundation of the 1946-1971 economy. It provided for no money down, federally-guaranteed mortgage loans (the GI Bill gave birth to the "modern" suburbs – see Mettler, pp.103-104), a stipend to live on and start a family, and paid tuition to go to school. This benefit made it possible for millions of ordinary people, who wouldn't have been able to afford it on their own, to go to college and professional schools, or trade schools. The GI Bill created a generation of professionals and trades-people, who in turn created more demand in the economy for more goods and services due to their higher incomes (the multiplier effect). The barber who cut my hair when I was a boy went to Barber School on the GI Bill, and he had a nice little house for his family to live in.

From 1946 through 1971, the capital gains tax averaged 25.8%, and the marginal tax on income over $200,000 (about $1.4million in today's dollars) averaged 80%. And during this time, the Federal debt *dropped* from 120% of GDP to only 37% of GDP, and GDP *grew* an average of 4% per year.

FINDING SOLID GROUND IN POLITICS AND THE ECONOMY

Below is my summary of economic indicators:

	1946-1971	1972-2012
Federal debt as % of GDP:	***DECREASED* 69%** (from 120% to 37%)	***INCREASED* 175%** (from 37% to 102%)

www.whitehouse.gov/omb/budget/historicals (Table 7.1)

Average annual Federal budget deficit: 1.8%   14%
www.presidency.ucsb.edu/data/budget.php

Average annual unemployment rate: 4.6%   6.4%
www.bls.gov/data or www.infoplease.com "unemployment rates for previous years"

Number of Federal budget surpluses: 8   4
www.presidency.ucsb.edu./data/budget.php

Average number of people on the Federal payroll: 5.8 million   4.7 million
NOTE: comprehensive data collection started in 1962
www.opm.gov/feddata/HistoricalTables/TotalGovernmentSince1962.asp

Average annual GDP growth rate (adjusted for inflation): 4%   2.8%
www.multpl.com/us-real-gdp-growth-rate/table/by-year

Average annual inflation rate:	3.4%	4.3%
www.multpl.com/inflation/table		
Average marginal tax rate on highest incomes:	80%	44%
www.taxpolicycenter.org		
Average capital gains tax rate:	25.8%	18.9%
www.taxpolicycenter.org		
Average annual corporate tax revenue as % of GDP:	4%	1.9%
www.taxpolicycenter.org		
Average annual rate of per capita GDP growth:	2.46%	1.74%
www.multpl.com/us-real-gdp-per-capita/table/by-year		

<u>Broad Data on Income Trends</u>

Average annual income of the **Top 20%** of households as a percentage of the average annual income of the **Middle 20%** of households:	**152%**	**211%**
	(1967-1971)	(1972-2013)

Census Bureau: Current Population Survey, Annual Social and Economic Supplements. **This means that the average income gap between the TOP 20% and the MIDDLE 20% was 152% from 1967 to 1971. Since 1971 the average gap is 211%—a 39%** *increase* **in the income gap between these two groups.**

Average annual income of the **Middle 20%** of households as a percentage of the average annual income of the **Bottom 20%** of households: 335%   323%
                                    (1967-1971)   (1972-2013)

Census Bureau: Current Population Survey, Annual Social and Economic Supplements. **This means that the average income gap between the MIDDLE 20% and the BOTTOM 20% was 335% from 1967 to 1971. Since 1971 the average gap is 323%—a 3.6%** *decrease* **in the income gap between these two groups.**

Average annual income of the **Top 5%** of households as a percentage of the average annual income of the **Bottom 20%** of households: 1,558%   2,195%
                                    (1967-1971)   (1972-2013)

Census Bureau: Current Population Survey, Annual Social and Economic Supplements. **This means that the average income gap between the TOP 5% and the BOTTOM 20% was 1,558% from 1967 to 1971. Since 1971 the average gap is 2,195%—a 41%** *increase* **in the very large gap between these groups.**

The facts show that the U.S. economy was better from 1946 to 1971 than it has been since 1972, and **with much less income inequality.** *(Too much income inequality weakens the whole economy because it reduces consumer demand for products and services, which means fewer jobs and lower pay.* There is more on income inequality below.)

QUESTION: WHICH ECONOMY WOULD YOU RATHER LIVE IN, AND PASS ON TO THE NEXT GENERATIONS?

The economy is an infinitely complex system of exchange of goods and services that is affected by every transaction that has an exchange value, and many other factors, too. (see Kuznets, and Deaton, in the Resources) It is therefore difficult, if not impossible, to prove economic causation beyond a reasonable doubt. This means that, for the average person, *the patterns of correlation of economic indicators, and the policies in place at a given time,* are the base-line economic facts available for us to use when we make economic policy decisions. It would be foolish to ignore patterns of correlation of economic indicators and economic policies.

What are economic policies? Some examples of economic policy are: fiscal policy (government spending and revenue); monetary policy (interest rates and the money supply); and labor policy (labor law).

Corporate policy is also crucial to the economy. In the stronger economy between WWII and the early 1980s, big corporations governed themselves according to the *stakeholder* policy. They saw their workers, the community, their shareholders, and the government as having a "stake" in corporate policy and behavior. In the weaker economy since the early 1980s, big corporations see themselves as answerable only to the short-term interest of their owners, their *shareholders.* (see Gomory and Sylla, 2013, for the history of post-war corporate policy).

Corporate taxation and subsidies are also economic policies.

The regulation of financial businesses is also an economic policy. For example, following the Wall Street crash of 1929, the Glass-Steagall Act of 1933 was enacted to prevent future finance business disasters. But, beginning with President Clinton in the 1990s, Glass-Steagall has been dismantled or diluted. This contributed to the Wall Street crash of 2008, and The Great Recession that followed.

Certainly, many things have happened in the past 70 years that have had an impact on the economy. I think **the single most important _policy factor_ is the Federal tax code:**

-Under **President Nixon** in 1972, the capital gains tax was cut in half—while the "official" tax _rate_ on capital gains increased slightly "on paper," the tax code made 50% of capital gains tax exempt!

-Under **President Carter**, the capital gains tax _rate_ was cut and the 50% exemption remained.

-Under **President Reagan**, up until 1987, the capital gains _rate_ was cut even further, the exemption was increased to 60%, and the marginal tax rate on the highest incomes was also cut. **Federal debt soared by almost 43%**—rising from 35% of GDP at the end of 1981, to 50% of GDP by the end of 1986.

Starting in 1972, **manipulation of the federal tax code became the primary _policy_ means _to redistribute wealth_ FROM the lower and middle income taxpayers TO the wealthy taxpayers.**

This use of the tax code to redistribute wealth from lower and middle income taxpayers to the higher income taxpayers, along with the suppression of wages (see Broad Data on Income Trends, above), has a name: "_trickle-down economics._" (See Fiction #5, below).

It is not a random coincidence that, *beginning* in the 1970s, trickle-down economics' suppression of wages roughly coincides with the flood of cheaper goods made outside the U.S., the widespread use of the credit card, the use of the home equity loan to take that cruise, buy the new car, or try to put the kids through college, and the reverse mortgage. (Many workers have lost their pensions due to "vulture capitalism." The reverse mortgage helped cushion the blow.)

<u>Fictions</u>

1. IF YOU RAISE TAXES ON THE HIGH INCOME JOB CREATORS YOU KILL JOBS. *NOT TRUE!* The fact is that *higher* taxes on the wealthy have coincided with *lower* unemployment.

2. WE HAVE TO BALANCE THE FEDERAL BUDGET TO CREATE JOBS AND GROW THE ECONOMY. *NOT TRUE!* The fact is that since 1921, we have had two balanced budgets—in 1938 and 1960. Federal spending was cut 8.2% in the "austerity" budget of 1938. This budget cut coincided with a 2.4% *drop* in GDP, and a 32.6% *increase* in unemployment. In 1960, Federal spending was cut 4.8%. The GDP growth rate *dropped* from 4.5% to 0.8%, and *unemployment did not go down.*

3. FEDERAL SPENDING CAUSES FEDERAL DEBT. WE HAVE TO REDUCE FEDERAL SPENDING TO REDUCE FEDERAL DEBT. *NOT TRUE!* The fact is that **higher levels of Federal spending have not coincided with increased Federal debt**, and lower levels of Federal spending have not coincided with decreased Federal debt. **Lower tax rates on the wealthy have coincided with increasing Federal debt.** Federal spending creates demand in the economy, but <u>***INSUFFICIENT FEDERAL REVENUE CORRELATES WITH HIGHER FEDERAL DEBT!***</u>

4. PRIVATE ENTERPRISE IS ALWAYS ABLE TO DO EVERYTHING BETTER, CHEAPER, AND FASTER. *NOT TRUE!*

FINDING SOLID GROUND IN POLITICS AND THE ECONOMY

There are *many* examples of the fact that private enterprise is NOT always able to do everything better, cheaper, and faster. Healthcare is a good example. (see Stiglitz, pp.172-186) And don't forget the catastrophic oil spills.

Another example is long-term care for the frail elderly and the disabled. I have personal experience and knowledge of for-profits and not-for-profits operating medical adult day care and residential care facilities. Low quality care costs less than high quality care. We must remember that *for-profit operators exist to make a profit.* The way they make a profit is usually to minimize their staff expense.

According to a study of nursing home care (*New York State Nursing Homes: Sponsorship as a Defining Factor in Outcomes,* LeadingAge, 2012), **not-for-profits receive higher marks for quality care than the for-profits.** Not-for-profits usually have more direct-care staff than the for-profits. This means that not-for-profits give better care (and create more local jobs) than the for-profits.

But it seems to me that the payment system, and the threats to Medicaid, are putting pressure on the not-for-profits to reduce direct-care staff, so that the for-profit *lower* quality of care will become "the industry standard."

Do we really want to nickel-and-dime our frail elderly and disabled, to save some tax dollars? Do we really want to help the for-profits, which may legally make political "donations," make a profit on public dollars? Shouldn't we just pay what it costs to treat the nursing home residents as well as we would like to be treated? How do we want these facilities to be operating when we get there? And when our children get there? *We will get what we are willing to pay for.*

5. TRICKLE-DOWN ECONOMICS WORKS. *NOT TRUE!* In 1974, CEO pay was 35x (times) higher than the average worker's pay. In 1980, CEO pay was 40x higher than the average worker. In 1995, it was 150x higher, and in 2011 it was 400x higher.

From 1977 to 1989, CEO pay increased 104% while worker pay increased 7%. Since 1990, CEO pay has increased 298% and worker pay has increased 4.3%.

Fact: our economy has had a *declining growth rate* since 1981. From 1951 to 1981, the economy grew at an annual average rate of 3.6%; from 1982 to 2011, the economy grew at an annual average rate of 2.8% (Federal Reserve Bank of St. Louis, cited in Stiglitz, p.298, note 19).

According to Cornell economist Robert Frank, "...when researchers examine the data within individual countries over time, they find a negative correlation between [economic] growth rates and [income] inequality." (Frank, 2011, p.159) **This means that HIGHER INCOME INEQUALITY = LOWER ECONOMIC GROWTH.** Income inequality's negative impact on the global economy is featured in *The Economist* magazine, Oct. 13, 2012, Vol. 405, No. 8806.

"Inequality's apologists argue that giving more money to the top will benefit everyone because it will lead to more growth. This is an idea called trickle-down economics. It has a long pedigree—and has long been discredited... higher inequality has not led to more growth, and most Americans have actually seen their incomes sink or stagnate. What America has been experiencing is the opposite of trickle-down economics: the riches accruing to the top come at the expense of those below." (Stiglitz, p.6. See also the Congressional Budget Office Report, *Trends in the Distribution of Household Income*.)

Lower wages = less demand for products and services, and a weaker economy.

FURTHER, I think it's clear that income inequality is aggravating the racial and gender tensions that have always existed in American society. Low wages and poverty are most common among women of all colors, and non-white males. When there is less to go around because the wealthy are taking too much, everyone else fights over what hasn't been taken.

The Way Forward

Most of what I hear that passes for economic common sense—like the Fictions on the previous pages—is really nonsense.

But the Fictions have powerful and persuasive champions in government and the media. In my opinion, **Representative Paul Ryan is probably the best-known representative of economic nonsense in government today**. Some people think he tells "the truth, the whole truth, and nothing but the truth" about the Federal budget and the economy. But his pronouncements about taxing and spending, and especially his pronouncements about Social Security, Medicare, and other public benefits, are based on *nothing* but his own ideological assumptions—which, I believe, have been informed mainly by Ayn Rand's *fiction*. I think Mr. Ryan is probably a firm believer in the Fictions listed above.

When fictions of *any* kind guide policy—that is, when "simple-minded phrases are uttered by the powers that be" (Minsky, p.321)—*the consequences are tragic for all of us.*

It would be foolish to throw away opportunities to protect ourselves and the next generations from unnecessary hardship because someone says we should *protect their ideological economic fiction*. According to Article 1, Section 8 of our Constitution, **IF WE WANT THE BENEFITS OF THE VARIOUS FORMS OF SOCIAL INSURANCE, ALL WE HAVE TO DO IS TO REQUIRE OURSELVES TO PAY FOR THEM!**

What can *we, the people*, do when the economic "information" we hear is often nonsense disguised as common sense? We need a way forward that 1) relies on facts, not fiction that sounds like common sense, and 2) maintains the balance of our core values expressed in The Preamble.

We need a Preamble way to think about the economy.

Neither unregulated free market economies nor centralized command economies work well over time. Neither system is able to provide for the well-being of the entire population. Both systems hurt a lot of people.

My own research shows that the U.S. economy has worked best when it has achieved a productive mix of the government *and* private sectors (a **Mixed Economy**). The government and private sectors NEED each other to function at their best. (See the Resources on Mixed Economy at the end of the book.)

I offer to you **the view of the economy that I use**: I think of the economy as *a circulation system with a heart* that has *four chambers*—**the private and the government sectors, and supply and demand** (see the diagram below). The heart won't work well if any of the chambers is too small to do its job well. And the entire economic system suffers when the circulation system is not nourishing ALL parts of the social body because the heart is not pumping well.

The diagram below *roughly* illustrates the concept of the four chambers of the heart of the economic circulation system:

THE "HEART" OF THE ECONOMY

Private Sector Supply	Government Sector Supply
Private Sector Demand	Government Sector Demand

A healthy economic circulation system is inclusive and infusive of ALL parts of the social body. (Acemoglu and Robinson,

FINDING SOLID GROUND IN POLITICS AND THE ECONOMY

pp.428-431) "A full-employment economy is bound to expand..." (Minsky, p.325)

From the private sector perspective, *government spending is necessary for at least two reasons:* **1)** markets "boom" and "bust." When they bust in a big way, the Invisible Hand does NOT self-adjust. The private sector will not risk its capital to create demand by increasing capacity or raising wages. Dr. Mott has written, "...there can too easily be insufficient spending out of profits to keep the economy growing..." (Mott, p.134); and, **2)** the maintenance and improvement of fixed and human capital—for example, government spending on infrastructure, education, and health care—are good for the economy because spending creates demand, and demand can create shared prosperity *for all*, and shared prosperity creates more demand for more supply. "Tax revenue [Dr. Mott recommends a wealth tax] can be used to finance socially-useful spending *to maintain employment and profitability* if investment spending is too low to do so." (Mott, p.136, emphasis added) **Government spending provides a base-line of demand in the economy.**

Why would anyone in government and media say things about the economy and the Federal budget that have no factual basis?

Ever since the New Deal was enacted, there have been those who want to end it because they want to minimize government. In the 1930s, a group called **The American Liberty League** was formed and funded by wealthy interests. The purpose of the group was to promote the idea that things like Social Security, and government "interference" in the economy, are "un-American." (Rudolph, *The American Liberty League, 1934-1940*)

The group failed because their message didn't get any traction with the public. Most people remembered the Great Depression that was caused by *unregulated* financial markets, and most people had *personally experienced* the moral and economic value of the New Deal.

Note: *Unregulated "free" markets tend to create monopolies*, and monopoly markets are not free markets. Here is a paradox: **markets can be free only when they are regulated** to prevent catastrophic risk, fraud, and to maintain fair competition. "The experience of 1890 [The Sherman Act antitrust law] is ample warning that the people will not submit to a reign of license wherein their economic and social welfare...are at the mercy of a few powerful and designing men." (see "Anti-Trust Laws or Socialism," an address by Abram F. Myers, published in the May, 1927 issue of *Association Management*.)

The spirit and agenda of The American Liberty League live on today, represented in segments of the media and government, still funded by *very* wealthy interests. *The "new" Liberty League tells us that government is bad. And they want to end the New Deal* (especially Social Security), and now Medicare, too. If they are unable to end these public benefits, they want to at least *privatize them for profit*.

Since there is no evidence that private enterprise can always do everything better, cheaper, and faster, I think there are two *real* reasons for the push for privatization:

1) through privatization, more profit can be made on public money; and,

2) for-profits can make political "donations," but not-for-profits and government agencies cannot.

Privatization is a way for some elected officials *and* private enterprise to use *more* public dollars to serve their own political interests and to increase profit.

FINDING SOLID GROUND IN POLITICS AND THE ECONOMY

The New Liberty League wants any and ALL governments that could inhibit their profit-making to be too *small* to be effective. And they still believe that one of the best ways to increase profit is to minimize labor costs. This strategy contradicts Adam Smith.

THE NEW LIBERTY LEAGUE WANTS US TO BELIEVE THAT *THE MAIN PURPOSE* OF THE UNITED STATES IS TO HELP INDIVIDUALS AND BUSINESSES TO GET RICH—AND HELP THOSE WHO ARE ALREADY RICH TO GET RICHER. In one of his State of The Union addresses, President Obama said that people come to America to get rich. I was disappointed to hear him say that. That statement violates The Preamble. Many people come to the United States because they want to be members, and they want their children to be members, of a civil and democratic society. They want to contribute to, and receive, the benefits—like public education and civil liberty—which a democratic government in a civil society *can* provide for its members.

The "government is bad" message can also be heard on Main Street. This seems, at best, short-sighted, because **all of us are the beneficiaries of the government spending that *built* the post-WWII economy, including many of the houses that millions of baby-boomers grew up in and inherited. The GI Bill and other government spending created *inheritable* wealth for millions of Baby-Boomers and their children.**

Here is another Main Street mystery: as I recall, the Tea Party movement began as a protest against the fact that "Wall Street" —the people responsible for the Great Recession—got an immediate and generous bailout from the Federal government (do you remember TARP?), but ordinary people on Main Street did not get an immediate and generous bailout from the Federal government (which was supposed to be worried about them, too). *Their outrage was turned against the Federal government itself*—they turned against the goose that refused to lay the golden egg *for them*. By turning against government itself, Tea-Partiers became agents of the New Liberty League's agenda, which is to make government too small to effectively regulate business, or otherwise inhibit their profits. *The "government is bad" mentality serves the New Liberty League's agenda very well.*

In my opinion, the Tea Party movement and the Occupy movement both wanted government to address the interests of ordinary people—like we did with the GI Bill—not just the wealthy and the corporations.

Maybe the pre-2008 "sub-prime" homebuyers didn't realize that they were being lured into a complicated shell game called *mortgage-backed securities*. When the shell game went bankrupt, so did many on Main Street. (It's interesting to note that Canadian banks didn't crash in The Great Recession, and Canada has a *higher percentage* of homeowners than the U.S. Maybe someone could do some research on that.)

And maybe students couldn't imagine that their loans would definitely be a big money-maker for the schools and some loan vendors—but not necessarily for them. When the Great Recession hit, students were left holding the bag. But the conventional schools (and the FOR-PROFIT SCHOOLS—something new on the education scene) have been able to make money on student loans.

The Tea Party and Occupy movements could have formed a very powerful political alliance, but our bankrupt ideological divisions made that impossible. Maintaining animosity among the various factions of "the commoners" is necessary for the success of the New Liberty League's agenda. (see "The Commercial Society" below)

If we starve the goose that lays the golden eggs (*our* government), the average person will NEVER have a voice in managing our economy. *The economy is ours. It is an expression of our union in action.* The New Deal, the GI Bill, and other "big government" programs have demonstrated their moral, political, and economic value for ordinary people.

The real problem is not government that is too BIG to care about ordinary people. The problem is BAD government—government which responds first and foremost to the interests of those who use their financial power to control elected officials, and the political and economic agenda.

Remember: BAD GOVERNMENTS COME IN ALL SIZES!

<u>The Principles of a Preamble Economy</u>
THE ECONOMY IS THE SOCIAL BODY'S CIRCULATION SYSTEM
A Preamble economy means finding the best mix of individual liberty *and* the general welfare, the private *and* government sectors. All four chambers of our economic heart need to be pumping well, so that vital economic nourishment can reach all parts of the social body. **We all do better when everyone does better.**

Finding the best mix of government and private sector supply and demand should be an ongoing, pragmatic experiment. We *could* find the best mix, because our Preamble values are complementary, NOT contradictory.

We could even learn how to adjust the mix from time to time as needed because "...a program for full employment, price stability, and greater equity is not a simple one-shot affair." (Minsky, p.326)

But it's hard to find the best mix if too many people believe our core values are contradictory—that is, if **too many people believe *government is always the problem*** and private enterprise is the solution, **and too many people believe *private enterprise is always the problem*** and government is the solution. Both of these views are bankrupt and divisive ideologies. They have NO factual basis. Both views sabotage The Preamble and our economic well-being.

We have the best chance of achieving *civil* liberty, and *economic and political* justice for all, if we are able to see that

1) our economy is a circulation system that can and should nourish all parts of the social body and,

2) the economic circulation system is driven by a heart with FOUR chambers and,

3) *we can use our hearts and minds to adjust the system from time to time. "**The primary aim is a humane economy as a first step toward a humane society**.*" (Minsky, p.326, emphasis added)

The circulation system model of the economy—with a heart with four chambers—is consistent with The Preamble because it includes both the private and government sectors. The general welfare *and* liberty are both essential to the economy.

THOUGHTS ON SOME CURRENT CHALLENGES
The Commercial Society

As stated above, in 1705 Mandeville said that "... fraud, luxury, and pride are necessary in what we might call a **business civilization**." (Heilbroner, TWP, p.22, emphasis added)

And in 1755, Cantillon depicted "the workings of a **market-driven society**." (Heilbroner, TWP, p.30, emphasis added)

"...the grandfather of the **modern welfare state** was neither a socialist nor a liberal of any sort. [The Prussian Prime Minister] Otto von Bismarck (1815-1898), the ardently antisocialist 'Iron Chancellor'... believed that the welfare state was the best way to oppose socialism. Through a state-sponsored system of taxing employers and employees to support ill, injured, and unemployed workers, the German state stole the thunder of the socialists..." (Ball and Dagger, PIDI, p.78, emphasis added) {Would it be going too far to suggest that Bismarck had some knowledge of the bloodbath of the French Revolution, less than

FINDING SOLID GROUND IN POLITICS AND THE ECONOMY

a hundred years before, and the uprisings of 1848, and these events may have figured into his thinking?}

In the U.S., the harsh working conditions that resulted from the unregulated practices of the Social Darwinist business leaders, like Rockefeller and Carnegie, *naturally* led to the legal abolition of child labor, the formation of labor unions, and The Sherman Act. Between 1901 and 1913, Presidents Theodore Roosevelt and William H. Taft brought 120 cases against the monopolies under The Sherman Act. To repeat the quotation from Abram Myers: "The experience of 1890 is ample warning that the people will not submit to a reign of license wherein their economic and social welfare...are at the mercy of a few powerful and designing men."

In his Address to the American Society of Newspaper Editors on January 17, 1925, President Calvin Coolidge made this somewhat famous statement: "After all, **the chief business of the American people is business**. They are profoundly concerned with producing, buying, selling, investing and prospering in the world." (emphasis added)

President Coolidge was a strong advocate of *laissez-faire*, but his speech also contained references to "the general welfare." This short speech is worth reading.

His statement that "the chief business of the American people is business" expressed the spirit of The Roaring Twenties, which ended with the Wall Street crash and The Great Depression.

There is evidence of an awareness of The Commercial Society since the 1700s (for example, Mandeville, Cantillon, Marx, Bismarck, the Sherman Act, and the speeches by Coolidge and Myers, cited above). And, given the fact that The American Liberty League actually existed in the 1930s and early '40s, I do not think it's a case of conspiracy theory to suggest that **there**

is a New Liberty League, discussed above, who are still trying to establish a Commercial Society in the U.S.—people like the Koch brothers, the Mercer family, and Rep. Paul Ryan come to mind.

The New Liberty League's vision of The Commercial Society has four goals. <u>The primary goal is to *maximize quarterly profits*</u>. *There are three secondary goals supporting this goal:*

-minimize business costs;
-minimize government;
-minimize effective public opposition to their agenda.

Here are some of the tactics used by The New Liberty League to achieve their goals:

-<u>Low wages for low and middle income workers</u>. This will help *minimize business costs;*

-<u>Easy credit for middle income workers, and the "payday loan" for the working poor</u>. This makes it possible for banks and other credit companies to *maximize profits by <u>charging interest on the workers' purchasing power</u>* which they would have if they had higher wages;

-<u>Low taxes for everyone, but *especially* for the wealthy</u>. This will help *minimize government:* **the FALSE ASSERTION that we have to cut taxes to stimulate economic growth is used to support the FALSE ASSERTION that we have to reduce the size of government—in other words, we have to cut government spending—to reduce the budget deficit and the national debt;**

-<u>Eliminate, or minimize, or at least privatize government spending</u>, especially on entitlements and benefits. This will *minimize government* and *reduce business costs*, by freeing businesses from paying their share of the Social Security payroll tax. *Plus*, privatizing public services, entitlements, and benefits help *maximize profit;*

-Destroy public and private sector labor unions and weaken labor laws. This will *minimize benefit and wage costs;*

-Make the regulation of commerce minimal and ineffective. This will *minimize government*, and help corporations fulfill their self-assigned main purpose, which is to *maximize quarterly profits;* (see Gomory and Sylla, 2013)

-Bribe the kleptocrats who rule non-democratic countries to gain access to their human and natural resources to *reduce business costs and maximize profits* (my thanks to Dr. Dambisa Moyo for the term "kleptocrats" – Moyo, p.53);

-Establish trade agreements which can "legally" overrule national governments*** in countries which cannot be quietly controlled through bribery. This will *maximize profits and minimize government;*

***Under NAFTA's Investment Rights and Protection provisions, as of February, 2014, **U.S. tax payers have already paid $430million in claims of lost revenue.** (See Public Citizen, "TABLE OF FOREIGN INVESTOR-STATE CASES AND CLAIMS UNDER NAFTA AND OTHER U.S. TRADE DEALS, Feb. 14, 2014.) ***FURTHER, as of this writing, TransCanada Corp. is suing the U.S. for $15*billion* of "lost revenue" under NAFTA, because we have not approved the Keystone XL pipeline! (See Bloomberg.com, "TransCanada Fights Keystone Denial With $15 Billion Appeal" by Rebecca Penty, January 6, 2016.)

-Influence law-makers and media to protect and promote their agenda;

–Establish a global Commercial Oligarchy, governed by the deals made among the wealthiest of the wealthy in every nation. The global Commercial Oligarchy will *minimize civil government and democracy in every nation.* The achievement of this Grand Goal will realize all four goals of The Commercial Society.

Oligarchs control a nation's wealth, and they try to control, or spin, information. Commercial oligarchies, and countries that are becoming commercial oligarchies, have existed for a long time. U.S. foreign policy has been creating and sustaining oppressive commercial oligarchies around the world for a long time. (See Mowbray, and Kleveman, in the Resources.)

Putin's Russia is a commercial oligarchy. Putin and the other Russian oligarchs control the government and information, and they make deals with the wealthy in other countries. Those who expose or oppose them are brutally silenced. Ordinary people (the commoners) have to get by the best they can.

It is not unreasonable to assume that the Grand Goal of The Commercial Society strategy would be to *effectively* privatize government itself. This minimal government would be the security service, to protect commercial activity in "the homeland" and abroad, and eliminate civil restraints on commercial activity. Does this sound like any of the ideologies discussed above?

Consider this *thought experiment:* Let's assume for a moment that everyone agrees that we should think of the United States as a business—The United States of America, Inc. Does the following sound like a good business plan for The U.S.A., Inc.?

-A workforce that can only afford to buy *less* of the products and services that are for sale?

-Outdated and crumbling infrastructure?

-A workforce that is in poor health and poorly educated?

-A workforce that is not as productive as it could be because we *avoid* using the talents of some workers because of their gender, skin color, ethnicity, native language, religion, or gender-orientation?

-An environment with severe storms, droughts, floods, wildfires, and a rising sea level? (Maybe now is a good time to get in on the ground floor of the **New Coastline** real estate market. Can you guess where it will be? Remember, *location is everything*.)

BUT, *even if we see ourselves as a commercial society, we still have to invest in the general welfare of our business!* Good human resources policy says we should develop and use everyone's talents, even people from groups we look down on, in order to *maximize profits*. And it makes sense to have a healthy, stable environment with good infrastructure, because this will give us greater control of our markets and production operations, and *reduce catastrophic expenses*. And it doesn't make sense to make our labor force sick from the ways we produce energy, food, and other commodities.

A good business plan for The U.S.A., Inc. would have to include the goals of The Preamble. If it doesn't, then either the highest hopes of the Libertarian Anarchists, or the worst fears of Otto von Bismarck, will come to pass. Neither of those outcomes would be good for business.

In The Commercial Society, material wealth is the highest human value. Money determines the importance of everything, and decides everything. *People, the earth, and animals are just factors of commerce.* Money is the commercial society's religion, and *the wealthiest of the wealthy are the commercial society's monarchs and aristocrats*. Those who **preach, teach, and legislate** the commercial society are its **clergy, philosophers, and clerks.**

But there is no evidence that the people of The United States intended to establish a commercial society. The word *commerce* does not appear in The Preamble.

The Commercial Society is a reactionary idea. It is a regression to the medieval social, political, and economic systems of feudalism and mercantilism.

If we don't learn from history, history _naturally_ repeats itself—we have to go through all the suffering and conflict again, to reach the level where we stopped making progress, and started to go backwards.

I don't want to live in a Commercial Society. I want to live in a <u>humane civil society</u> in which I can exercise my freedom and social responsibilities, and in a <u>civil state</u> that strives to fulfill The Preamble.

Which kind of society do you want to live in, and pass along to the next generations?

Citizens United

We have laws against foreign governments, businesses, and other foreign interests influencing U.S. elections. But is it illegal for government officials to receive donations, favors, and gifts *indirectly* from foreign entities? I DON'T KNOW THE ANSWER TO THIS QUESTION. DO YOU?

If a U.S. corporation has *any* investments, operations, or facilities outside the U.S., it should be *illegal* for them to even *try* to influence our elections and officials in any way.

And **"dark money"** from undisclosed sources (WHICH IS NOW LEGAL!) must be made illegal—we should know if government officials are taking money, gifts, bribes, or any other favors, help, or benefits from *any* entity, foreign or domestic, that **secretly** may be using our government to further their own interests.

Corporate Taxation

The economic indicator data show that **corporate taxes were a larger share of government revenue** in the stronger economy of 1946 to '71 than it has been since 1972, and **with less income inequality**. This would suggest that higher corporate taxes are not the *cause* of lower wages and greater income inequality. It seems more likely that **the shareholder corporate** *philosophy* causes lower wages and greater income inequality. (see Gomory and Sylla, 2013)

But in an August 14, 2016 article in *The Wall Street Journal* titled "The Cure for Wage Stagnation", Kevin A. Hassett and Aparna Mathur say that **higher corporate taxes = lower wages, and lower corporate taxes = higher wages**. "Our empirical analysis, which used data we gathered on international tax rates and manufacturing wages in 72 countries over 22 years, confirmed that the corporate tax is for the most part paid by workers."

If that is true, I think we should eliminate taxes on corporations' profits.

Federal income tax exempt status *should* **substantially limit corporations' political influence, because income tax exempt corporations (like not-for-profits) cannot make political donations.** (Should we ask corporations if they want to be exempt from paying Federal income tax?) Plus, the elimination of the corporate income tax *could* make more funds available for the employees and shareholders. But even small business owners should pay income taxes on the business revenue they *use for themselves.*

Federal, state, and local governments could make up for lost revenue by taxing individuals and families, using *the same tax rates* **on capital gains and marginal income** *that worked well from 1946-1971*, when our economy was better. Then, the average capital gains tax rate was **25.8%**; the average tax rate on the amount of wage and salary ("earned") income over about $1.4million (in today's dollars) was **82.2%**; and the average tax rate on "unearned" income (from rent, for example) was **83.7%** on amounts over about $1.4million (in today's dollars).

Adam Smith said that *those who enjoy the most prosperity should pay more than their "fair share" of the public expense.* (Smith, Bk.5, Ch.2, Pt.2) This principle should apply *especially* to taxes businesses pay to local and state governments for the police, fire, schools, and other public services and amenities that strengthen communities and benefit businesses.

The state and local race to the bottom of the tax scale is a very bad idea. It increases company profits, executive salaries, and stockholders' capital gains, but it hurts everyone else.

I have heard spokespersons for property owners say that a reduction in property taxes would help create affordable housing (presumably, the tax savings would be passed along to tenants). **I doubt that very much.** I think the lower taxes would probably result in higher profits for the owners, and less public services and institutions.

It should be a felony for individuals, families, and businesses to evade paying taxes by hiding money offshore. States that collude in this practice are co-conspirators in tax evasion.

Global Trade

My friend Dr. Ralph Gomory, and Dr. William J. Baumol have written on global trade as follows: "It does not require special training to see that foreign competition can put some domestic jobs in danger, or that once-vibrant home-grown industries sometimes succumb to foreign competitors... International trade sometimes leads to the contraction or even loss of some industries, even significant ones... *there are in fact inherent conflicts in international trade.*" (Gomory and Baumol, GT, p.3-4, emphasis added)

And, "...what is the effect of the activities of a multinational corporation on its home country? Suppose that one of the advanced nation's leading companies decides to build manufacturing capacity in a foreign country... If that new capacity takes the form of a production facility, its establishment may send both knowledge and capital abroad ... This overseas investment decision may then prove to be very good for that multinational firm. But ...the question is: Is the decision good for its own country? ... It is important to realize that... the interests of a company and of its home country...can diverge sharply... if a nation loses its share of world industries... national income and the nation's wage-earners are apt to be the ultimate victims." (Gomory and Baumol, GT, pp.71-72, emphasis added)

Given the reality of global trade as stated above, consider this: Certainly, trade has always existed, and can be beneficial to people in rich and poor nations. It's good for *everyone* to be *able* to have prosperity, education, and health care. But the resources generated through trade that should be used to provide these social benefits are often stolen by the bullies and kleptocrats of poor *and* rich countries.

I have the impression that most people think globalization and trade is either all good, or all bad. This is probably because trade agreements have been structured by the traders, to benefit themselves. But in and of itself, global trade is neither all good nor all bad. It is beneficial *and* harmful. It must be structured and regulated to maximize its benefits and minimize its harms to *the people of a nation,* not just the wealthy and corporations.

Of course I could be wrong about this because this idea may disagree with Gomory and Baumol's findings, but maybe a multi-level economic "tier" trade system would work better than what we have now. Rich tier countries could trade with middle tier countries, and middle tier countries could trade with poor tier countries. But the companies in rich tier countries should be prohibited from purchasing the cheapest labor in the world.

Maybe a policy like this could help shield people who live in poor countries that are ruled by kleptocrats—who probably benefit the most from global trade with their countries—from exploitive labor practices and environmental degradation. And it might slow down the rate of job loss in rich countries, allowing for *more gradual change in their work force.*

The Power of Individuals in the Economy

If we want to see who is most responsible for what has gone wrong with our economy, we have to look in the mirror.

Unfortunately, *we the people* have *ignored* Adam Smith's advice. We have failed to pay *suspicious attention* to what we are told by elected officials and experts—maybe because we have been mesmerized by our beloved and bankrupt ideologies.

And we have to be aware of two major issues: corporations' practice of increasing profit by using the *cheapest labor* in other countries, and *creative destruction*.

The Cheapest Labor: As individuals, we have three ways to influence economic policy: our vote, our voice, and our patterns of consumption. If we don't use our three forms of influence, *for example, if we always go for the lowest prices* (maybe because we haven't had a raise in years, and the credit cards are maxed-out), *sooner or later we have to expect low wages and lost jobs.* We need to realize that the cheapest (and probably the most exploited) labor in the world will always give us a lower price and hurt jobs in the U.S.

We should know the consequences when we make our consumer choices.

I remember the International Ladies' Garment Workers Union TV ad decades ago: "Look for the union label." They were trying to save their jobs. American consumers put them out of work. In my opinion, all nations would benefit if workforces everywhere were unionized. My own experience growing up tells me that unions bring some prosperity to ordinary people. **Even though labor unions can be just as selfish, corrupt, and short-sighted as business owners can be,** *labor unions are just as essential to the American Dream as businesses are.*

As I see it, this is the inherent conflict between businesses' short-term and long-term interests: the less they pay to their workforce, the more short-term profit they make; BUT,

in order to make profit in the long run, they need customers with purchasing power.

Henry Ford paid higher wages because he knew that *consumers need enough purchasing power to buy his cars.* **Businesses can't operate and grow without customers with purchasing power.** This means that, *even as we continue to lose jobs to automation due to the relentless drive to increase short-term profits,* <u>products must have purchasers</u>!

Businesses need to get purchasing power into the hands of consumers. If they don't, our whole economy weakens. When businesses pay the lowest possible wages, they work against their own long-term self-interest. The smart thing for any business to do to protect their long-term interest would be to pay the highest possible wages, as Adam Smith said. Like government spending, **WAGES ARE A BASE-LINE OF DEMAND FOR PRODUCTS AND SERVICES.** *Higher wages are good for business because wages are an investment in the whole economy.*

But we should realize that the main purpose of corporations' use of the cheapest labor is NOT to supply cheaper products to the U.S. consumer, or to help the poor people of the "host" country. The main purpose is to maximize short-term profits.

<u>Creative Destruction</u> has always been a necessary part of economic development. It's about finding better ways to do things. And it *always* destroys jobs in old industries, and creates jobs in new industries.

A good example of creative destruction is the whale oil industry. Can you imagine if we had not advanced beyond using whale oil to light our buildings and streets? We would be sitting in the dark, because we would have brutally killed all the whales on earth a long time ago.

"When the [whaling] industry peaked in 1847, nearly 700 whaling ships operated on the oceans of the world. Whaling was the fifth largest industry in the United States, employing 70,000 people, and harvesting nearly 8,000 whales a year ... Whales that remained near the coast were soon decimated... Whalers began undertaking longer voyages into the South Atlantic and Pacific..." (Lind, pp.76-78)

Incidentally, the story of the whaling ship *Essex* is very interesting. On November 20, 1820, the *Essex* encountered a whale that fought back. "The enraged creature rammed the ship and crushed its bow, causing it to sink. The captain and surviving crew in lifeboats traveled thousands of miles across the open water for three months, surviving by cannibalizing the dead... The story of the *Essex* and a legend about a whale called Mocha Dick, that haunted the waters around Mocha Island near Chile... inspired a young whaler named Herman Melville...to write his masterpiece, *Moby Dick*." (Lind, p.76)

"...on August 28, 1859, oil was struck in Titusville, Pennsylvania... Kerosene lamps soon replaced whale oil... [and after that]...the development of electricity ended the age of kerosene lamps..." (Lind, p.161) And now, non-toxic and perpetual energy sources are beginning to replace finite, dirty, and dangerous fuels.

We *always* need to find *better and more humane* ways to do things. For example, for a lot of reasons, we need to stop using fossil fuels YESTERDAY. This means we should be investing much more on research and development of non-toxic energy sources that are *not* based on finite and dirty commodities, like coal, oil, and gas, or dangerous fuels, like nuclear. When I visit back home, I am glad to see windmills on some of the mountains.

In the past, government funding of research and development has been essential to finding better ways to do things. And this is the case today. Further, government funding should be used to prepare adults who lose their jobs due to creative destruction to participate in the new industries, as Adam Smith said. (See the Resources for information on the historical role of government spending in research and development.)

But creative destruction is NOT the same as using the cheapest labor in the world. Creative destruction is NOT about creating more profit on conventional products by exploiting the cheapest labor in the world in unsafe and inhumane conditions.

The general public's strategy must be to use our suspicious attention, and our votes, voices, and patterns of consumption, to establish and maintain *moral and effective* policy principles. Gomory and Baumol emphasize Adam Smith's insight: "…we should not forget…a very tangible matter: the wages that a country can pay to its working men and women." (Gomory and Baumol, GT, p.72)

The Economy and The Environment

Regardless of how wealth is created, **the economy's purpose is to serve human well-being.** (Erdal and Whiten, pp.141-144) We can't serve human well-being if we are destroying the earth's ability to supply our food, air, and water.

On January 3, 2017, BBC World Service (radio) reported on studies showing that natural methane gas (which is produced by the animals in our food industry, and by "fracking") is worse for our environment than the carbon dioxide produced by fossil fuels. I recommend the documentary film *Cowspiracy* on this subject.

THE PREAMBLE WAY FORWARD

FIRST STEP: <u>Realize</u> that all of The Preamble goals are necessary and interdependent, and that the ideological and party preferences that favor only one or two of the goals violate *the general will of the people* of the United States.

<u>Reject</u> ALL of the current ideologies and political and economic labels, including party labels, because there is NO EVIDENCE to support ANY of them apart from the others. As prescriptions for how we should govern ourselves, they are all bankrupt now—they can't help us anymore.

In his Farewell Address to the nation, published on September 19, 1796, George Washington gave us this advice: "...you should properly estimate the immense value of your national union to your *collective and individual happiness* ... associations...become potent engines, by which cunning, ambitious, and unprincipled men will be enabled to subvert the power of the people and to *usurp for themselves the reins of government... Let me now warn you in the most solemn manner against...the spirit of party generally...* The alternate domination of one faction over another, sharpened by the spirit of revenge... is itself a frightful despotism... *The disorders and miseries that result gradually incline men to seek security and repose in the absolute power of an individual...* [who] *turns this disposition to the purposes of his own elevation... the mischiefs of the spirit of party are sufficient to make it the interest and duty of a wise people to discourage and restrain it.*" (emphasis added)

George Washington was right about this.

<u>*Check*</u> our thinking for slogans and assumptions. Be on guard against the powerful ideological "residue" in our thinking (it's hard to break bad mental habits). This part is especially tricky because, I suspect, our "knee-jerk" preferences have a strong psychological dimension—this could explain the strong feelings, like anger, that we have when we engage in "discussions" with people who *won't* agree with us. A friend of mine once said, "If two people disagree about something, it doesn't mean that either one of them is right."

When we have beliefs and opinions that are accompanied by very strong feelings, but no set of facts to support them, this means that our beliefs are serving a psychological need that is dominating our thinking. For example, maybe some of the anti-government individualists have a *psychological need* to live "outside" society, <u>even if the society is democratic</u>. And maybe some of the reactionary neo-noble conservatives, socialists, and communists have a *psychological need* to live within the security and control of "their" society, <u>even if the society is not democratic</u>. In the long run, neither pattern promotes the survival and well-being of individuals or society.

If we have psychological motives for our social, political, and economic beliefs, then *we need to at least be aware of that*, so we can try to reduce the psychological influences on our thinking and actions. For example, in my opinion, when elected officials like **Senator Mitch McConnell** declare that their primary goal is to defeat another official in every possible way, this probably means that **their psychological motives and personal biases are more important to them than their oath of office.**

Good self-governance requires clear thinking that is based on our Preamble goals and facts—not on our psychological needs and personal biases.

SECOND STEP: <u>*Work*</u> **for political consensus on *goals*.** What can we, the people, do in our generation to further the goals of The Preamble for ourselves, and the next generations? <u>*We must trade in our beloved ideologies for goals*</u>. Do we want *consistently* lower unemployment and higher wages? A government that works well for all of us? Healthcare for everyone (our economy's "human capital")? Equal rights and opportunity for everyone? Free, or at least actually affordable, quality higher education (something like the GI Bill) for everyone? Do we want a healthy environment that isn't over-heating? Do we want laws and policies that respect other sentient beings? Do we want Social Security, Medicare, Medicaid, food stamps, and affordable housing?

We have the right and duty to democratically set our goals, and we have the right and duty to use our government to serve our interests, and the interests of the next generations.

Most people I know already agree on some goals:

-to revive The American Dream for ordinary people now, and for the next generations. They want some financial surplus and leisure (some *real* prosperity), and the possibility of owning their own home. (According to the March, 2017 *AARP Bulletin*, Millennials earn an average *20% less* than their parents did at their age, adjusted for inflation-see "Are The Kids Alright?", p.6); -an equal opportunity for everyone to get a good public school education;

-good healthcare for everyone;

-financial security when we reach retirement (not being *forced* to work until the day we die just to cover basic expenses); -the help we need when we suffer "the slings and arrows of outrageous fortune";

-no more Wall Street "emergencies";

-food and product safety;

-respect and caring for other sentient beings;

-better enforcement of more responsible gun laws; and,

-a healthy environment that isn't over-heating.

But our agreements are often ignored or distorted by our government officials. My personal experience with elected officials tells me that many of them respond best to the desires of people who can help them or hurt them the most. I think they should spend more time working for us, holding public meetings and hearings on our goals, laws, and policies, and less time raising money for themselves. **Sometimes I feel that some (many? most?) of our elected officials are the best that money can buy.**

Outside the office of EVERY elected official, and every policy maker, should be posted the list of ALL of their financial and "perq" donors, including speaking and "consulting" fees and honoraria, with a value over $500 in a calendar year: what was received (cash, favors, and/or perqs), from whom, and when and how much was received, beginning with their FIRST elected office or government job. Failure to disclose this information completely and "voluntarily" to the public should be a felony.

Talk to the people you know, and see what they want for themselves and for the young people growing up now. Do you want any of the things they want? *Why not work together for the things we want?*

THIRD STEP: A Preamble Ideology - Democratic Pragmatism

-use *our* government to establish *our* Preamble-based goals democratically;

-use facts—NOT BANKRUPT AND DIVISIVE IDEOLOGIES—to develop policies to achieve our goals;

-use facts to judge how well policies achieve goals; and,

-make fact-based revisions to goals and policies as needed.

The work of the American philosopher John Dewey (1859-1952) can help us with this. "Dewey presents freedom as the ability to make intelligent choices, and act on them ... planning [can be] an application of intelligence [which] can provide the conditions for freedom." (see Reese, "Dewey, John")

If we want Social Security, Medicare, Medicaid, and food stamps, but some experts and elected officials are telling us that we can't afford such things, we should **make them prove their case with a comprehensive presentation of facts, not slogans and assumptions that they** *present as if they were facts.*

And we should *carefully examine their assumptions.* **For example, are they assuming that we should never ever raise taxes to pay for what we want?** How many elected officials receive financial and political support from special interests in exchange for agreeing to never increase taxes, no matter how bad things get? (Look up the name *Grover Norquist*.)

Tax cuts are not a substitute for wage increases for the middle class and working poor. Tax cuts and trickle-down economics are a dead-end for people who aren't already wealthy.

Strong institutions and effective democratic government make civil and humane society possible. Insufficient tax revenue weakens institutions and government. We must pay for what we want to pass on to the next generations. This means that **WE HAVE TO CHANGE OUR NEGATIVE ATTITUDES TOWARD PAYING TAXES!** The idea that lowering taxes is always good for the economy is false, and it is a real danger to our democracy and civil society. When we pay what it costs to protect and promote our Preamble goals, *we are actually helping ourselves* and the next generations.

We the people can build a better economy if we use our democratic political process to establish our goals, tax ourselves to pay for what WE want, and use facts to evaluate our policies. The tax rates we used from 1946-1971 worked very well.

Conclusion

The inherited ideologies and familiar parties that divide us are no longer useful. They have brought us to a dead-end. But we can change the way we think about our politics and economy. We can follow George Washington's advice and govern ourselves without party labels and bankrupt, divisive ideologies. Labels and ideologies only distort the task at hand, waste time and money, make a few people rich(er), and divide us by causing unnecessary and unproductive conflicts that feed on anger, fear, and ignorance.

The Preamble is the established American philosophy that brings us together. *Our Preamble binds and benefits all of us.*

The Preamble NEGATES these divisive beliefs:

-the belief that the social order should benefit one group more than others;

-the belief that government is always an obstacle to individuals' liberty; and,

-the belief that private enterprise is always an obstacle to the general welfare.

These divisive beliefs have been forming a *less perfect union* for us and the next generations.

We have to keep our Preamble goals in mind when we talk about issues, and we have to be factual when we talk about policies. This will open our eyes to reality, and will help us become well-informed, rational, moral, self-governing adults.

We have a lot of hard work to do to find the best policies to achieve our goals. And we must realize that the best policies may change from time to time, depending on circumstances.

But a firm commitment to The Preamble, that is grounded in knowledge of our history and informed by facts, will change the way we think and feel about our politics and economy.

Personally, I would like to join what would be, in effect, a Preamble "party." The Preamble party would defend and promote democracy, and civil and humane society. It would not pretend to have the answers to all of our problems right now. But it would create a more respectful, tradition-based frame for responsible discussion and policy-making. (I think George Washington would approve of a Preamble Party.)

Because the Preamble integrates all the themes and forces in our history and current circumstances, the Preamble Party would not be about "win-lose." It would be about building *together* on the solid ground we established in 1789.

The most important question before us is NOT, "Which of our bankrupt and divisive inherited ideologies and political parties should we pass along to future generations?" The most important question is, "How can we, the people, use The Preamble to help us form the way of life that we want to pass forward to the next generations?"

The questions listed at the beginning of this book are essential. The best approach to answering our questions can be found in *The Preamble perspective*—not in our bankrupt and divisive ideologies and parties. The Preamble moves us forward, beyond the dead-end. The Preamble moves us toward "the best of all possible <u>nations</u>."

I would be proud to pass The Preamble Way forward to the next generations. How about you?

PART TWO
FINDING SOLID GROUND IN JESUS' TEACHING

PART TWO IS the story of how I came to believe that Christianity should be grounded in Jesus' teaching, and to see the consistency between Jesus' teaching and The Preamble. Part Two also discusses traditional Christianity's turning away from Jesus' teaching. Part Two has four sections: The Background, Jesus' Teaching, What Traditional Christianity Says, and Jesus' Teaching and The Preamble.

The background presents the concrete experience that led me to focus on the importance of Jesus' teaching.

The Background

I was appointed Pastor of Bay Ridge United Methodist Church (BRUMC) in Brooklyn, N.Y., in February, 2005. The congregation occupied a big, beautiful, century-old green stone building that stood on the corner of 4th and Ovington Avenues. This was the congregation's fourth location in what is now Brooklyn. The congregation was incorporated in 1830, in the town of New Utrecht, before Brooklyn existed. The congregation existed at least 15 years before it incorporated.

Like many congregations, BRUMC's active membership had dwindled over the years, and the Sunday offerings were insufficient to meet expenses. So, like many congregations, BRUMC housed a not-for-profit community service program that received public funds. This helped them meet basic expenses, but they would not have been able to afford a new roof.

The building was known in Bay Ridge as The Green Church. It featured a clock tower that overlooked the spacious intersection. The tower was part of the memory of Bay Ridge. Many people said to me, "I know I'm in Bay Ridge when I see the clock tower." The clock's mechanism needed expensive repair.

In the 1990s, a large chunk of stone fell from the tower. Fortunately, no one was struck by the stone. With encouragement from the community, BRUMC launched a drive to raise money to Save The Clock Tower. The drive raised just enough money to conduct a study, which found that the stone was disintegrating, and separating from the brick anchor wall behind it. A further study found that the building's entire exterior was in the same condition.

This was hard for many in the congregation to face, because they had stories of special times there, and memories of weddings, baptisms, and saying good-bye to loved ones.

An expensive net was wrapped around the tower, and a fence was put around the building, to prevent injuries from falling chunks of stone. When the net began to disintegrate, expensive scaffolding was put up to catch falling stone.

The building sat on a large parcel of valuable land, and there was a newer brick education building next to the church. Some community residents thought that some of the land could be sold or leased, and the proceeds would be used to continuously repair the old building.

The congregation talked about whether spending so much money to try to maintain the beautiful old building would be the right thing to do—maybe most of the property could be sold, and a smaller church building could be built on the remaining property. The interest on the unused proceeds could help the congregation keep going indefinitely, even if the offerings were inadequate, and public (government) funds for community-based human service programs were cut, or "phased out."

I wanted to work with a congregation that was willing to consider selling its beloved building, if that's what was necessary to continue as a congregation in ministry. (For many years, the congregation had housed an over-night shelter for homeless women in the education building, which was staffed by volunteers from the congregation and the community. But the congregation had recently received notice that the facility was no longer needed.)

Even before a decision was made, word got out that the congregation was considering demolishing The Green Church, and selling most of the property. Many in the community said they would miss the building, but they understood the situation.

In March of 2005, the congregation voted unanimously to sell most of the property, and build a smaller building on the unsold property. Assemblymember Jim Brennan offered to help the congregation apply for assistance to install solar power.

A few church members who had not attended services for many years, and some members of the community, voiced their opposition to this plan. Contentious public meetings were held. We invited the community to come and take a piece of the stone, to see for themselves that the stone was disintegrating—it could be removed with your bare hands. (See the *New York Times* article, NEIGHBORHOOD REPORT: BAY RIDGE; "This Flock Wants The Walls to Tumble Down," by Peter Ritter, October 5, 2005.)

No one took up the offer. Instead, they mounted a campaign to "Save The Green Church." Their campaign included an effort to have the building landmarked. The Landmarks Commission denied their request. (See the *New York Daily News* article, "Reverend: Let Us Tear Down Our Church," by Matthew Lysiak, January 24, 2008.)

And there was vicious opposition from a small, but politically influential, group in the community. I say this group's opposition was vicious because it included slanderous attacks on me, the trustees, and the entire congregation. Some well-known columnists in the local press joined in the slander.

I was involved in community conflicts when I was a Pastor

on the Upper West Side in Manhattan in the late 1970s and early '80s. But I had never seen anything like the behavior of this group in Bay Ridge. They held protest demonstrations in front of the church and my home, complete with drums, and nasty signs and slogans.

In a way, I could sympathize with them. They were acting out their feelings of loss of familiar surroundings. They couldn't understand that church buildings are different from the old schoolhouse of their childhood. They couldn't see the larger perspective on The Church's unique value in a community because, as you will see below, The Church has not understood and represented its true mission in the world.

More Save The Green Church meetings were held by "the community" to consider *what they should do about The Green Church* (see the front page article, "NABE [i.e., 'neighborhood']: 'SAVE OUR CHURCH'", *Bay Ridge Courier*, February 21, 2008). All of this after the congregation had taken a full page ad in one of the local papers to declare that the sale of the property, and a new, smaller building, would enable the congregation to remain active in ministry in Bay Ridge indefinitely, and do more of the work that Jesus calls The Church to do—that is, to help those who need help (The Gospel of Matthew, Ch.25, vs.31-45).

The intensity of these events raised questions for me: Where did people get the idea that the community has the right to decide how a religious institution should use its resources? Is it possible they are right—why shouldn't the congregation do everything possible to keep the building going, even if it takes all of the congregation's resources?

These questions led me to think about The Church's purpose—why it exists. Does The Church belong to the community? Is The Church really just a social amenity? Is it just a building where religious services are held? Who has the legal right, and the moral and spiritual authority, to determine The Church's purpose—the community, the congregation, the institutional

FINDING SOLID GROUND IN JESUS' TEACHING

Church? **Does Jesus have any authority to establish The Church's purpose? Would Jesus want us to keep the building going because it is a comforting fixture in the community?**

Should The Church say and do things that are not prescribed in Jesus' teaching?

From my own experience as a life-long church member, I knew that many congregations seem to identify very much with their building. Some members of other local congregations supported the Save The Green Church campaign.

[Here, I want to say "thank you" to the pastors in Bay Ridge who publicly supported BRUMC during this difficult time: Rev. David Rommereim (now retired from The Lutheran Church of The Good Shepherd), Rev. Khader El-Yateem (Salam Arabic Lutheran Church), and Rev. Craig Miller (now retired from Our Saviour's Lutheran Church).]

Above all, I wondered what Jesus would say to all of us.

With the above questions in mind, I decided to study Jesus' teaching in the quotes attributed to him in the four Gospels. (This may sound strange, but *I doubt that seminaries offer courses specifically on Jesus' teaching*.) My method was very simple, and can be used by anyone. I slowly, carefully, and thoughtfully read the four Gospels again, focusing on the quotes attributed to Jesus. Reading his words in this way helped me to not "skip" through passages, assuming that I already knew what they meant because they were familiar to me. **I looked for his recurring words and topics, and for what *he* said is most important.** After that review, I compared his teaching to the subjects The Church emphasizes that are found in the other books of The New Testament (such as sin and salvation), and to The Church's creeds.

The two most important things I discovered *about* Jesus' teaching are: **1) most of his core principles can be embraced by any person of good will, regardless of their religious background (or no religious background at all); and, 2) Jesus' main topic is very different from the topics emphasized in the other New Testament books, The Church's creeds, and the generally-accepted understandings of Christianity.**

NOTE: I MUST TELL YOU THAT I AM NOT A PROFESSIONAL BIBLE SCHOLAR OR THEOLOGIAN. It would be impossible for me to write a respectable scholarly paper on the material below. Some scholars may find much to object to in the following material. I am sharing with you what I discovered while trying to be faithful to Jesus under the circumstances "in the field," with the knowledge available to me. I take some comfort in knowing that no one knows everything about anything.

ANOTHER NOTE: I DO NOT ASK ANYONE TO TAKE MY WORD FOR ANYTHING. I INVITE YOU TO READ AND THINK FOR YOURSELF. For your convenience, Eleanor Ruth Geryk, a member of BRUMC, has compiled the quotes attributed to Jesus in the Gospels. See "The Jesus Quotes in The Four Gospels" at the end of Part Two.

<u>Jesus' Teaching</u>

Context: As is the case with every religion, there is disagreement over the substance and meaning of Christianity.

There are two main views on this subject. One is the institutional view, addressed in the <u>What Traditional Christianity Says</u> section, below. This view says that Christian faith is what The Church says it is—The Church has authority to *define* Christian faith.

The second is the Biblical view, which says that the substance and meaning of Christian faith is found in *The Bible*, and it is therefore possible that the institutional Church's understanding of Christian faith may be mistaken.

And there is a relatively recent variation of the second view which says Christian faith should include Jesus' teaching and actions, but it is not easy to be *historically certain* of what he said and did. Some of the scholars of this view say the four official Gospels in The New Testament, Matthew, Mark, Luke, and John, are copies of recorded verbal memories with layers of material added over time, and copies of those copies. Therefore, the four Gospels may not be trustworthy accounts of Jesus' words and actions. (For more information on this view, search "The Historical Jesus.")

I TAKE THE QUOTES OF JESUS IN THE FOUR GOSPELS AS *GENERAL EVIDENCE* OF WHAT HE SAID. By *general evidence,* I mean to say that I do think it's possible that some of the words in the Jesus quotes may not be his, but may be words the Gospel authors attributed to him because they wanted to present *their* best understanding of the *meaning* of Jesus.

But if some of the words in the quotes may not have been spoken by Jesus, how can we know which words are authentic? How can we establish a trustworthy understanding of Jesus' teaching, especially since Jesus is quoted as saying that some scripture is of greater importance than other scripture? If some scripture passages are more important than others, accuracy and authenticity become even more important—we may not need to struggle with sayings attributed to him that are not likely to be authentic, and may not be as important as other passages.

I THINK THE BEST WAY TO FIND WHAT IS AUTHENTIC IN JESUS' QUOTES IS TO SEE IF WE CAN DISCOVER HIS <u>CORE PRINCIPLES</u>. These principles will give us a vision of the substance of his teaching. This vision can serve as our guide and standard, to help us see the implications of his teaching.

If you carefully read his quotes, while putting aside your learned assumptions about what his words mean, you can see for yourself what he talked about the most, and what he said is most important. This will help you identify Jesus' core principles. When you have identified his core principles, you can judge the meaning and importance of his other quotes for yourself. ***This approach will promote a life-long process of spiritual and moral development, based on Jesus' teaching.***

In my opinion, **five key passages carry Jesus' core principles**:

1. When asked by religious authorities what is the most important scripture, Jesus answers by quoting from The Torah (Deuteronomy 6:5): **Love God with all our mind, heart, soul, and strength.** (Mark 12:30 and Matthew 22:37. In Luke 10:27, this reference is spoken by a teacher of the Law, and is confirmed by Jesus.)

2. In the same scene in these three Gospels, Jesus continues his answer by again quoting from The Torah (Leviticus 19:18): the second most important scripture *is like the first:* **love your neighbor as yourself**.

3. Jesus says **we should treat others as we want to be treated**. (Matthew 7:12, and Luke 6:31)

4. Jesus gives us a new commandment: we should **love one another as he loves us**. (John 13:34 and 15:12)

5. When his disciples ask him how they should pray to God, Jesus includes these words in his brief "model" prayer: **Your kingdom come, your will be done on earth as it is in heaven**. (Matthew 6:10)

Let's briefly look at each of these principles.

LOVE GOD WITH ALL OUR MIND, HEART, SOUL, AND STRENGTH. What does this mean? Is it possible to do this? What if a person doesn't believe in God and/or love?

Surely, there are as many feelings and thoughts on the meaning of "love" and "God" as there are people on the earth. These would involve each person's own thoughts and feelings *about* "God" and "love," including whether God and/or love really exist, based on their own life experience and learning.

We have to be careful about this. Theology matters. *What we believe about "God" and "love" matters.* For example, should we believe in, and love, a "God" who is a judge who thinks cruelty and violence are OK? Or, should we believe in, and love, a "God" who is obsessed with his majesty and power, and who harms those who don't "properly" adore him enough?

I realize that my personal experience and understanding of "God" and "love" are inadequate. My own thoughts and experience do NOT tell me everything I want and need to know about "God" and "love."

I believe Jesus loved God much better than I do. I believe Jesus the human person *did* love God with all his heart, mind, soul, and strength. Therefore, I *choose* to take Jesus as my authority on what it means to love God. For me, *loving God with all our heart, mind, soul, and strength means **loving God as Jesus loved God***. But how can we know what this meant for him? For clues to this, we can read what Jesus said about God. From what he said, I conclude that Jesus believed that God is loving and good. Loving God is good if we believe God is loving and good.

If God is loving and good, then **loving God with all our heart, mind, soul, and strength means loving goodness and love completely.** It may sound odd to say we should "love love." But sometimes we may reject or ignore love because it has brought pain, or it feels like weakness, or seems "childish."

Jesus' love is love without danger, sorrow, anxiety, fear,

dominance, or submission. At the least, it means having *good will toward God*. We *can* love God as Jesus did. *We can start by wanting to love goodness and love.*

This includes loving God's nature within us. (Genesis 1:26, 27) I believe the soul is God's nature within us. ***Our soul's goodness and love is our direct experience of God.***

Learning to love God as Jesus did is a pleasurable and wrenching life-long spiritual practice.

LOVE YOUR NEIGHBOR AS YOURSELF. What does this mean? What if we don't even like our neighbor, or our self? Most of us have mixed feelings about ourselves and others—like and dislike, compassion and indifference, love and sometimes even hate.

In the Luke version of this passage, the teacher of the Law asks Jesus, "Who is my neighbor?" Jesus shows the meaning of this scripture by telling the Parable of the Good Samaritan. (Luke 10:29-37)

Apparently, neighbors are anyone, even people from different groups. And loving the neighbor as one's self means having good will for the neighbor—desiring, and *acting like* we desire, their well-being, even if we don't like them. This principle applies to *all* others—people we don't know, don't care about, don't like, or maybe even hate. Everyone can act like a neighbor, and anyone can be a neighbor.

Learning to care about others as much as we care about ourselves is a pleasurable and wrenching life-long spiritual practice.

TREAT OTHERS AS WE WANT TO BE TREATED. This is an expression of the "love your neighbor" principle, and variations of it are found in some other philosophies and religions. But it may not be a perfect principle. For example, it may not be a good principle for self-destructive people to use in their treatment of others.

But in spite of its imperfections, this principle intends to

<u>validate the best in all of us</u>, by validating empathy and sympathy for *all* sentient beings: if we don't want poverty, sickness, and ignorance in our own life or our children's lives, we should *strive* to eliminate those things in others' lives; and if we don't want to be treated brutally, we shouldn't treat other beings brutally. And in our spiritual imagination, we can also apply this principle to the way we treat the earth.

At the very least, this principle <u>invalidates the worst in us</u>. It means there is no place for hatred, violence, discrimination of any kind, or indifference to the well-being of others, our fellow creatures, or the planet that supplies our food, air, and water.

Learning to live this way is a pleasurable and wrenching lifelong spiritual practice.

LOVE ONE ANOTHER AS JESUS LOVES US. This teaching is unique to Jesus. He tells us that he is our trustworthy example of God's goodness and love. **Jesus' love wants the well-being of Creation, because it is the Creator's love of the Created.**

If we are self-aware enough to have doubts about the "purity" of our love of God and neighbor, or if we are open-minded enough to have doubts about our comfort-zone thinking on *any* topic, we can learn from Jesus.

<u>Jesus' teaching applies to all dimensions of living</u>. What does Jesus' love want and do? This love wants the very best for *all* of creation. This means doing our best to transform the whole world into a good and safe place for everyone. It means changing the things that hurt creation (including people), and creating those things that will help creation (including people). As John Wesley said, we should <u>*do all the good we can, in every way we can*</u>. **Jesus' public opposition to corruption, exploitation, and injustice** (Matthew 21:12-14) **is just as much an expression of goodness and love as his blessing, "Your sins are forgiven, go and sin no more."** (John 8:11)

When Jesus told the teacher of the law that the commandment

to love the neighbor is *like* the commandment to love God, he was telling us that *the way we love and treat each other is the way we love and treat God.* It is *impossible* to love God and hate, or even be indifferent to, anyone. The Creator's love—Jesus' love—applies to *all* of creation. Therefore, this principle also applies to ourselves—**Jesus wants us to *love ourselves as he loves us*.**

Jesus teaches us to trust his example, and to have faith in his teaching. We can *entrust ourselves, our children, and the whole world,* to his teaching. We can put our usual thinking about *everything* on the shelf, and seek first God's Way of Life (the kingdom of God). (Matthew 6:33) This is not easy. We have to be *willing* to allow his teaching to change our hearts and minds, and that is VERY hard to do. But it is not a waste of time: Jesus said, "Seek, and you will find." (Matthew 7:7)

Learning to love as Jesus loves is a pleasurable and wrenching life-long spiritual practice.

GOD'S KINGDOM COME...ON EARTH AS IT IS IN HEAVEN. The interchangeable terms "kingdom of God" and "kingdom of heaven" appear 94 times in Jesus' quotes. And Chapter one, verse three of the Book of Acts (the first New Testament book after the Gospels), says, "For forty days after his death he appeared to them...and talked with them about *the Kingdom of God*." (Today's English Version, emphasis added) But this term appears only 19 times in the other 23 New Testament books, and those passages speak of the kingdom in a different way than Jesus did. Those passages seem to see the kingdom as something that will be established in the "Second Coming."

The Second Coming interpretation of the kingdom of God is common even today. In various settings, I hear some Christians say that sin, sorrow, suffering, and violence are the way of the world. It has always been so, and will continue to be so, until The Messiah comes again—and that's THE TRUTH about life in *this* world. <u>*The Second Coming view of the kingdom of God distorts Jesus' teaching*</u>.

JESUS TALKED ABOUT THE KINGDOM OF GOD/HEAVEN <u>ON EARTH</u> MORE THAN ANY OTHER TOPIC. What did Jesus say about it? How can we understand it? If you comb through Jesus' quotes, you will see that he uses many images to describe it. For example, he says it is like yeast acting in dough; and it is like a pearl of great price—a merchant would sell everything he has in order to possess it.

And in an amazing passage that reminds me of the first creation story in Genesis, which says that we have the image of God within us (Genesis 1:1-2:4), Jesus says **the kingdom of God is already within and among us.** (Luke 17:21) This means we don't have to reach above or beyond ourselves to find it. **Love and goodness *already* live within and among us. The Church's doctrine of original sin was NOT taught by Jesus.**

God is loving and good. Heaven is *all* the times and places—*<u>now and forever</u>*—where God's Way of Life is lived. *Making heaven on earth <u>now</u>* is the vision and purpose that integrate Jesus' moral, spiritual, and theological principles. The purpose of his principles is to show us *how* to make heaven on earth *now*—the *kinds* of thoughts, feelings, motives, and actions that make Heaven on Earth. For example, if hatred, indifference, and brutality are not present in heaven "above" or "hereafter," then such things should not be present here and now.

This is <u>supremely</u> important. Many religions have a notion of heaven, paradise, or nirvana in another world, *after the death of the body*. And some religions have teachings on justice and compassion that would certainly lead to a *better* life on earth. And in Socrates, Plato, and Aristotle, there is the notion that human beings can use our ability to reason to achieve justice.

Jesus is unique NOT because he was a moral and wise teacher. He is unique because he was the world's first *utopian*. He was the first—and perhaps the only—ancient teacher to say specifically that *our* PRIMARY GOAL should be to make Heaven on Earth—*the best of all possible worlds in this life, here and now.* (I hope someone will look into this, and correct me if I'm wrong.)

What does "utopian" mean? If Jesus is utopian, does that mean his teaching is neither attainable nor practical in the *real* world?

"...the concept of utopia at first appears straightforward... a perfect but imaginary place... And yet on closer inspection this term reveals itself to be rather more ambiguous. *Utopia* is, of course, the name Sir Thomas More created for his book of 1516. But More's title combines two Greek neologisms, *<u>ou</u>topia*, meaning no place, and *<u>eu</u>topia*, meaning good place..." (Coverly, p.9; see also Rebhorn, p.xxxiv, emphasis added) ("topia" means place)

Utopia does not exist yet, and it may or may not be a perfect place. <u>But at the very least, it is a good place</u>. I think Jesus' teaching about God's Way of Life says that the world can and should at least be *<u>a good place for everyone</u>*.

In the first creation story, cited above, **The Creator declares that all of creation is good**. The declaration *specifically* includes humankind, our fellow creatures, and the earth itself. HEAVEN ON EARTH comes when we live The Creator's goodness that already lives in us.

Striving to make life "on earth as it is in heaven" is a pleasurable and wrenching life-long spiritual practice.

<u>What Traditional Christianity Says</u>

Traditional Christianity has a long history of maintaining that The Church is the authority on the truth and meaning of

Christian faith. The scriptural authority for this "apostolic faith" is The Gospel of Matthew, Ch.16, vs.18 and 19, where Jesus says to Peter, "...you are Peter ["petros" means "rock" - Peter's other name was Simon], and upon this rock I will build my church... I will give you the keys of the kingdom of heaven; and whatever you bind on earth shall be bound in heaven, and whatever you loose on earth shall be loosed in heaven."

But if you read Peter's first public speeches—the first one was on the day of Pentecost (Acts 2:14-40), and the second one was soon after that (Acts 3:12-26)—you will see that Peter never mentions making the kingdom of God on earth, or *any* of the other principles of Jesus' teaching. Peter says nothing about loving God and neighbor, nothing about treating others as we want to be treated, and nothing about loving as Jesus loves.

Jesus apparently had great confidence in Peter. But **I DO NOT BELIEVE PETER WAS GIVEN AUTHORITY TO CHANGE JESUS' TEACHING.**

Peter focused on who Jesus was, NOT on Jesus' teaching. And the oldest and most generally-accepted creeds we know of, The Nicene Creed and The Apostle's Creed, did not even mention Jesus' teaching. These ancient Creeds can be found in most hymn and worship books. They are quoted below from The United Methodist Hymnal, so you can judge for yourself whether or not they state Jesus' teaching.

The Nicene Creed:
"We believe in one God, the Father, the Almighty, maker of heaven and earth, of all that is, seen and unseen. "We believe in one Lord, Jesus Christ, the only Son of God, eternally begotten of the Father, God from God, Light from Light, true God from true God, begotten, not made, of one Being with the Father; through him all things were made. "For us and our salvation he came down from heaven, was incarnate of the Holy Spirit and the Virgin Mary and became truly human. For our sake he was

crucified under Pontius Pilate; he suffered death and was buried. On the third day he rose again in accordance with the Scriptures; he ascended into heaven and is seated at the right hand of the Father. He will come again in glory to judge the living and the dead, and his kingdom will have no end.

"We believe in the Holy Spirit, the Lord, the giver of life, who proceeds from the Father and the Son, who with the Father and the Son is worshiped and glorified, who has spoken through the prophets.

"We believe in the one holy catholic and apostolic church. We acknowledge one baptism for the forgiveness of sins. We look for the resurrection of the dead, and the life of the world to come. Amen."

<u>The Apostles' Creed:</u>

"I believe in God the Father Almighty, maker of heaven and earth;

"And in Jesus Christ his only Son our Lord; who was conceived by the Holy Spirit, born of the Virgin Mary, suffered under Pontius Pilate, was crucified, dead, and buried; [he descended into hell]; he ascended into heaven, and sitteth at the right hand of God the Father Almighty; from thence he shall come to judge the quick [the living] and the dead.

"I believe in the Holy Spirit, the holy catholic church, the communion of saints, the forgiveness of sins, the resurrection of the body, and the life everlasting. Amen."

I don't find Jesus' teaching in The Church's foundation statements of belief. It seems they were saying what they believed <u>*about*</u> Jesus. But they did NOT say what Jesus said. The result has been that believing in Jesus' principles—or at least *wanting* to believe in his principles—has not been a requirement for membership in The Church.

The Church's creeds *could* have said, "We believe Jesus is

The Christ, whose teaching is the Word of God that saves the world." *But The Church never said that.*

Incredible.

Further, traditional Christianity has doctrines concerning *The Bible* **as a whole,** *but these doctrines do not give superior standing to Jesus' teaching!* **This makes it easy for The Church to preach and practice Old and New Testament scripture that does NOT conform to the letter and spirit of Jesus' principles.** This helps to explain why Jesus' principles have not been a dominant influence in The Church or in the world.

You, the reader, are also evidence of what traditional Christianity says. If you grew up in The Church, or you are currently a Church member, what is your own experience with Christianity? What does your Church teach? Are you <u>explicitly</u> taught Jesus' teaching as the core of Christian faith, or does your Church teach other things?

If you are not a Church member, or if you follow another religion, or no religion at all, what is your impression of what Christianity says and does?

If The Church is the authority on Jesus, but it doesn't follow his teaching, or if we cannot know what he said, we should close our churches and go home. We shouldn't use Jesus' name, and we shouldn't say things about him, to serve our own, or the Apostles', traditions and preferences. This is a subtle but effective betrayal of him.

When The Church does not focus on Jesus' teaching, especially in the buildings built in his name, we betray him. If we don't focus on his teaching, we should at least be honest with him and ourselves, and call ourselves religious clubs—for example,

FINDING SOLID GROUND

the Catholic Club, the Orthodox Club, the Lutheran Club, the Presbyterian Club, the United Methodist Club, the Baptist Club, the Pentecostal Club, etc.

The international efforts toward Church/Christian unity (the ecumenical movement) cannot succeed until The Church grounds itself in Jesus' teaching.

Since Christianity was adopted by the Roman Emperor Constantine about 1,700 years ago, The Church has often condoned, or directly engaged in, all types of brutality and war. I think the twentieth century will be known as the century of *brilliant discoveries and inventions, and mass murder* (the three are not unrelated). In World War I (known as "The Great War"), the nations of "Christendom" slaughtered each other by the millions *for no moral reason*. Did The Church demand, in one loud and continuous voice, in Jesus' name, that the carnage should stop immediately? Did The Church explain to the world *why* Jesus would say to stop the slaughter? The answer is NO. This is one of many examples of traditional Christianity's great distance from Jesus' teaching.

My experience in Bay Ridge taught me that **religious tradition is not Jesus; The Church is not Jesus; the community is not Jesus; and *The Bible* is not Jesus.** What BRUMC and I experienced with the small group in Bay Ridge is one of the results of traditional Christianity's ongoing betrayal of Jesus' teaching. *My experience is that traditional Christianity's "churchianity" generally will focus on <u>anything</u> but Jesus' teaching.*

In the opening pages of this book, I referred to the Pew research which shows that **a lower percentage of U.S. residents, and especially a low percentage of Millennials, identify with traditional Christianity.** And in 2015, only 55% of Millennials said that The Church has a positive impact on society—down from 73% in 2010. Further, **most Millennials don't believe in** *any* form of discrimination, but they do believe in the common good.

Can The Church grow in numbers by following Jesus' principles? I read somewhere that The Church is not declining in numbers, and may actually be growing, in the places in the world where Church-condoned *discrimination* (and sometimes murderous hatred) **and** *superstition* dominate people's attitudes and actions. This means that large numbers attending worship services is NOT proof that a Church is following Jesus. *Lots of things can draw a crowd.*

Whether we are many or few in number, **The Church's purpose is to proclaim and promote God's Way of Life as Jesus taught us, to the whole world—God's love for us, within us, among us, and through us, and to love God and each other as he loves.** This is the good news we have to proclaim.

I see many people, young and older, rejecting prejudice and discrimination, and joining with others at the grassroots to make a more humane society and a better world. They are doing God's will. **They are acting on the goodness and love that live within them. But they may not connect this goodness and love with God, Jesus, or The Church, because The Church has NOT taught Jesus' principles as the authentic core of Christian faith.**

The Church should proclaim what Jesus taught us: THE GOODNESS AND LOVE WE FEEL WITHIN AND AMONG US *IS* GOD'S WAY OF LIFE—THE KINGDOM OF GOD—WITHIN AND AMONG US. The Church should stop validating hatred, cruelty, discrimination, and indifference, because such things betray Jesus' teaching and God's nature within us.

At the very least, churches should provide meeting space to local groups that are striving, in a manner consistent with Jesus' teaching, to make the world a better place.

FINDING SOLID GROUND

[Here, I want to say again that after all the conflict with some in the community, and in spite of the congregation's grief over their loss, BRUMC decided they could serve Jesus better by selling most of the property, and building a smaller, solar-powered building—a new "green" church—that can serve as a platform for ministry and service to our community, city, nation, and world, for the next century, in Jesus' name. As of this writing, construction on the new building has not yet been completed, due to continuing challenges. But thanks to Pastor Rommereim and the Good Shepherd Lutheran Church Council, Good Shepherd Lutheran has been BRUMC's residence during the construction of the new building. THANK YOU!]

Jesus teaches the world that loving God and neighbor, treating others as we want to be treated, and loving as he loved, <u>create</u> heaven on earth, the best of all possible worlds.
JESUS' WAY OF LOVE IS GOD'S WAY OF LIFE.
As The Church enters our third Millennium, we should proclaim Jesus' principles as the solid ground of Christian faith.

Here is some good news for The Church: Jesus tells us that even those who come late to the work are welcome. (Matthew 20:1-7)

The Church's turning away from Jesus' teaching has been tragic for the whole world: for nations, for communities, for families, and especially for children. If the Church had been teaching Jesus' teaching all along, we would be much farther along in our ability to understand and value The Preamble.

<u>Jesus' Teaching and The Preamble</u>
The best of all possible worlds. Maybe not a perfect place, but certainly a good place for *everyone*. The Preamble points us toward *the best of all possible <u>nations</u>*. **"Heaven on earth" and**

"utopia" are similar concepts, and they resonate with "the ***best*** of all ***possible*** nations."

What are the characteristics of a place that we ALL feel proud to pass on to the next generations? What kinds of beliefs, values, ethics, politics, and economics would help us get there? Jesus' teaching and The Preamble agree on some basic points:

HEAVEN ON EARTH would need a more perfect union—a democratic and effective union that the inhabitants would use to make their lives, and the children's lives, better. This would be consistent with Jesus' principles.

HEAVEN ON EARTH would establish equal justice and rights for all. This would show divine love and good will. This would be consistent with Jesus' principles.

HEAVEN ON EARTH would insure domestic tranquility. Violence is not good for anyone. Insuring domestic tranquility would mean teaching non-violence as a way of life, and reaching out to help those who feel that violence is the only effective way they are able to express themselves. This would be consistent with Jesus' principles.

HEAVEN ON EARTH would provide for the common defense. From the perspective of Jesus' principles **this is a tough one, because Jesus does not condone violence.** *HOW CAN WE PROTECT THE GOOD THINGS WE HAVE, FOR OURSELVES AND THE CHILDREN, WITHOUT VIOLATING JESUS' PRINCIPLES?*

Maybe we should try pre-emptive good will as a strategy. We must find ways to make sure that our foreign policies do not create animosity against us because we exploit people in other nations. We have to make sure that we don't support tyrants who get rich by helping us exploit their nation's human and natural resources. (See Mowbray, *Dangerous Diplomacy*, and Kleveman, *The New Great Game*, listed in the Resources.)

When we look at other nations, we shouldn't see dollar signs, or opportunities to demonstrate our "we're-always-the-best-in-every-way-no-matter-what 'American Exceptionalism.'"

We Americans would benefit from more awareness of our nation's actions in other countries, and the consequences of our actions. In many ways, we have been our own worst enemy—we often create the threats to our national security. I think it is customary for U.S. foreign policy to serve commercial interests most of the time, even when those policies cost lives and money. We speculate about this. But our officials are never honest with us about it, even though *we the people* are paying for it with our lives and resources. (Again, see *Dangerous Diplomacy*, and *The New Great Game*.)

We should stop using bullies and kleptocrats in poor countries to do our bidding. We should do as much as we can to strengthen the civil institutions in other countries—the institutions which promote justice, tranquility, the general welfare, and the blessings of liberty. We haven't tried this approach to national security yet. We must try it, to see if it would work better than what we do now.

We don't have to give up our armed forces yet—they are employment and educational opportunities, and they can be of critical help in natural disasters.

But let us be clear: **JESUS DOES NOT TEACH VIOLENCE!** Jesus is *extremely* clear on this. He said, "**Blessed are the peacemakers...**" (Matthew 5:9) **Jesus does NOT teach the "Just War" doctrine!** If and when we engage in international violence, we must never say it's OK with Jesus. We must always look for nonviolent ways to defend ourselves by *preventing* wars. This would be consistent with Jesus' principles.

HEAVEN ON EARTH would promote the general welfare. We would use our resources and institutions to promote everyone's well-being. We would *strive* to end poverty, disease, and ignorance. We would strive to end indifference. We would strive to end all forms of brutality against other sentient beings. We would strive to help every person develop her or his capacity to make intelligent choices, and to act on those choices. We would make sure that all parts of the social body are able to contribute to, and receive, the benefits of the economic circulation system. Everyone should be able to enjoy living in the social body. Everyone can contribute to, and benefit from, the good things the social body has to offer—things like education, health care, justice, public safety, and security in our older age. Again, we all do better when everyone does better. This would be consistent with Jesus' principles.

HEAVEN ON EARTH would secure the blessings of liberty for its inhabitants and their posterity. Again, freedom is the ability to make intelligent choices, and liberty is the ability to act on those choices. When all of the Preamble goals are being pursued equally, in the spirit of Jesus' principles, each individual has the best chance of *enjoying self-development, informed freedom, and humane liberty*. This would be consistent with Jesus' principles.

Jesus' teaching is Preamble-friendly. Jesus' principles apply to all dimensions of living, including our self-governance. The Preamble goals are all essential to our individual and social well-being. Devotion to The Preamble goals—NOT to divisive parties and bankrupt ideologies—resonates with Jesus' principles.

Jesus said, "Seek first the kingdom of God." (Matthew 6:33) This means we should not put *any* ideology *above* his principles. **Political, social, and economic ideology must be consistent with Jesus' principles and The Preamble goals. Preamble-based democracy, and the circulation system model of the economy that nourishes all parts of the social body, are consistent with Jesus' principles.**

Again, we should use facts to make policies to serve those goals and principles, and we should use facts to evaluate how well our policies are working. This approach will lead us past our dead-end divisions in a wholesome way.

In my opinion, about 2,500 years ago the Greek philosopher Socrates (470-399 BCE) raised these questions that we still struggle with today: Can we use morality and reason to govern our life together? Can morality and reason take us beyond the harmful and limiting aspects of our "normal" way of life? Jesus' principles and The Preamble are extremely important to the long and wrenching process of answering **YES!** to those questions.

The best of all possible worlds—a good place for *everyone* to live—is achievable if we live by the best principles and goals in our tradition. Jesus' principles and The Preamble goals can help us become *very* proud of what we create and pass on to the next generations.

As a follower of Jesus, I *choose* to have faith in his principles.
As an American, I *choose* to have faith in The Preamble.

I welcome your comments: findingsolidground@aol.com

THE JESUS QUOTES IN THE FOUR GOSPELS
COMPILED BY
ELEANOR RUTH GERYK

THIS EFFORT BEGAN as a search for a source that presented just the words of Jesus, without analysis or undue editing, to help to understand his teachings. When that search proved fruitless, we decided to produce one ourselves. This document includes ONLY those quotations attributed to Jesus in the Christian Bible.

The purpose of this compilation is to sort out and present all of Jesus' quotes from the Bible in one document, separate from narration or interpretation, and allow the reader to ponder meanings for her/himself. Chapter and verse citations are included, to allow the reader to look into the context of the words, if interested.

The version we have used is the New American Standard Bible (NASB), published by The Lockman Foundation, La Habra, CA (listed in the Part Two Resources). All excerpts are as they appear in the NASB including uses of gender singular and/or plural (for example "Man" refers to all of humankind). NOTE: acting on the idea of "getting back to basics," any sentences or phrases identified in NASB footnotes as not appearing in early manuscripts of each book have been omitted.

A note about format: in order to keep Jesus' statements as straightforward as possible, verse citations are listed only at the end of each quotation; numbers are not specified within the passages. Also, if a partial verse is cited, a,b,c, or d follows the number (as in *verse 17b* in Chapter 1). Most of these partial excerpts simply reflect our leaving out phrases such as "And Jesus said." Please read the quotes and their context in the NASB.

The Gospels in this compilation appear chronologically, in the order in which they were written, according to L. Michael White, *From Jesus to Christianity*. See Resources for details.

Mark, dated 70-75 CE, author unknown. Audience: Greek-speaking Jews in the Jesus Movement. (White, p.233)

CHAPTER 1

"The time is fulfilled, and the kingdom of God is at hand; repent and believe in the gospel." *verse 15*

"Follow Me, and I will make you become fishers of men." *verse 17b*

"Be quiet, and come out of him!" *verse 21b*

"Let us go somewhere else to the towns nearby, so that I may preach there also; for that is what I came for." *verse 38b*

"I am willing; be cleansed." *verse 41b*

"See that you say nothing to anyone; but go, show yourself to the priest and offer for your cleansing what Moses commanded, as a testimony to them." *verse 44b*

CHAPTER 2

"Son, your sins are forgiven." *verse 5b*

"Why are you reasoning about these things in your hearts? Which is easier, to say to the paralytic, 'Your sins are forgiven'; or to say, 'Get up, and pick up your pallet and walk'? But so that you may know that the Son of Man has authority on earth to forgive sins, I say to you, get up, pick up your pallet and go home." *verses 8b-11*

"Follow Me!" *verse 14b*

"It is not those who are healthy who need a physician, but those who are sick; I did not come to call the righteous, but sinners." *verse 17b*

"While the bridegroom is with them, the attendants of the bridegroom cannot fast, can they? So long as they have the bridegroom with them, they cannot fast. But the days will come when the bridegroom is taken away from them, and then they will fast in that day." *verses 19b-20*

"No one sews a patch of unshrunk cloth on an old garment; otherwise the patch pulls away from it, the new from the old, and a worse tear results. No one puts new wine into old wineskins; otherwise the wine will burst the skins, and the wine is lost and the skins as well; but one puts new wine into fresh wineskins." *verses 21-22*

"Have you never read what David did when he was in need and he and his companions became hungry; how he entered the house of God in the time of Abiathar the high priest, and ate the consecrated bread, which is not lawful for anyone to eat except the priests, and he also gave it to those who were with him? The Sabbath was made for man, and not man for the Sabbath. So the Son of Man is Lord even of the Sabbath." *verses 25b-28*

CHAPTER 3

"Get up and come forward!" *verse 3b*

"Is it lawful to do good or to do harm on the Sabbath, to save a life or to kill?" *verse 4b*

"Stretch out your hand." *verse 5b*

"How can Satan cast out Satan? If a kingdom is divided against itself, that kingdom cannot stand. If a house is divided against itself, that house will not be able to stand. If Satan has risen up against himself and is divided, he cannot stand, but he is finished! But no one can enter the strong man's house and plunder his property unless he first binds the strong man, and then he will plunder his house. Truly I say to you, all sins shall be forgiven the sons of men, and whatever blasphemies they utter; but whoever blasphemes against the Holy Spirit never has forgiveness, but is guilty of an eternal sin." *verses 23b-29*

"Who are My mother and My brothers?

"Behold My mother and My brothers! For whoever does the will of God, he is My brother and sister and mother." *verses 33b, 34b-35*

CHAPTER 4

"Listen to this! Behold, the sower went out to sow; as he was sowing, some seed fell beside the road, and the birds came and ate it up. Other seed fell on the rocky ground where it did not have much soil; and immediately it sprang up because it had no depth of soil. And after the sun had risen, it was scorched; and because it had no root, it withered away. Other seed fell among the thorns, and the thorns came up and choked it, and it yielded no crop. Other seeds fell into the good soil, and as they grew up and increased, they yielded a crop and produced thirty, sixty, and a hundredfold." *verses 3-8*

"He who has ears to hear, let him hear." *verse 9b*

"To you has been given the mystery of the kingdom of God, but those who are outside get everything in parables, so that while seeing, they may see and not perceive, and while hearing, they may hear and not understand, otherwise they might return and be forgiven." *verses 11b-12*

"Do you not understand this parable? How will you understand all the parables? The sower sows the word. These are the ones who are beside the road where the word is sown; and when they hear, immediately Satan comes and takes away the word which has been sown in them. In a similar way these are the ones on whom seed was sown on the rocky places, who, when they hear the word, immediately receive it with joy; and they have no firm root in themselves, but are only temporary; then, when affliction or persecution arises because of the word, immediately they fall away. And others are the ones on whom seed was sown among the thorns; these are the ones who have heard the word, but the worries of the world, and the deceitfulness of riches, and the desires for other things enter in and choke the word, and it becomes unfruitful. And those are the ones on whom seed was sown on the good soil; and they hear the word and accept it and bear fruit, thirty, sixty, and a hundredfold." *verses 13b-20*

"A lamp is not brought to be put under a basket, is it, or under a bed? Is it not brought to be put on the lampstand? For nothing is hidden, except to be revealed; nor has anything been secret, but that it would come to light. If anyone has ears to hear, let him hear." *verses 21b-23*

"Take care what you listen to. By your standard of measure it will be measured to you; and more will be given you besides. For whoever has, to him more shall be given; and whoever does not have, even what he has shall be taken away from him." *verses 24-25*

"The kingdom of God is like a man who casts seed upon the soil; and he goes to bed at night and gets up by day, and the seed sprouts and grows—how, he himself does not know. The soil produces crops by itself; first the blade, then the head, then the mature grain in the head. But when the crop permits, he immediately puts in the sickle, because the harvest has come." *verses 26b-29*

"How shall we picture the kingdom of God, or by what parable shall we present it? It is like a mustard seed, which, when sown upon the soil, though it is smaller than all the seeds that are upon the soil, yet when it is sown, it grows up and becomes larger than all the garden plants and forms large branches; so that the birds of the air can nest under its shade." *verses 30b-32*

"Let us go over to the other side." *verse 35b*

"Hush, be still." *verse 39b*

"Why are you afraid? Do you still have no faith?" *verse 40b*

CHAPTER 5

"Come out of the man, you unclean spirit!" *verse 8b*

"What is your name?" *verse 9b*

"Go home to your people and report to them what great things the Lord has done for you, and how He had mercy on you." *verse 19b*

"Who touched My garments?" *verse 30b*

"Daughter, your faith has made you well; go in peace and be healed of your affliction." *verse 34b*

"Do not be afraid any longer, only believe." *verse 36b*

"Why make a commotion and weep? The child has not died, but is asleep." *verse 39b*

"Talitha kum!" ("Little girl, I say to you, get up!"). *verse 41b*

CHAPTER 6

"A prophet is not without honor except in his hometown and among his own relatives and in his own household." *verse 4b*

"Do not put on two tunics." *verse 9c*

"Wherever you enter a house, stay there until you leave town. Any place that does not receive you or listen to you, as you go out from there, shake the dust off the soles of your feet for a testimony against them." *verses 10b-11*

"Come away by yourselves to a secluded place and rest a while." *verse 31b*

"You give them something to eat!" *verse 37b*

"How many loaves do you have? Go look!" *verse 38b*

"Take courage; it is I, do not be afraid." *verse 50c*

CHAPTER 7

"Rightly did Isaiah prophesy of you hypocrites, as it is written: 'This people honors Me with their lips, but their heart is far away from Me. But in vain do they worship Me, teaching as doctrines the precepts of men.' Neglecting the commandment of God, you hold to the tradition of men." *verses 6b-8*

"You are experts at setting aside the commandment of God in order to keep your tradition. For Moses said, 'Honor your father and your mother'; and, 'He who speaks evil of father or mother, is to be put to death'; but you say, 'If a man says to his father or his mother, whatever I have that would help you is Corban (that is to say, given to God),' you no longer permit him to do anything for his father or his mother; thus invalidating the word of God by your tradition which you have handed down; and you do many things such as that." *verses 9b-13*

"Listen to Me, all of you, and understand: there is nothing outside the man which can defile him if it goes into him; but the things which proceed out of the man are what defile the man." *verses 14b-16*

"Are you so lacking in understanding also? Do you not understand that whatever goes into the man from outside cannot defile him, because it does not go into his heart, but into his stomach, and is eliminated?" *verses 18b-19*

"That which proceeds out of the man, that is what defiles the man. For from within, out of the heart of men, proceed the evil thoughts, fornications, thefts, murders, adulteries, deeds of coveting and wickedness, as well as deceit, sensuality, envy, slander, pride and foolishness. All these evil things proceed from within and defile the man." *verses 20b-23*

"Let the children be satisfied first, for it is not good to take the children's bread and throw it to the dogs." verse 27b

"Because of this answer go; the demon has gone out of your daughter." *verse 29b*

"Ephphatha!" ("Be opened!") *verse 34c*

CHAPTER 8

"I feel compassion for the people because they have remained with Me now three days and have nothing to eat. If I send them away hungry to their homes, they will faint on the way; and some of them have come from a great distance." *verses 2-3*

"How many loaves do you have?" *verse 5b*

"Why does this generation seek for a sign? Truly I say to you, no sign will be given to this generation." *verse 12b*

"Watch out! Beware of the leaven of the Pharisees and the leaven of Herod." *verse 15b*

"Why do you discuss the fact that you have no bread? Do you not yet see or understand? Do you have a hardened heart? Having eyes, do you not see? And having ears, do you not hear? And do you not remember, when I broke the five loaves for the five thousand, how many baskets full of broken pieces you picked up? When I broke the seven for the four thousand, how many large baskets full of broken pieces did you pick up? Do you not yet understand?" *verses 17b-21b*

"Do you see anything?" *verse 23c*

"Do not even enter the village." *verse 26b*

"Who do people say that I am?" *verse 27c*

"But who do you say that I am?" *verse 29b*

"Get behind Me, Satan; for you are not setting your mind on God's interests, but man's." *verse 33b*

"If anyone wishes to come after Me, he must deny himself, and take up his cross and follow Me. For whoever wishes to save his life will lose it, but whoever loses his life for My sake and the gospel's will save it. For what does it profit a man to gain the whole world, and forfeit his soul? For what will a man give in exchange for his soul? For whoever is ashamed of Me and My words in this adulterous and sinful generation, the Son of Man will also be ashamed of him when He comes in the glory of His Father with the holy angels." *verses 34b-38*

CHAPTER 9

"Truly I say to you, there are some of those who are standing here who will not taste death until they see the kingdom of God after it has come with power." *verse 1b*

"Elijah does first come and restore all things. And yet how is it written of the Son of Man that He will suffer many things and be treated with contempt? But I say to you that Elijah has indeed come, and they did to him whatever they wished, just as it is written of him." *verses 12b-13*

"What are you discussing with them?" *verse 16b*

"O unbelieving generation, how long shall I be with you? How long shall I put up with you? Bring him to Me!" *verse 19b*

"How long has this been happening to him?" *verse 21b*

"'If You can?' All things are possible to him who believes." *verse 23b*

"You deaf and mute spirit, I command you, come out of him and do not enter him again." *verse 25c*

"This kind cannot come out by anything but prayer." *verse 29b*

"The Son of Man is to be delivered into the hands of men, and they will kill Him; and when He has been killed, He will rise three days later." *verse 31b*

"What were you discussing on the way?" *verse 33c*

"If anyone wants to be first, he shall be last of all and servant of all." *verse 36b*

"Whoever receives one child like this in My name receives Me; and whoever receives Me does not receive Me, but Him who sent Me." *verse 37*

"Do not hinder him, for there is no one who will perform a miracle in My name, and be able soon afterward to speak evil of Me. For he who is not against us is for us. For whoever gives you a cup of water to drink because of your name as followers of Christ, truly I say to you, he will not lose his reward." *verses 39b-41*

"Whoever causes one of these little ones who believe to stumble, it would be better for him if, with a heavy millstone hung around his neck, he had been cast into the sea. If your hand causes you to stumble, cut it off; it is better for you to enter life crippled, than, having your two hands, to go into hell, into the unquenchable fire. If your foot causes you to stumble, cut it off; it is better for you to enter life lame, than, having your two feet, to be cast into hell. If your eye causes you to stumble, throw it out; it is better for you to enter the kingdom of God with one eye, than, having two eyes, to be cast into hell, where their worm does not die, and the fire is not quenched. For everyone will be salted with fire." *verses 42-49*

"Salt is good; but if the salt becomes unsalty, with what will you make it salty *again*? Have salt in yourselves, and be at peace with one another." *verse 50*

CHAPTER 10
"What did Moses command you?" *verse 3b*

"Because of your hardness of heart he wrote you this commandment. But from the beginning of creation, God made them male and female. For this reason a man shall leave his father and mother, and the two shall become one flesh; so they are no longer two, but one flesh. What therefore God has joined together, let no man separate." *verses 5b-9*

"Whoever divorces his wife and marries another woman commits adultery against her; and if she herself divorces her husband and marries another man, she is committing adultery." *verses 11b-12*

"Permit the children to come to Me; do not hinder them; for the kingdom of God belongs to such as these. Truly I say to you, whoever does not receive the kingdom of God like a child will not enter it at all." *verses 14b-15*

"Why do you call Me good? No one is good except God alone. You know the commandments, 'Do not murder, Do not commit adultery, Do not steal, Do not bear false witness, Do not defraud, Honor your father and mother.'" *verses 18b-19*

"One thing you lack: go and sell all you possess and give to the poor, and you will have treasure in heaven; and come, follow Me." *verse 21c*

"How hard it will be for those who are wealthy to enter the kingdom of God!" *verse 23b*

"Children, how hard it is to enter the kingdom of God! It is easier for a camel to go through the eye of a needle than for a rich man to enter the kingdom of God." *verses 24c-25*

"With people it is impossible, but not with God; for all things are possible with God." *verse 27b*

"Truly I say to you, there is no one who has left house or brothers or sisters or mother or father or children or farms, for My sake and for the gospel's sake, but that he will receive a hundred times as much now in the present age, houses and brothers and sisters and mothers and children and farms, along with persecutions; and in the age to come, eternal life. But many who are first will be last, and the last, first." *verses 29b-31*

"Behold, we are going up to Jerusalem, and the Son of Man will be delivered to the chief priests and the scribes; and they will condemn Him to death and will hand Him over to the Gentiles. They will mock Him and spit on Him, and scourge Him and kill Him, and three days later He will rise again." *verses 33b-34*

"What do you want Me to do for you?" *verse 36b*

"You do not know what you are asking. Are you able to drink the cup that I drink, or to be baptized with the baptism with which I am baptized?" *verse 38b*

"The cup that I drink you shall drink; and you shall be baptized with the baptism with which I am baptized. But to sit on My right or on My left, this is not Mine to give; but it is for those for whom it has been prepared." *verses 39c-40*

"You know that those who are recognized as rulers of the Gentiles lord it over them; and their great men exercise authority over them. But it is not this way among you, but whoever wishes to become great among you shall be your servant; and whoever wishes to be first among you shall be slave of all. For even the Son of Man did not come to be served, but to serve, and to give His life a ransom for many." *verses 42b-45*

"Call him here." *verse 49b*

"What do you want Me to do for you?" *verse 51b*

"Go; your faith has made you well." *verse 52b*

CHAPTER 11

"Go into the village opposite you, and immediately as you enter it, you will find a colt tied there, on which no one yet has ever sat; untie it and bring it here. If anyone says to you, 'Why are you doing this?' you say, 'The Lord has need of it'; and immediately he will send it back here." *verses 2b-3*

"May no one ever eat fruit from you again!" *verse 14b*

"Is it not written, 'My house shall be called a house of prayer for all the nations'? But you have made it a robbers' den." *verse 17b*

"Have faith in God. Truly I say to you, whoever says to this mountain, 'Be taken up and cast into the sea,' and does not doubt in his heart, but believes that what he says is going to happen, it will be granted him. Therefore I say to you, all things for which you pray and ask, believe that you have received them, and they will be granted you. Whenever you stand praying, forgive, if you have anything against anyone, so that your Father who is in heaven will also forgive you your transgressions." *verses 22b-25*

"I will ask you one question, and you answer Me, and then I will tell you by what authority I do these things. Was the baptism of John from heaven, or from men? Answer Me." *verses 29b-30*

"Nor will I tell you by what authority I do these things." *verse 33c*

CHAPTER 12

"A man planted a vineyard and put a wall around it, and dug a vat under the wine press and built a tower, and rented it out to vine-growers and went on a journey. At the harvest time he sent a slave to the vine-growers, in order to receive some of the produce of the vineyard from the vine-growers. They took him, and beat him and sent him away empty-handed. Again he sent them another slave, and they wounded him in the head, and treated him shamefully. And he sent another, and that one they killed; and so with many others, beating some and killing others. He had one more to send, a beloved son; he sent him last of all to them, saying, 'They will respect my son.' But those vine-growers said to one another, 'This is the heir; come, let us kill him, and the inheritance will be ours!' They took him, and killed him and threw him out of the vineyard. What will the owner of the vineyard do? He will come and destroy the vine-growers, and will give the vineyard to others.

"Have you not even read this Scripture: 'The stone which the builders rejected, this became the chief corner stone; this came about from the Lord, and it is marvelous in our eyes'?" *verses 1b-11*

"Why are you testing Me? Bring Me a denarius to look at. Whose likeness and inscription is this? Render to Caesar the things that are Caesar's, and to God the things that are God's." *verses 15c, 16c, and 17b*

"Is this not the reason you are mistaken, that you do not understand the Scriptures or the power of God? For when they rise from the dead, they neither marry nor are given in marriage, but are like angels in heaven. But regarding the fact that the dead rise again, have you not read in the book of Moses, in the passage about the burning bush, how God spoke to him, saying, 'I am the God of Abraham, and the God of Isaac, and the God of Jacob'? He is not the God of the dead, but of the living; you are greatly mistaken." *verses 24b-27*

"The foremost is, 'Hear, O Israel! The Lord our God is one Lord; and you shall love the Lord your God with all your heart, and with all your soul, and with all your mind, and with all your strength.' The second is this, 'You shall love your neighbor as yourself.' There is no other commandment greater than these." *verses 29b-31*

"You are not far from the kingdom of God." *verse 34b*

"How is it that the scribes say that the Christ is the son of David? David himself said in the Holy Spirit, 'The Lord said to my Lord, "Sit at My right hand, until I put Your enemies beneath Your feet."' David himself calls Him 'Lord'; so in what sense is He his son?" *verse 35b*

"Beware of the scribes who like to walk around in long robes, and like respectful greetings in the market places, and chief seats in the synagogues and places of honor at banquets, who devour widows' houses, and for appearance's sake offer long prayers; these will receive greater condemnation." *verses 38b-40*

"Truly I say to you, this poor widow put in more than all the contributors to the treasury; for they all put in out of their surplus, but she, out of her poverty, put in all she owned, all she had to live on." *verse 43b*

CHAPTER 13

"Do you see these great buildings? Not one stone will be left upon another which will not be torn down." *verse 2b*

"See to it that no one misleads you. Many will come in My name, saying, 'I am He!' and will mislead many. When you hear of wars and rumors of wars, do not be frightened; those things must take place; but that is not yet the end. For nation will rise up against nation, and kingdom against kingdom; there will be earthquakes in various places; there will also be famines. These things are merely the beginning of birth pangs. But be on your guard; for they will deliver you to the courts, and you will be flogged in the synagogues, and you will stand before governors and kings for My sake, as a testimony to them.

"The gospel must first be preached to all the nations. When they arrest you and hand you over, do not worry beforehand about what you are to say, but say whatever is given you in that hour; for it is not you who speak, but it is the Holy Spirit. Brother will betray brother to death, and a father his child; and children will rise up against parents and have them put to death. You will be hated by all because of My name, but the one who endures to the end, he will be saved.

"But when you see the abomination of desolation standing where it should not be then those who are in Judea must flee to the mountains. The one who is on the housetop must not go down, or go in to get anything out of his house; and the one who is in the field must not turn back to get his coat. But woe to those who are pregnant and to those who are nursing babies in those days! But pray that it may not happen in the winter. For those days will be a time of tribulation such as has not occurred since the beginning of the creation which God created until now, and never will. Unless the Lord had shortened those days, no life would have been saved; but for the sake of the elect, whom He chose, He shortened the days. "And then if anyone says to you,

'Behold, here is the Christ'; or, 'Behold, He is there'; do not believe him; for false Christs and false prophets will arise, and will show signs and wonders, in order to lead astray, if possible, the elect.

"But take heed; behold, I have told you everything in advance. But in those days, after that tribulation, the sun will be darkened and the moon will not give its light, and the stars will be falling from heaven, and the powers that are in the heavens will be shaken. Then they will see the Son of Man coming in clouds with great power and glory. And then He will send forth the angels, and will gather together His elect from the four winds, from the farthest end of the earth to the farthest end of heaven. "Now learn the parable from the fig tree: when its branch has already become tender and puts forth its leaves, you know that summer is near. Even so, you too, when you see these things happening, recognize that He is near, right at the door. Truly I say to you, this generation will not pass away until all these things take place. Heaven and earth will pass away, but My words will not pass away.

"But of that day or hour no one knows, not even the angels in heaven, nor the Son, but the Father alone. Take heed, keep on the alert; for you do not know when the appointed time will come. It is like a man away on a journey, who upon leaving his house and putting his slaves in charge, assigning to each one his task, also commanded the doorkeeper to stay on the alert. Therefore, be on the alert—for you do not know when the master of the house is coming, whether in the evening, at midnight, or when the rooster crows, or in the morning—in case he should come suddenly and find you asleep. What I say to you I say to all, 'Be on the alert!'" *verses 5b-37*

CHAPTER 14

"Let her alone; why do you bother her? She has done a good deed to Me. For you always have the poor with you, and whenever you wish you can do good to them; but you do not always have Me. She has done what she could; she has anointed My body beforehand for the burial. Truly I say to you, wherever the gospel is preached in the whole world, what this woman has done will also be spoken of in memory of her." *verses 6b-9*

"Go into the city, and a man will meet you carrying a pitcher of water; follow him; and wherever he enters, say to the owner of the house, 'The Teacher says, "Where is My guest room in which I may eat the Passover with My disciples?"' And he himself will show you a large upper room furnished and ready; prepare for us there." *verses 13b-15*

"Truly I say to you that one of you will betray Me—one who is eating with Me." *verse 18b*

"It is one of the twelve, one who dips with Me in the bowl. For the Son of Man is to go just as it is written of Him; but woe to that man by whom the Son of Man is betrayed! It would have been good for that man if he had not been born." *verses 20b-21*

"Take it; this is My body." *verse 22c*

"This is My blood of the covenant, which is poured out for many. Truly I say to you, I will never again drink of the fruit of the vine until that day when I drink it new in the kingdom of God." *verses 24b-25*

"You will all fall away, because it is written, 'I will strike down the shepherd, and the sheep shall be scattered.' But after I have been raised, I will go ahead of you to Galilee." *verses 27b-28*

"Truly I say to you, that this very night, before a rooster crows twice, you yourself will deny Me three times." *verse 30b*

"Sit here until I have prayed." *verse 32c*

"My soul is deeply grieved to the point of death; remain here and keep watch." *verse 34b*

"Abba! Father! All things are possible for You; remove this cup from Me; yet not what I will, but what You will." *verse 36b*

"Simon, are you asleep? Could you not keep watch for one hour? Keep watching and praying that you may not come into temptation; the spirit is willing, but the flesh is weak." *verses 37c-38*

"Are you still sleeping and resting? It is enough; the hour has come; behold, the Son of Man is being betrayed into the hands of sinners. Get up, let us be going; behold, the one who betrays Me is at hand!" *verses 41b-42*

"Have you come out with swords and clubs to arrest Me, as you would against a robber? Every day I was with you in the temple teaching, and you did not seize Me; but this has taken place to fulfill the Scriptures." *verses 48b-49*

"I am; and you shall see the Son of Man sitting at the right hand of Power, and coming with the clouds of heaven." *verse 62b*

CHAPTER 15

"It is as you say." *verse 2c*

"Eloi, Eloi, lama sabachthani?" ("My God, My God, why have You forsaken Me?") *verse 34b*

Chapter 16 – NOTE: all of the Jesus quotes in this chapter are said to have been added in later manuscripts. For this reason, they are not included here.

Matthew, dated 80-90 CE, author unknown. Audience: Greek-speaking Jews in the Jesus Movement. (White, p. 244)

CHAPTERS 1 and 2: Jesus is not quoted.

CHAPTER 3

"Permit it at this time; for in this way it is fitting for us to fulfill all righteousness." *verse 15b*

CHAPTER 4

"It is written, 'Man shall not live on bread alone, but on every word that proceeds out of the mouth of God.'" *verse 4b*

"On the other hand, it is written, 'You shall not put the Lord your God to the test.'" *verse 7b*

"Go, Satan! For it is written, 'You shall worship the Lord your God, and serve Him only.'" *verse 10b*

"Repent, for the kingdom of heaven is at hand." *verse 17b*

"Follow Me, and I will make you fishers of men." *verse 19b*

CHAPTER 5

"Blessed are the poor in spirit, for theirs is the kingdom of heaven.

"Blessed are those who mourn, for they shall be comforted.

"Blessed are the gentle, for they shall inherit the earth.

"Blessed are those who hunger and thirst for righteousness, for they shall be satisfied.

"Blessed are the merciful, for they shall receive mercy.

"Blessed are the pure in heart, for they shall see God.

"Blessed are the peacemakers, for they shall be called sons of God.

"Blessed are those who have been persecuted for the sake of righteousness, for theirs is the kingdom of heaven.

"Blessed are you when people insult you and persecute you, and falsely say all kinds of evil against you because of Me. Rejoice and be glad, for your reward in heaven is great; for in the same way they persecuted the prophets who were before you. "You are the salt of the earth; but if the salt has become tasteless, how can it be made salty again? It is no longer good for anything, except to be thrown out and trampled under foot by men. You are the light of the world. A city set on a hill cannot be hidden; nor does anyone light a lamp and put it under a basket, but on the lampstand, and it gives light to all who are in the house. Let your light shine before men in such a way that they may see your good works, and glorify your Father who is in heaven.

"Do not think that I came to abolish the Law or the Prophets; I did not come to abolish but to fulfill. For truly I say to you, until heaven and earth pass away, not the smallest letter or stroke shall pass from the Law until all is accomplished. Whoever then annuls one of the least of these commandments, and teaches others to do the same, shall be called least in the kingdom of heaven; but whoever keeps and teaches them, he shall be called great in the kingdom of heaven. For I say to you that unless your righteousness surpasses that of the scribes and Pharisees, you will not enter the kingdom of heaven. You have heard that the ancients were told, 'You shall not commit murder' and 'Whoever commits murder shall be liable to the court.' But I say to you that everyone who is angry with his brother shall be guilty before the court; and whoever says to his brother, 'You good-for-nothing,' shall be guilty before the supreme court; and whoever says, 'You fool,' shall be guilty enough to go into the fiery hell. Therefore if you are presenting your offering at the altar, and there remember that your brother has something against you, leave your offering there before the altar and go; first be reconciled to your brother, and then come and present your offering. Make friends quickly with your opponent at law while you are with him on the way, so that your opponent may not hand you over to the judge, and the judge to the officer, and you be thrown into prison. Truly I say to you, you will not come out of there until you have paid up the last cent. You have heard that it was said, 'You shall not commit adultery'; but I say to you that everyone who looks at a woman with lust for her has already committed adultery with her in his heart. If your right eye makes you stumble, tear it out and throw it from you; for it is better for you to lose one of the parts of your body, than for your whole body to be thrown into hell. If your right hand makes you stumble, cut it off and throw it from you; for it is better for you to lose one of the parts of your body, than for your whole body to go into hell.

"It was said, 'Whoever sends his wife away, let him give her a certificate of divorce'; but I say to you that everyone who divorces his wife, except for the reason of unchastity, makes her commit adultery; and whoever marries a divorced woman commits adultery.

"Again, you have heard that the ancients were told, 'You shall not make false vows, but shall fulfill your vows to the Lord.' But I say to you, make no oath at all, either by heaven, for it is the throne of God, or by the earth, for it is the footstool of His feet, or by Jerusalem, for it is the city of the great King. Nor shall you make an oath by your head, for you cannot make one hair white or black. But let your statement be, 'Yes, yes' or 'No, no'; anything beyond these is of evil. You have heard that it was said, 'An eye for an eye, and a tooth for a tooth.' But I say to you, do not resist an evil person; but whoever slaps you on your right cheek, turn the other to him also. If anyone wants to sue you and take your shirt, let him have your coat also. Whoever forces you to go one mile, go with him two. Give to him who asks of you, and do not turn away from him who wants to borrow from you.

"You have heard that it was said, 'You shall love your neighbor and hate your enemy.' But I say to you, love your enemies and pray for those who persecute you, so that you may be sons of your Father who is in heaven; for He causes His sun to rise on the evil and the good, and sends rain on the righteous and the unrighteous. For if you love those who love you, what reward do you have? Do not even the tax collectors do the same? If you greet only your brothers, what more are you doing than others? Do not even the Gentiles do the same? Therefore you are to be perfect, as your heavenly Father is perfect." *verses 4-48*

CHAPTER 6

"Beware of practicing your righteousness before men to be noticed by them; otherwise you have no reward with your Father who is in heaven. So when you give to the poor, do not sound a trumpet before you, as the hypocrites do in the synagogues and in the streets, so that they may be honored by men. Truly I say to you, they have their reward in full. But when you give to the poor, do not let your left hand know what your right hand is doing, so that your giving will be in secret; and your Father who sees what is done in secret will reward you. When you pray, you are not to be like the hypocrites; for they love to stand and pray in the synagogues and on the street corners so that they may be seen by men. Truly I say to you, they have their reward in full. But you, when you pray, go into your inner room, close your door and pray to your Father who is in secret, and your Father who sees what is done in secret will reward you. And when you are praying, do not use meaningless repetition as the Gentiles do, for they suppose that they will be heard for their many words. So do not be like them; for your Father knows what you need before you ask Him. Pray, then, in this way:

"Our Father who is in heaven, hallowed be Your name. Your kingdom come. Your will be done, on earth as it is in heaven. Give us this day our daily bread. And forgive us our debts, as we also have forgiven our debtors. And do not lead us into temptation, but deliver us from evil.

"For if you forgive others for their transgressions, your heavenly Father will also forgive you. But if you do not forgive others, then your Father will not forgive your transgressions. Whenever you fast, do not put on a gloomy face as the hypocrites do, for they neglect their appearance so that they will be noticed by men when they are fasting. Truly I say to you, they have their reward in full. But you, when you fast, anoint your head and wash your face so that your fasting will not be noticed by men, but by your Father who is in secret; and your Father who sees what is done in secret will reward you. Do not store up for yourselves treasures on earth, where moth and rust destroy, and where thieves break in and steal. But store up for yourselves treasures in heaven, where neither moth nor rust destroys, and where thieves do not break in or steal; for where your treasure is, there your heart will be also.

"The eye is the lamp of the body; so then if your eye is clear, your whole body will be full of light. But if your eye is bad, your whole body will be full of darkness. If then the light that is in you is darkness, how great is the darkness!

"No one can serve two masters; for either he will hate the one and love the other, or he will be devoted to one and despise the other. You cannot serve God and wealth. For this reason I say to you, do not be worried about your life, as to what you will eat or what you will drink; nor for your body, as to what you will put on. Is not life more than food, and the body more than clothing? Look at the birds of the air, that they do not sow, nor reap nor gather into barns, and yet your heavenly Father feeds them. Are you not worth much more than they? And who of you by being worried can add a single hour to his life? And why are you worried about clothing? Observe how the lilies of the field grow; they do not toil nor do they spin, yet I say to you that not even Solomon in all his glory clothed himself like one of these. But if God so clothes the grass of the field, which is alive today and tomorrow is thrown into the furnace, will He not much more clothe you? You of little faith! Do not worry then, saying, 'What will we eat?' or 'What will we drink?' or 'What will we wear for clothing?' For the Gentiles eagerly seek all these things; for your heavenly Father knows that you need all these things. But seek first His kingdom and His righteousness, and all these things will be added to you. So do not worry about tomorrow; for tomorrow will care for itself. Each day has enough trouble of its own." *verses 1-34*

CHAPTER 7

"Do not judge so that you will not be judged. For in the way you judge, you will be judged; and by your standard of measure, it will be measured to you. Why do you look at the speck that is in your brother's eye, but do not notice the log that is in your own eye? Or how can you say to your brother, 'Let me take the speck out of your eye,' and behold, the log is in your own eye? You hypocrite, first take the log out of your own eye, and then you will see clearly to take the speck out of your brother's eye.

"Do not give what is holy to dogs, and do not throw your pearls before swine, or they will trample them under their feet, and turn and tear you to pieces.

"Ask, and it will be given to you; seek, and you will find; knock, and it will be opened to you. For everyone who asks receives, and he who seeks finds, and to him who knocks it will be opened. Or what man is there among you who, when his son asks for a loaf, will give him a stone? Or if he asks for a fish, he will not give him a snake, will he? If you then, being evil, know how to give good gifts to your children, how much more will your Father who is in heaven give what is good to those who ask Him! In everything, therefore, treat people the same way you want them to treat you, for this is the Law and the Prophets. "Enter through the narrow gate; for the gate is wide and the way is broad that leads to destruction, and there are many who enter through it. For the gate is small and the way is narrow that leads to life, and there are few who find it.

"Beware of the false prophets, who come to you in sheep's clothing, but inwardly are ravenous wolves. You will know them by their fruits. Grapes are not gathered from thorn bushes nor figs from thistles, are they? So every good tree bears good fruit, but the bad tree bears bad fruit. A good tree cannot produce bad fruit, nor can a bad tree produce good fruit. Every tree that does not bear good fruit is cut down and thrown into the fire. So then, you will know them by their fruits. "Not everyone who says to Me, 'Lord, Lord,' will enter the kingdom of heaven, but he who does the will of My Father who is in heaven will enter. Many will say to Me on that day, 'Lord, Lord, did we not prophesy in Your name, and in Your name cast out demons, and in Your name perform many miracles?' And then I will declare to them, 'I never knew you; depart from Me, you who practice lawlessness.' Therefore everyone who hears these words of Mine and acts on them, may be compared to a wise man who built his house on the rock. And the rain fell, and the floods came, and the winds blew and slammed against that house; and yet it did not fall, for it had been founded on the rock. Everyone who hears these words of Mine and does not act on them, will be like a foolish man who built his house on the sand. The rain fell, and the floods came, and the winds blew and slammed against that house; and it fell—and great was its fall." *verses 1-27*

CHAPTER 8

"I am willing; be cleansed." *verse 3b*

"See that you tell no one; but go, show yourself to the priest and present the offering that Moses commanded, as a testimony to them." *verse 4b*

"I will come and heal him." *verse 7b*

"Truly I say to you, I have not found such great faith with anyone in Israel. I say to you that many will come from east and west, and recline at the table with Abraham, Isaac and Jacob in the kingdom of heaven; but the sons of the kingdom will be cast out into the outer darkness; in that place there will be weeping and gnashing of teeth." *verses 10b-12*

"Go; it shall be done for you as you have believed." *verse 13b*

"The foxes have holes and the birds of the air have nests, but the Son of Man has nowhere to lay His head." *verse 20b*

"Follow Me, and allow the dead to bury their own dead." *verse 22b*

"Why are you afraid, you men of little faith?" *verse 26b*

"Go!" *verse 32b*

CHAPTER 9

"Take courage, son; your sins are forgiven." *verse 2c*

"Why are you thinking evil in your hearts? Which is easier, to say, 'Your sins are forgiven,' or to say, 'Get up, and walk'? But so that you may know that the Son of Man has authority on earth to forgive sins" *verses 4b-6a*

"Get up, pick up your bed and go home." *verse 6c*

"Follow Me!" *verse 9c*

"It is not those who are healthy who need a physician, but those who are sick. But go and learn what this means: 'I desire compassion, and not sacrifice,' for I did not come to call the righteous, but sinners." *verses 12b-13*

"The attendants of the bridegroom cannot mourn as long as the bridegroom is with them, can they? But the days will come when the bridegroom is taken away from them, and then they will fast.

"But no one puts a patch of unshrunk cloth on an old garment; for the patch pulls away from the garment, and a worse tear results. Nor do people put new wine into old wineskins; otherwise the wineskins burst, and the wine pours out and the wineskins are ruined; but they put new wine into fresh wineskins, and both are preserved." *verses 15b-17*

"Daughter, take courage; your faith has made you well." *verse 22b*

"Leave; for the girl has not died, but is asleep." *verse 24b*

"Do you believe that I am able to do this?" *verse 28c*

"It shall be done to you according to your faith." *verse 29b*

"See that no one knows about this!" *verse 30c*

"The harvest is plentiful, but the workers are few. Therefore beseech the Lord of the harvest to send out workers into His harvest." *verse 37b*

CHAPTER 10

"Do not go in the way of the Gentiles, and do not enter any city of the Samaritans; but rather go to the lost sheep of the house of Israel. And as you go, preach, saying, 'The kingdom of heaven is at hand.' Heal the sick, raise the dead, cleanse the lepers, cast out demons. Freely you received, freely give. Do not acquire gold, or silver, or copper for your money belts, or a bag for your journey, or even two coats, or sandals, or a staff; for the worker is worthy of his support. And whatever city or village you enter, inquire who is worthy in it, and stay at his house until you leave that city. As you enter the house, give it your greeting. If the house is worthy, give it your blessing of peace. But if it is not worthy, take back your blessing of peace. Whoever does not receive you, nor heed your words, as you go out of that house or that city, shake the dust off your feet. Truly I say to you, it will be more tolerable for the land of Sodom and Gomorrah in the day of judgment than for that city.

"Behold, I send you out as sheep in the midst of wolves; so be shrewd as serpents and innocent as doves. But beware of men, for they will hand you over to the courts and scourge you in their synagogues; and you will even be brought before governors and kings for My sake, as a testimony to them and to the Gentiles. But when they hand you over, do not worry about how or what you are to say; for it will be given you in that hour what you are to say. For it is not you who speak, but it is the Spirit of your Father who speaks in you. Brother will betray brother to death, and a father his child; and children will rise up against parents and cause them to be put to death. You will be hated by all because of My name, but it is the one who has endured to the end who will be saved. But whenever they persecute you in one city, flee to the next; for truly I say to you, you will not finish going through the cities of Israel until the Son of Man comes. A disciple is not above his teacher, nor a slave above his master. It is enough for the disciple that he become like his teacher, and the slave like his master. If they have called the head of the house Beelzebul, how much more will they malign the members of his household! Therefore do not fear them, for there is nothing concealed that will not be revealed, or hidden that will not be known. What I tell you in the darkness, speak in the light; and what you hear whispered in your ear, proclaim upon the housetops. Do not fear those who kill the body but are unable to kill the soul; but rather fear Him who is able to destroy both soul and body in hell.

"Are not two sparrows sold for a cent? And yet not one of them will fall to the ground apart from your Father. But the very hairs of your head are all numbered. So do not fear; you are more valuable than many sparrows. Therefore everyone who confesses Me before men, I will also confess him before My Father who is in heaven. But whoever denies Me before men, I will also deny him before My Father who is in heaven.

"Do not think that I came to bring peace on the earth; I did not come to bring peace, but a sword. For I came to set a man against his father, and a daughter against her mother, and a daughter-in-law against her mother-in-law; and a man's enemies will be the members of his household. He who loves father or mother more than Me is not worthy of Me; and he who loves son or daughter more than Me is not worthy of Me. And he who does not take his cross and follow after Me is not worthy of Me. He who has found his life will lose it, and he who has lost his life for My sake will find it.

"He who receives you receives Me, and he who receives Me receives Him who sent Me. He who receives a prophet in the name of a prophet shall receive a prophet's reward; and he who receives a righteous man in the name of a righteous man shall receive a righteous man's reward. And whoever in the name of a disciple gives to one of these little ones even a cup of cold water to drink, truly I say to you, he shall not lose his reward." *verses 5b-42*

CHAPTER 11

"Go and report to John what you hear and see: the blind receive sight and the lame walk, the lepers are cleansed and the deaf hear, the dead are raised up, and the poor have the gospel preached to them. And blessed is he who does not take offense at Me." *verses 4b-6*

"What did you go out into the wilderness to see? A reed shaken by the wind? But what did you go out to see? A man dressed in soft clothing? Those who wear soft clothing are in kings' palaces! But what did you go out to see? A prophet? Yes, I tell you, and one who is more than a prophet. This is the one about whom it is written, 'Behold, I send My messenger ahead of You, Who will prepare Your way before You.' Truly I say to you, among those born of women there has not arisen anyone greater than John the Baptist! Yet the one who is least in the kingdom of heaven is greater than he. From the days of John the Baptist until now the kingdom of heaven suffers violence, and violent men take it by force. For all the prophets and the Law prophesied until John. And if you are willing to accept it, John himself is Elijah who was to come. He who has ears to hear, let him hear.

"But to what shall I compare this generation? It is like children sitting in the market places, who call out to the other children, and say, 'We played the flute for you, and you did not dance; we sang a dirge, and you did not mourn.' For John came neither eating nor drinking, and they say, 'He has a demon!' The Son of Man came eating and drinking, and they say, 'Behold, a gluttonous man and a drunkard, a friend of tax collectors and sinners!' Yet wisdom is vindicated by her deeds." *verses 7b-19*

"Woe to you, Chorazin! Woe to you, Bethsaida! For if the miracles had occurred in Tyre and Sidon which occurred in you, they would have repented long ago in sackcloth and ashes. Nevertheless I say to you, it will be more tolerable for Tyre and Sidon in the day of judgment than for you. And you, Capernaum, will not be exalted to heaven, will you? You will descend to Hades; for if the miracles had occurred in Sodom which occurred in you, it would have remained to this day. Nevertheless I say to you that it will be more tolerable for the land of Sodom in the day of judgment, than for you." *verses 21-24*

"I praise You, Father, Lord of heaven and earth, that You have hidden these things from the wise and intelligent and have revealed them to infants. Yes, Father, for this way was well-pleasing in Your sight. All things have been handed over to Me by My Father; and no one knows the Son except the Father; nor does anyone know the Father except the Son, and anyone to whom the Son wills to reveal Him. Come to Me, all who are weary and heavy-laden, and I will give you rest. Take My yoke upon you and learn from Me, for I am gentle and humble in heart, and you will find rest for your souls. For My yoke is easy and My burden is light." *verses 25b-30*

CHAPTER 12

"Have you not read what David did when he became hungry, he and his companions, how he entered the house of God, and they ate the consecrated bread, which was not lawful for him to eat nor for those with him, but for the priests alone? Or have you not read in the Law, that on the Sabbath the priests in the temple break the Sabbath and are innocent? But I say to you that something greater than the temple is here. But if you had known what this means, 'I desire compassion, and not a sacrifice,' you would not have condemned the innocent. For the Son of Man is Lord of the Sabbath." *verses 3b-8*

"What man is there among you who has a sheep, and if it falls into a pit on the Sabbath, will he not take hold of it and lift it out? How much more valuable then is a man than a sheep! So then, it is lawful to do good on the Sabbath." *verses 11b-12*

"Stretch out your hand!" *verse 13b*

"Any kingdom divided against itself is laid waste; and any city or house divided against itself will not stand. If Satan casts out Satan, he is divided against himself; how then will his kingdom stand? If I by Beelzebul cast out demons, by whom do your sons cast them out? For this reason they will be your judges. But if I cast out demons by the Spirit of God, then the kingdom of God has come upon you. Or how can anyone enter the strong man's house and carry off his property, unless he first binds the strong man? And then he will plunder his house. He who is not with Me is against Me; and he who does not gather with Me scatters. Therefore I say to you, any sin and blasphemy shall be forgiven people, but blasphemy against the Spirit shall not be forgiven. Whoever speaks a word against the Son of Man, it shall be forgiven him; but whoever speaks against the Holy Spirit, it shall not be forgiven him, either in this age or in the age to come. Either make the tree good and its fruit good, or make the tree bad and its fruit bad; for the tree is known by its fruit. You brood of vipers, how can you, being evil, speak what is good? For the mouth speaks out of that which fills the heart. The good man brings out of his good treasure what is good; and the evil man brings out of his evil treasure what is evil. But I tell you that every careless word that people speak, they shall give an accounting for it in the day of judgment. For by your words you will be justified, and by your words you will be condemned." *verses 25b-37*

"An evil and adulterous generation craves for a sign; and yet no sign will be given to it but the sign of Jonah the prophet; for just as Jonah was three days and three nights in the belly of the sea monster, so will the Son of Man be three days and three nights in the heart of the earth. The men of Nineveh will stand up with this generation at the judgment, and will condemn it because they repented at the preaching of Jonah; and behold, something greater than Jonah is here. The Queen of the South will rise up with this generation at the judgment and will condemn it, because she came from the ends of the earth to hear the wisdom of Solomon; and behold, something greater than Solomon is here.

"Now when the unclean spirit goes out of a man, it passes through waterless places seeking rest, and does not find it. Then it says, 'I will return to my house from which I came'; and when it comes, it finds it unoccupied, swept, and put in order. Then it goes and takes along with it seven other spirits more wicked than itself, and they go in and live there; and the last state of that man becomes worse than the first. That is the way it will also be with this evil generation." *verses 39b-45*

"Who is My mother and who are My brothers? Behold My mother and My brothers! For whoever does the will of My Father who is in heaven, he is My brother and sister and mother." *verses 48b and 49b-50*

CHAPTER 13

"Behold, the sower went out to sow; and as he sowed, some seeds fell beside the road, and the birds came and ate them up. Others fell on the rocky places, where they did not have much soil; and immediately they sprang up, because they had no depth of soil. But when the sun had risen, they were scorched; and because they had no root, they withered away. Others fell among the thorns, and the thorns came up and choked them out. And others fell on the good soil and yielded a crop, some a hundredfold, some sixty, and some thirty. He who has ears, let him hear." *verses 3b-9*

"To you it has been granted to know the mysteries of the kingdom of heaven, but to them it has not been granted. For whoever has, to him more shall be given, and he will have an abundance; but whoever does not have, even what he has shall be taken away from him. Therefore I speak to them in parables; because while seeing they do not see, and while hearing they do not hear, nor do they understand. In their case the prophecy of Isaiah is being fulfilled, which says, 'You will keep on hearing, but will not understand; You will keep on seeing, but will not perceive; For the heart of this people has become dull, With their ears they scarcely hear, And they have closed their eyes, Otherwise they would see with their eyes, Hear with their ears, And understand with their heart and return, And I would heal them.' But blessed are your eyes, because they see; and your ears, because they hear. For truly I say to you that many prophets and righteous men desired to see what you see, and did not see it, and to hear what you hear, and did not hear it. Hear then the parable of the sower. When anyone hears the word of the kingdom and does not understand it, the evil one comes and snatches away what has been sown in his heart. This is the one on whom seed was sown beside the road. The one on whom seed was sown on the rocky places, this is the man who hears the word and immediately receives it with joy; yet he has no firm root in himself, but is only temporary, and when affliction or persecution arises because of the word, immediately he falls away. And the one on whom seed was sown among the thorns, this is the man who hears the word, and the worry of the world and the deceitfulness of wealth choke the word, and it becomes unfruitful. And the one on whom seed was sown on the good soil, this is the man who hears the word and understands it; who indeed bears fruit and brings forth, some a hundredfold, some sixty, and some thirty." *verses 11b-23*

"The kingdom of heaven may be compared to a man who sowed good seed in his field. But while his men were sleeping, his enemy came and sowed tares among the wheat, and went away. But when the wheat sprouted and bore grain, then the tares became evident also. The slaves of the landowner came and said to him, 'Sir, did you not sow good seed in your field? How then does it have tares?' And he said to them, 'An enemy has done this!' The slaves said to him, 'Do you want us, then, to go and gather them up?' But he said, 'No; for while you are gathering up the tares, you may uproot the wheat with them. Allow both to grow together until the harvest; and in the time of the harvest I will say to the reapers, 'First gather up the tares and bind them in bundles to burn them up; but gather the wheat into my barn.'" *verses 24b-30*

"The kingdom of heaven is like a mustard seed, which a man took and sowed in his field; and this is smaller than all other seeds, but when it is full grown, it is larger than the garden plants and becomes a tree, so that the birds of the air come and nest in its branches." *verses 31b-32*

"The kingdom of heaven is like leaven, which a woman took and hid in three pecks of flour until it was all leavened." *verse 33b*

"The one who sows the good seed is the Son of Man, and the field is the world; and as for the good seed, these are the sons of the kingdom; and the tares are the sons of the evil one; and the enemy who sowed them is the devil, and the harvest is the end of the age; and the reapers are angels. So just as the tares are gathered up and burned with fire, so shall it be at the end of the age. The Son of Man will send forth His angels, and they will gather out of His kingdom all stumbling blocks, and those who commit lawlessness, and will throw them into the furnace of fire; in that place there will be weeping and gnashing of teeth. Then the righteous will shine forth as the sun in the kingdom of their Father. He who has ears, let him hear. The kingdom of heaven is like a treasure hidden in the field, which a man found and hid again; and from joy over it he goes and sells all that he has and buys that field.

"Again, the kingdom of heaven is like a merchant seeking fine pearls, and upon finding one pearl of great value, he went and sold all that he had and bought it.

"Again, the kingdom of heaven is like a dragnet cast into the sea, and gathering fish of every kind; and when it was filled, they drew it up on the beach; and they sat down and gathered the good fish into containers, but the bad they threw away. So it will be at the end of the age; the angels will come forth and take out the wicked from among the righteous, and will throw them into the furnace of fire; in that place there will be weeping and gnashing of teeth. Have you understood all these things?" *verses 37b-51a*

"Therefore every scribe who has become a disciple of the kingdom of heaven is like a head of a household, who brings out of his treasure things new and old." *verse 52b*

"A prophet is not without honor except in his hometown and in his own household." *verse 57c*

CHAPTER 14

"They do not need to go away; you give them something to eat!" *verse 16b*

"Bring them here to Me." *verse 18b*

"Take courage, it is I; do not be afraid." *verse 27b*

"Come!" *verse 29b*

"You of little faith, why did you doubt?" *verse 31b*

CHAPTER 15

"Why do you yourselves transgress the commandment of God for the sake of your tradition? For God said, 'Honor your father and mother,' and, 'He who speaks evil of father or mother is to be put to death.' But you say, 'Whoever says to his father or mother, "Whatever I have that would help you has been given to God," he is not to honor his father or his mother.' And by this you invalidated the word of God for the sake of your tradition. You hypocrites, rightly did Isaiah prophesy of you: 'This people honors Me with their lips, But their heart is far away from Me.

But in vain do they worship Me, teaching as doctrines the precepts of men.'" *verses 3b-9*

"Hear and understand. It is not what enters into the mouth that defiles the man, but what proceeds out of the mouth, this defiles the man." *verses 10b-11*

"Every plant which My heavenly Father did not plant shall be uprooted. Let them alone; they are blind guides of the blind. And if a blind man guides a blind man, both will fall into a pit." *verses 13b-14*

"Are you still lacking in understanding also? Do you not understand that everything that goes into the mouth passes into the stomach, and is eliminated? But the things that proceed out of the mouth come from the heart, and those defile the man. For out of the heart come evil thoughts, murders, adulteries, fornications, thefts, false witness, slanders. These are the things which defile the man; but to eat with unwashed hands does not defile the man." *verses 16b-20*

"I was sent only to the lost sheep of the house of Israel." *verse 24b*

"It is not good to take the children's bread and throw it to the dogs." *verse 26b*

"O woman, your faith is great; it shall be done for you as you wish." *verse 28b*

"I feel compassion for the people, because they have remained with Me now three days and have nothing to eat; and I do not want to send them away hungry, for they might faint on the way. How many loaves do you have?" *verses 32b and 34b*

CHAPTER 16

"An evil and adulterous generation seeks after a sign; and a sign will not be given it, except the sign of Jonah." *verse 4*

"Watch out and beware of the leaven of the Pharisees and Sadducees." *verse 6b*

"You men of little faith, why do you discuss among yourselves that you have no bread? Do you not yet understand or remember the five loaves of the five thousand, and how many baskets full you picked up? Or the seven loaves of the four thousand, and how many large baskets full you picked up? How is it that you do not understand that I did not speak to you concerning bread? But beware of the leaven of the Pharisees and Sadducees." *verses 8b-11*

"Who do people say that the Son of Man is?" verse 13c

"But who do you say that I am?" *verse 15b*

"Blessed are you, Simon Barjona, because flesh and blood did not reveal this to you, but My Father who is in heaven. I also say to you that you are Peter, and upon this rock I will build My church; and the gates of Hades will not overpower it. I will give you the keys of the kingdom of heaven; and whatever you bind on earth shall have been bound in heaven, and whatever you loose on earth shall have been loosed in heaven." *verses 17b-19*

"Get behind Me, Satan! You are a stumbling block to Me; for you are not setting your mind on God's interests, but man's." *verse 23b*

"If anyone wishes to come after Me, he must deny himself, and take up his cross and follow Me. For whoever wishes to save his life will lose it; but whoever loses his life for My sake will find it. For what will it profit a man if he gains the whole world and forfeits his soul? Or what will a man give in exchange for his soul? For the Son of Man is going to come in the glory of His Father

FINDING SOLID GROUND

with His angels, and will then repay every man according to his deeds. Truly I say to you, there are some of those who are standing here who will not taste death until they see the Son of Man coming in His kingdom." *verses 24b-28*

CHAPTER 17

"Get up, and do not be afraid." *verse 7b*

"Tell the vision to no one until the Son of Man has risen from the dead." *verse 9c*

"Elijah is coming and will restore all things; but I say to you that Elijah already came, and they did not recognize him, but did to him whatever they wished. So also the Son of Man is going to suffer at their hands." *verses 11b-12*

"You unbelieving and perverted generation, how long shall I be with you? How long shall I put up with you? Bring him here to Me." *verse 17b*

"Because of the littleness of your faith; for truly I say to you, if you have faith the size of a mustard seed, you will say to this mountain, 'Move from here to there,' and it will move; and nothing will be impossible to you." *verse 20b*

"The Son of Man is going to be delivered into the hands of men; and they will kill Him, and He will be raised on the third day." *verses 22c-23*

"What do you think, Simon? From whom do the kings of the earth collect customs or poll-tax, from their sons or from strangers? Then the sons are exempt. However, so that we do not offend them, go to the sea and throw in a hook, and take the first fish that comes up; and when you open its mouth, you will find a shekel. Take that and give it to them for you and Me." *verses 25c and 26c*

CHAPTER 18

"Truly I say to you, unless you are converted and become like children, you will not enter the kingdom of heaven. Whoever then humbles himself as this child, he is the greatest in the kingdom of heaven. And whoever receives one such child in My name receives Me; but whoever causes one of these little ones who believe in Me to stumble, it would be better for him to have a heavy millstone hung around his neck, and to be drowned in the depth of the sea. Woe to the world because of its stumbling blocks! For it is inevitable that stumbling blocks come; but woe to that man through whom the stumbling block comes! If your hand or your foot causes you to stumble, cut it off and throw it from you; it is better for you to enter life crippled or lame, than to have two hands or two feet and be cast into the eternal fire. If your eye causes you to stumble, pluck it out and throw it from you. It is better for you to enter life with one eye, than to have two eyes and be cast into the fiery hell. See that you do not despise one of these little ones, for I say to you that their angels in heaven continually see the face of My Father who is in heaven." *verses 2c-10*

"What do you think? If any man has a hundred sheep, and one of them has gone astray, does he not leave the ninety-nine on the mountains and go and search for the one that is straying? If it turns out that he finds it, truly I say to you, he rejoices over it more than over the ninety-nine which have not gone astray. So it is not the will of your Father who is in heaven that one of these little ones perish. If your brother sins, go and show him his fault in private; if he listens to you, you have won your brother. But if he does not listen to you, take one or two more with you, so that by the mouth of two or three witnesses every fact may be confirmed. If he refuses to listen to them, tell it to the church; and if he refuses to listen even to the church, let him be to you as a Gentile and a tax collector. Truly I say to you, whatever you bind on earth shall have been bound in heaven; and whatever you loose on earth shall have been loosed in heaven. Again I say to

FINDING SOLID GROUND

you, that if two of you agree on earth about anything that they may ask, it shall be done for them by My Father who is in heaven. For where two or three have gathered together in My name, I am there in their midst." *verses 12-20*

"I do not say to you, up to seven times, but up to seventy times seven. For this reason the kingdom of heaven may be compared to a king who wished to settle accounts with his slaves. When he had begun to settle them, one who owed him ten thousand talents was brought to him. But since he did not have the means to repay, his lord commanded him to be sold, along with his wife and children and all that he had, and repayment to be made. So the slave fell to the ground and prostrated himself before him, saying, 'Have patience with me and I will repay you everything.' And the lord of that slave felt compassion and released him and forgave him the debt. But that slave went out and found one of his fellow slaves who owed him a hundred denarii; and he seized him and began to choke him, saying, 'Pay back what you owe.' So his fellow slave fell to the ground and began to plead with him, saying, 'Have patience with me and I will repay you.' But he was unwilling and went and threw him in prison until he should pay back what was owed. So when his fellow slaves saw what had happened, they were deeply grieved and came and reported to their lord all that had happened. Then summoning him, his lord said to him, 'You wicked slave, I forgave you all that debt because you pleaded with me. Should you not also have had mercy on your fellow slave, in the same way that I had mercy on you?' And his lord, moved with anger, handed him over to the torturers until he should repay all that was owed him. My heavenly Father will also do the same to you, if each of you does not forgive his brother from your heart." *verses 22b-25*

CHAPTER 19

"Have you not read that He who created them from the beginning made them male and female, and said, 'For this reason a man shall leave his father and mother and be joined to his wife, and the two shall become one flesh'? So they are no longer two, but one flesh. What therefore God has joined together, let no man separate." *verses 4b-6*

"Because of your hardness of heart Moses permitted you to divorce your wives; but from the beginning it has not been this way. And I say to you, whoever divorces his wife, except for immorality, and marries another woman commits adultery." *verses 8b-9*

"Not all men can accept this statement, but only those to whom it has been given. For there are eunuchs who were born that way from their mother's womb; and there are eunuchs who were made eunuchs by men; and there are also eunuchs who made themselves eunuchs for the sake of the kingdom of heaven. He who is able to accept this, let him accept it." *verses 11b-12*

"Let the children alone, and do not hinder them from coming to Me; for the kingdom of heaven belongs to such as these." *verse 14b*

"Why are you asking Me about what is good? There is only One who is good; but if you wish to enter into life, keep the commandments." *verse 17b*

"You shall not commit murder; You shall not commit adultery; You shall not steal; You shall not bear false witness; Honor your father and mother; and You shall love your neighbor as yourself." *verses 18c-19*

"If you wish to be complete, go and sell your possessions and give to the poor, and you will have treasure in heaven; and come, follow Me." *verse 21b*

"Truly I say to you, it is hard for a rich man to enter the kingdom of heaven. Again I say to you, it is easier for a camel to go through the eye of a needle, than for a rich man to enter the kingdom of God." *verse 23b*

"With people this is impossible, but with God all things are possible." *verse 26b*

"Truly I say to you, that you who have followed Me, in the regeneration when the Son of Man will sit on His glorious throne, you also shall sit upon twelve thrones, judging the twelve tribes of Israel. And everyone who has left houses or brothers or sisters or father or mother or children or farms for My name's sake, will receive many times as much, and will inherit eternal life. But many who are first will be last; and the last, first. *verses 28b-30*

CHAPTER 20

"For the kingdom of heaven is like a landowner who went out early in the morning to hire laborers for his vineyard. When he had agreed with the laborers for a denarius for the day, he sent them into his vineyard. And he went out about the third hour and saw others standing idle in the market place; and to those he said, 'You also go into the vineyard, and whatever is right I will give you.' And so they went. Again he went out about the sixth and the ninth hour, and did the same thing. And about the eleventh hour he went out and found others standing around; and he said to them, 'Why have you been standing here idle all day long?' They said to him, 'Because no one hired us.' He said to them, 'You go into the vineyard too.' When evening came, the owner of the vineyard said to his foreman, 'Call the laborers and pay them their wages, beginning with the last group to the first.' When those hired about the eleventh hour came, each one received a denarius. When those hired first came, they thought that they would receive more; but each of them also received a denarius. When they received it, they grumbled at the landowner, saying, 'These last men have worked only one hour, and you have made them equal to us who have borne the burden and the scorching heat of the day.' But he answered and said to one of them, 'Friend, I am doing you no wrong; did you not agree with me for a denarius? Take what is yours and go, but I wish to give to this last man the same as to you. Is it not lawful for me to do what I wish with what is my own? Or is your eye envious because I am generous?' So the last shall be first, and the first last." *verses 1-16*

"Behold, we are going up to Jerusalem; and the Son of Man will be delivered to the chief priests and scribes, and they will condemn Him to death, and will hand Him over to the Gentiles to mock and scourge and crucify Him, and on the third day He will be raised up." *verses 18-19*

"What do you wish?" *verse 21b*

"You do not know what you are asking. Are you able to drink the cup that I am about to drink?" *verse 22b*

"My cup you shall drink; but to sit on My right and on My left, this is not Mine to give, but it is for those for whom it has been prepared by My Father." *verse 23b*

"You know that the rulers of the Gentiles lord it over them, and their great men exercise authority over them. It is not this way among you, but whoever wishes to become great among you shall be your servant, and whoever wishes to be first among you shall be your slave; just as the Son of Man did not come to be served, but to serve, and to give His life a ransom for many." *verses 25b-28*

"What do you want Me to do for you?" *verse 32b*

CHAPTER 21

"Go into the village opposite you, and immediately you will find a donkey tied there and a colt with her; untie them and bring them to Me. If anyone says anything to you, you shall say, 'The

Lord has need of them,' and immediately he will send them." *verses 2b-3*

"It is written, 'My house shall be called a house of prayer'; but you are making it a robbers' den." *verse 13b*

"Yes; have you never read, 'Out of the mouth of infants and nursing babies You have prepared praise for Yourself'?" *verse 16c*

"No longer shall there ever be any fruit from you." *verse 19c*

"Truly I say to you, if you have faith and do not doubt, you will not only do what was done to the fig tree, but even if you say to this mountain, 'Be taken up and cast into the sea,' it will happen. And all things you ask in prayer, believing, you will receive." *verses 21b-22*

"I will also ask you one thing, which if you tell Me, I will also tell you by what authority I do these things. The baptism of John was from what source, from heaven or from men?" *verses 24b-25*

"Neither will I tell you by what authority I do these things. But what do you think? A man had two sons, and he came to the first and said, 'Son, go work today in the vineyard.' And he answered, 'I will not'; but afterward he regretted it and went. The man came to the second and said the same thing; and he answered, 'I will, sir'; but he did not go. Which of the two did the will of his father?" They said, "The first." Jesus said to them, "Truly I say to you that the tax collectors and prostitutes will get into the kingdom of God before you. For John came to you in the way of righteousness and you did not believe him; but the tax collectors and prostitutes did believe him; and you, seeing this, did not even feel remorse afterward so as to believe him."

"Listen to another parable. There was a landowner who planted a vineyard and put a wall around it and dug a wine press in it, and built a tower, and rented it out to vine-growers and went on a journey. When the harvest time approached, he sent his slaves to the vine-growers to receive his produce. The vine-growers took his slaves and beat one, and killed another, and stoned a third. Again he sent another group of slaves larger than the first; and they did the same thing to them. But afterward he sent his son to them, saying, 'They will respect my son.' But when the vine-growers saw the son, they said among themselves, 'This is the heir; come, let us kill him and seize his inheritance.' They took him, and threw him out of the vineyard and killed him. Therefore when the owner of the vineyard comes, what will he do to those vine-growers?" They said to Him, "He will bring those wretches to a wretched end, and will rent out the vineyard to other vine-growers who will pay him the proceeds at the proper seasons." *verses 27c-41*

"Did you never read in the Scriptures, 'The stone which the builders rejected, this became the chief corner stone; This came about from the Lord, And it is marvelous in our eyes'? Therefore I say to you, the kingdom of God will be taken away from you and given to a people, producing the fruit of it. And he who falls on this stone will be broken to pieces; but on whomever it falls, it will scatter him like dust." *verses 42b-44*

CHAPTER 22

"The kingdom of heaven may be compared to a king who gave a wedding feast for his son. And he sent out his slaves to call those who had been invited to the wedding feast, and they were unwilling to come. Again he sent out other slaves saying, 'Tell those who have been invited, "Behold, I have prepared my dinner; my oxen and my fattened livestock are all butchered and everything is ready; come to the wedding feast."' But they paid no attention and went their way, one to his own farm, another to his business, and the rest seized his slaves and mistreated them and killed them. But the king was enraged, and he sent his armies and destroyed those murderers and set their city on fire. Then he said to his slaves, 'The wedding is ready, but those who were invited were not worthy. Go therefore to the main highways, and as many as you find there, invite to the wedding feast.' Those slaves went out into the streets and gathered together all they found, both evil and good; and the wedding hall was filled with dinner guests. But when the king came in to look over the dinner guests, he saw a man there who was not dressed in wedding clothes, and he said to him, 'Friend, how did you come in here without wedding clothes?' And the man was speechless. Then the king said to the servants, 'Bind him hand and foot, and throw him into the outer darkness; in that place there will be weeping and gnashing of teeth.' For many are called, but few are chosen." *verses 1b-14*

"Why are you testing Me, you hypocrites? Show Me the coin used for the poll-tax. Whose likeness and inscription is this? Then render to Caesar the things that are Caesar's; and to God the things that are God's." *verses 18b-19, 20b, and 21c*

"You are mistaken, not understanding the Scriptures nor the power of God. For in the resurrection they neither marry nor are given in marriage, but are like angels in heaven. But regarding the resurrection of the dead, have you not read what was spoken to you by God: 'I am the God of Abraham, and the God of Isaac, and the God of Jacob'? He is not the God of the dead but of the living." *verses 29b-32*

"'You shall love the Lord your God with all your heart, and with all your soul, and with all your mind.' This is the great and foremost commandment. The second is like it, 'You shall love your neighbor as yourself.' On these two commandments depend the whole Law and the Prophets." *verses 37b-39*

"What do you think about the Christ, whose son is He? Then how does David in the Spirit call Him 'Lord,' saying, 'The Lord said to my Lord, Sit at My right hand, Until I put Your enemies beneath

Your feet'"? If David then calls Him 'Lord,' how is He his son?" *verses 42a and 43b*

CHAPTER 23

"The scribes and the Pharisees have seated themselves in the chair of Moses; therefore all that they tell you, do and observe, but do not do according to their deeds; for they say things and do not do them. They tie up heavy burdens and lay them on men's shoulders, but they themselves are unwilling to move them with so much as a finger. But they do all their deeds to be noticed by men; for they broaden their phylacteries and lengthen the tassels of their garments. They love the place of honor at banquets and the chief seats in the synagogues, and respectful greetings in the market places, and being called Rabbi by men. But do not be called Rabbi; for One is your Teacher, and you are all brothers. Do not call anyone on earth your father; for One is your Father, He who is in heaven. Do not be called leaders; for One is your Leader, that is, Christ. But the greatest among you shall be your servant. Whoever exalts himself shall be humbled; and whoever humbles himself shall be exalted. But woe to you, scribes and Pharisees, hypocrites, because you shut off the kingdom of heaven from people; for you do not enter in yourselves, nor do you allow those who are entering to go in." *verses 2b-13*

"Woe to you, scribes and Pharisees, hypocrites, because you travel around on sea and land to make one proselyte; and when he becomes one, you make him twice as much a son of hell as yourselves. Woe to you, blind guides, who say, 'Whoever swears by the temple, that is nothing; but whoever swears by the gold of the temple is obligated.' You fools and blind men! Which is more important, the gold or the temple that sanctified the gold? And, 'Whoever swears by the altar, that is nothing, but whoever swears by the offering on it, he is obligated.' You blind men, which is more important, the offering, or the altar that sanctifies the offering? Therefore, whoever swears by the altar, swears both by the altar and by everything on it. And whoever swears by the temple, swears both by the temple and by Him who dwells within it. And whoever swears by heaven, swears both by the throne of God and by Him who sits upon it.

"Woe to you, scribes and Pharisees, hypocrites! For you tithe mint and dill and cummin, and have neglected the weightier provisions of the law: justice and mercy and faithfulness; but these are the things you should have done without neglecting the others. You blind guides, who strain out a gnat and swallow a camel! Woe to you, scribes and Pharisees, hypocrites! For you clean the outside of the cup and of the dish, but inside they are full of robbery and self-indulgence. You blind Pharisee, first clean the inside of the cup and of the dish, so that the outside of it may become clean also. Woe to you, scribes and Pharisees, hypocrites! For you are like whitewashed tombs which on the outside appear beautiful, but inside they are full of dead men's bones and all uncleanness. So you, too, outwardly appear righteous to men, but inwardly you are full of hypocrisy and lawlessness. Woe to you, scribes and Pharisees, hypocrites! For you build the tombs of the prophets and adorn the monuments of the righteous, and say, 'If we had been living in the days of our fathers, we would not have been partners with them in shedding the blood of the prophets.' So you testify against yourselves, that you are sons of those who murdered the prophets. Fill up, then, the measure of the guilt of your fathers. You serpents, you brood of vipers, how will you escape the sentence of hell? Therefore, behold, I am sending you prophets and wise men and scribes; some of them you will kill and crucify, and some of them you will scourge in your synagogues, and persecute from city to city, so that upon you may fall the guilt of all the righteous blood shed on earth, from the blood of righteous Abel to the blood of Zechariah, the son of Berechiah, whom you murdered between the temple and the altar. Truly I say to you, all these things will come upon this generation. Jerusalem, Jerusalem, who kills the prophets and stones those who are sent to her!

How often I wanted to gather your children together, the way a hen gathers her chicks under her wings, and you were unwilling. Behold, your house is being left to you desolate! For I say to you, from now on you will not see Me until you say, 'Blessed is He who comes in the name of the Lord!'" *verses 15-39*

CHAPTER 24

"Do you not see all these things? Truly I say to you, not one stone here will be left upon another, which will not be torn down." *verse 2b*

"See to it that no one misleads you. For many will come in My name, saying, 'I am the Christ,' and will mislead many. You will be hearing of wars and rumors of wars. See that you are not frightened, for those things must take place, but that is not yet the end. For nation will rise against nation, and kingdom against kingdom, and in various places there will be famines and earthquakes. But all these things are merely the beginning of birth pangs. Then they will deliver you to tribulation, and will kill you, and you will be hated by all nations because of My name. At that time many will fall away and will betray one another and hate one another. Many false prophets will arise and will mislead many. Because lawlessness is increased, most people's love will grow cold. But the one who endures to the end, he will be saved. This gospel of the kingdom shall be preached in the whole world as a testimony to all the nations, and then the end will come.

"Therefore when you see the abomination of desolation which was spoken of through Daniel the prophet, standing in the holy place, then those who are in Judea must flee to the mountains. Whoever is on the housetop must not go down to get the things out that are in his house. Whoever is in the field must not turn back to get his cloak. But woe to those who are pregnant and to those who are nursing babies in those days! But pray that your flight will not be in the winter, or on a Sabbath. For then there will be a great tribulation, such as has not occurred since the beginning of the world until now, nor ever will. Unless those days had been cut short, no life would have been saved; but for the sake of the elect those days will be cut short. Then if anyone says to you, 'Behold, here is the Christ,' or 'There He is,' do not believe him. For false Christs and false prophets will arise and will show great signs and wonders, so as to mislead, if possible, even the elect. Behold, I have told you in advance. So if they say to you, 'Behold, He is in the wilderness,' do not go out, or, 'Behold, He is in the inner rooms,' do not believe them. For just as the lightning comes from the east and flashes even to the west, so will the coming of the Son of Man be. Wherever the corpse is, there the vultures will gather.

"But immediately after the tribulation of those days the sun will be darkened, and the moon will not give its light, and the stars will fall from the sky, and the powers of the heavens will be shaken. And then the sign of the Son of Man will appear in the sky, and then all the tribes of the earth will mourn, and they will see the Son of Man coming on the clouds of the sky with power and great glory. And He will send forth His angels with a great trumpet and they will gather together His elect from the four winds, from one end of the sky to the other.

"Now learn the parable from the fig tree: when its branch has already become tender and puts forth its leaves, you know that summer is near; so, you too, when you see all these things, recognize that He is near, right at the door. Truly I say to you, this generation will not pass away until all these things take place. Heaven and earth will pass away, but My words will not pass away. But of that day and hour no one knows, not even the angels of heaven, nor the Son, but the Father alone. For the coming of the Son of Man will be just like the days of Noah. For as in those days before the flood they were eating and drinking, marrying and giving in marriage, until the day that Noah entered the ark, and they did not understand until the flood came and took them all away; so will the coming of the Son of Man be. Then there will be two men in the field; one will be taken and one will be left. Two women will be grinding at the mill; one will be taken and one will be left. Therefore be on the alert, for you do not know which day your Lord is coming. "But be sure of this, that if the head of the house had known at what time of the night the thief was coming, he would have been on the alert and would not have allowed his house to be broken into. For this reason you also must be ready; for the Son of Man is coming at an hour when you do not think He will. Who then is the faithful and sensible slave whom his master put in charge of his household to give them their food at the proper time? Blessed is that slave whom his master finds so doing when he comes. Truly I say to you that he will put him in charge of all his possessions. But if that evil slave says in his heart, 'My master is not coming for a long time,' and begins to beat his fellow slaves and eat and drink with drunkards; the master of that slave will come on a day when he does not expect him and at an hour which he does not know, and will cut him in pieces and assign him a place with the hypocrites; in that place there will be weeping and gnashing of teeth." *verses 4b-51*

CHAPTER 25

"Then the kingdom of heaven will be comparable to ten virgins, who took their lamps and went out to meet the bridegroom. Five of them were foolish, and five were prudent. For when the foolish took their lamps, they took no oil with them, but the prudent took oil in flasks along with their lamps. Now while the bridegroom was delaying, they all got drowsy and began to sleep. But at midnight there was a shout, 'Behold, the bridegroom! Come out to meet him.' Then all those virgins rose and trimmed their lamps. The foolish said to the prudent, 'Give us some of your oil, for our lamps are going out.' But the prudent answered, 'No, there will not be enough for us and you too; go instead to the dealers and buy some for yourselves.' And while they were going away to make the purchase, the bridegroom came, and those who were ready went in with him to the wedding feast; and the door was shut. Later the other virgins also came, saying, 'Lord, lord, open up for us.' But he answered, 'Truly I say to you, I do not know you.' Be on the alert then, for you do not know the day nor the hour. "For it is just like a man about to go on a journey, who called his own slaves and entrusted his possessions to them. To one he gave five talents, to another, two, and to another, one, each according to his own ability; and he went on his journey. Immediately the one who had received the five talents went and traded with them, and gained five more talents. In the same manner the one who had received the two talents gained two more. But he who received the one talent went away, and dug a hole in the ground and hid his master's money. Now after a long time the master of those slaves came and settled accounts with them. The one who had received the five talents came up and brought five more talents, saying, 'Master, you entrusted five talents to me. See, I have gained five more talents.' His master said to him, 'Well done, good and faithful slave. You were faithful with a few things, I will put you in charge of many things; enter into the joy of your master.' Also the one who had received the two talents came up and said, 'Master, you entrusted two talents to me. See, I have gained two more talents.' His master said to him, 'Well done, good and faithful slave. You were faithful with a few things, I will put you in charge of many things; enter into the joy of your master.' And the one also who had received the one talent came up and said, 'Master, I knew you to be a hard man, reaping where you did not sow and gathering where you scattered no seed. And I was afraid, and went away and hid your talent in the ground. See, you have what is yours.' But his master answered and said to him, 'You wicked, lazy slave, you knew that I reap where I did not sow and gather where I scattered no seed. Then you ought to have put my money in the bank, and on my arrival

I would have received my money back with interest. Therefore take away the talent from him, and give it to the one who has the ten talents.' For to everyone who has, more shall be given, and he will have an abundance; but from the one who does not have, even what he does have shall be taken away. Throw out the worthless slave into the outer darkness; in that place there will be weeping and gnashing of teeth.

"But when the Son of Man comes in His glory, and all the angels with Him, then He will sit on His glorious throne. All the nations will be gathered before Him; and He will separate them from one another, as the shepherd separates the sheep from the goats; and He will put the sheep on His right, and the goats on the left. Then the King will say to those on His right, 'Come, you who are blessed of My Father, inherit the kingdom prepared for you from the foundation of the world. For I was hungry, and you gave Me something to eat; I was thirsty, and you gave Me something to drink; I was a stranger, and you invited Me in; naked, and you clothed Me; I was sick, and you visited Me; I was in prison, and you came to Me.' Then the righteous will answer Him, 'Lord, when did we see You hungry, and feed You, or thirsty, and give You something to drink? And when did we see You a stranger, and invite You in, or naked, and clothe You? When did we see You sick, or in prison, and come to You?' The King will answer and say to them, 'Truly I say to you, to the extent that you did it to one of these brothers of Mine, even the least of them, you did it to Me.' Then He will also say to those on His left, 'Depart from Me, accursed ones, into the eternal fire which has been prepared for the devil and his angels; for I was hungry, and you gave Me nothing to eat; I was thirsty, and you gave Me nothing to drink; I was a stranger, and you did not invite Me in; naked, and you did not clothe Me; sick, and in prison, and you did not visit Me.' Then they themselves also will answer, 'Lord, when did we see You hungry, or thirsty, or a stranger, or naked, or sick, or in prison, and did not take care of You?' Then He will answer them, 'Truly I say to you, to the extent that you did not do it to

FINDING SOLID GROUND

one of the least of these, you did not do it to Me.' These will go away into eternal punishment, but the righteous into eternal life." *verses 1-46*

CHAPTER 26

"You know that after two days the Passover is coming, and the Son of Man is to be handed over for crucifixion." *verse 2*

"Why do you bother the woman? For she has done a good deed to Me. For you always have the poor with you; but you do not always have Me. For when she poured this perfume on My body, she did it to prepare Me for burial. Truly I say to you, wherever this gospel is preached in the whole world, what this woman has done will also be spoken of in memory of her." *verses 10b-13*

"Go into the city to a certain man, and say to him, The Teacher says, 'My time is near; I am to keep the Passover at your house with My disciples.'" *verse 18b*

"Truly I say to you that one of you will betray Me." *verse 21b*

"He who dipped his hand with Me in the bowl is the one who will betray Me. The Son of Man is to go, just as it is written of Him; but woe to that man by whom the Son of Man is betrayed! It would have been good for that man if he had not been born." *verses 23b-24*

"You have said it yourself." *verse 25c*

"Take, eat; this is My body." *verse 26d*

"Drink from it, all of you; for this is My blood of the covenant, which is poured out for many for forgiveness of sins. But I say to you, I will not drink of this fruit of the vine from now on until that day when I drink it new with you in My Father's kingdom." *verses 27c-29*

"You will all fall away because of Me this night, for it is written, 'I will strike down the shepherd, and the sheep of the flock shall be scattered.' But after I have been raised, I will go ahead of you to Galilee." *verses 31b-32*

"Truly I say to you that this very night, before a rooster crows, you will deny Me three times." *verse 34b*

"Sit here while I go over there and pray." *verse 36b*

"My soul is deeply grieved, to the point of death; remain here and keep watch with Me." *verse 38b*

"My Father, if it is possible, let this cup pass from Me; yet not as I will, but as You will." *verse 39b*

"So, you men could not keep watch with Me for one hour? Keep watching and praying that you may not enter into temptation; the spirit is willing, but the flesh is weak." *verses 40b-41*

"My Father, if this cannot pass away unless I drink it, Your will be done." *verse 42b*

"Are you still sleeping and resting? Behold, the hour is at hand and the Son of Man is being betrayed into the hands of sinners. Get up, let us be going; behold, the one who betrays Me is at hand!" *verses 45b-46*

"Friend, do what you have come for." *verse 50b*

"Put your sword back into its place; for all those who take up the sword shall perish by the sword. Or do you think that I cannot appeal to My Father, and He will at once put at My disposal more than twelve legions of angels? How then will the Scriptures be fulfilled, which say that it must happen this way?" *verses 52b-54*

"Have you come out with swords and clubs to arrest Me as you would against a robber? Every day I used to sit in the temple teaching and you did not seize Me. But all this has taken place to fulfill the Scriptures of the prophets." *verses 55b-56*

"You have said it yourself; nevertheless I tell you, hereafter you will see the Son of Man sitting at the right hand of Power, and coming on the clouds of heaven." *verse 64b*

CHAPTER 27

"It is as you say." *verse 11c*

"Eli, Eli, lama sabachthani?" ("My God, My God, why have You forsaken Me?") *verse 46b*

CHAPTER 28

"Do not be afraid; go and take word to My brethren to leave for Galilee, and there they will see Me." *verse 10b*

"All authority has been given to Me in heaven and on earth. Go therefore and make disciples of all the nations, baptizing them in the name of the Father and the Son and the Holy Spirit, teaching them to observe all that I commanded you; and lo, I am with you always, even to the end of the age." *verses 18b-20*

Luke, dated 90-100 CE, author uncertain. Audience: mostly gentile, Pauline influence, Aegean region. (White, p. 252)

CHAPTER 1- Jesus is not quoted.

CHAPTER 2

"Why is it that you were looking for Me? Did you not know that I had to be in My Father's house?" *verse 49b*

CHAPTER 3- Jesus is not quoted.

CHAPTER 4

"It is written, 'Man shall not live on bread alone.'" *verse 4b*

"It is written, 'You shall worship the Lord your God and serve Him only.'" *verse 8b*

"It is said, 'You shall not put the Lord your God to the test.'" *verse 12b*

"Today this Scripture has been fulfilled in your hearing." *verse 21b*

"No doubt you will quote this proverb to Me, 'Physician, heal yourself! Whatever we heard was done at Capernaum, do here in your hometown as well.'" *verse 23b*

"Truly I say to you, no prophet is welcome in his hometown. But I say to you in truth, there were many widows in Israel in the days of Elijah, when the sky was shut up for three years and six months, when a great famine came over all the land; and yet Elijah was sent to none of them, but only to Zarephath, in the land of Sidon, to a woman who was a widow. And there were many lepers in Israel in the time of Elisha the prophet; and none of them was cleansed, but only Naaman the Syrian." *verses 24b-27*

"Be quiet and come out of him!" *verse 35b*

"I must preach the kingdom of God to the other cities also, for I was sent for this purpose." *verse 43b*

CHAPTER 5

"Put out into the deep water and let down your nets for a catch." *verse 4b*

"Do not fear, from now on you will be catching men." *verse 10c*

"I am willing; be cleansed." *verse 13b*

"But go and show yourself to the priest and make an offering for your cleansing, just as Moses commanded, as a testimony to them." *verse 14b*

"Friend, your sins are forgiven you." *verse 20b*

"Why are you reasoning in your hearts? Which is easier, to say, 'Your sins have been forgiven you,' or to say, 'Get up and walk'? But, so that you may know that the Son of Man has authority on earth to forgive sins..." *verses 22b-24a*

"I say to you, get up, and pick up your stretcher and go home." *verse 24c*

"Follow Me." *verse 27c*

"It is not those who are well who need a physician, but those who are sick. I have not come to call the righteous but sinners to repentance." *verses 31b-32*

"You cannot make the attendants of the bridegroom fast while the bridegroom is with them, can you? But the days will come; and when the bridegroom is taken away from them, then they will fast in those days." *verses 34b-35*

"No one tears a piece of cloth from a new garment and puts it on an old garment; otherwise he will both tear the new, and the piece from the new will not match the old. And no one puts new wine into old wineskins; otherwise the new wine will burst the skins and it will be spilled out, and the skins will be ruined. But new wine must be put into fresh wineskins. And no one, after drinking old wine wishes for new; for he says, 'The old is good enough.'" *verses 36b-39*

CHAPTER 6

"Have you not even read what David did when he was hungry, he and those who were with him, how he entered the house of God, and took and ate the consecrated bread which is not lawful for any to eat except the priests alone, and gave it to his companions?" *verses 3b-4*

"The Son of Man is Lord of the Sabbath." *verse 5b*

"Get up and come forward!" *verse 8c*

"I ask you, is it lawful to do good or to do harm on the Sabbath, to save a life or to destroy it?" *verse 9b*

"Stretch out your hand!" *verse 10b*

"Blessed are you who are poor, for yours is the kingdom of God. Blessed are you who hunger now, for you shall be satisfied. Blessed are you who weep now, for you shall laugh. Blessed are you when men hate you, and ostracize you, and insult you, and scorn your name as evil, for the sake of the Son of Man. Be glad in that day and leap for joy, for behold, your reward is great in heaven. For in the same way their fathers used to treat the prophets. But woe to you who are rich, for you are receiving your comfort in full. Woe to you who are well-fed now, for you shall be hungry. Woe to you who laugh now, for you shall mourn and weep. Woe to you when all men speak well of you, for their fathers used to treat the false prophets in the same way.

"But I say to you who hear, love your enemies, do good to those who hate you, bless those who curse you, pray for those who mistreat you. Whoever hits you on the cheek, offer him the other also; and whoever takes away your coat, do not withhold your shirt from him either. Give to everyone who asks of you, and whoever takes away what is yours, do not demand it back. Treat others the same way you want them to treat you. If you love those who love you, what credit is that to you? For even sinners love those who love them. If you do good to those who do good to you, what credit is that to you? For even sinners do the same. If you lend to those from whom you expect to receive, what credit is that to you? Even sinners lend to sinners in order to receive back the same amount. But love your enemies, and do good, and lend, expecting nothing in return; and your reward will be great, and you will be sons of the Most High; for He Himself is kind to ungrateful and evil men. Be merciful, just as your Father is merciful.

"Do not judge, and you will not be judged; and do not condemn, and you will not be condemned; pardon, and you will be pardoned. Give, and it will be given to you. They will pour into your lap a good measure—pressed down, shaken together, and running over. For by your standard of measure it will be measured to you in return." *verses 20b-38*

"A blind man cannot guide a blind man, can he? Will they not both fall into a pit? A pupil is not above his teacher; but everyone, after he has been fully trained, will be like his teacher. Why do you look at the speck that is in your brother's eye, but do not notice the log that is in your own eye? Or how can you say to your brother, 'Brother, let me take out the speck that is in your eye,' when you yourself do not see the log that is in your own eye? You hypocrite, first take the log out of your own eye, and then you will see clearly to take out the speck that is in your brother's eye.

"For there is no good tree which produces bad fruit, nor, on the other hand, a bad tree which produces good fruit. For each tree is known by its own fruit. For men do not gather figs from thorns, nor do they pick grapes from a briar bush. The good man out of the good treasure of his heart brings forth what is good; and the evil man out of the evil treasure brings forth what is evil; for his mouth speaks from that which fills his heart.

"Why do you call Me, 'Lord, Lord,' and do not do what I say? Everyone who comes to Me and hears My words and acts on them, I will show you whom he is like: he is like a man building a house, who dug deep and laid a foundation on the rock; and when a flood occurred, the torrent burst against that house and could not shake it, because it had been well built. But the one who has heard and has not acted accordingly, is like a man who built a house on the ground without any foundation; and the torrent burst against it and immediately it collapsed, and the ruin of that house was great." *verses 39b-49*

CHAPTER 7

"I say to you, not even in Israel have I found such great faith." *verse 9c*

"Do not weep." *verse 13c*

"Young man, I say to you, arise!" *verse 14c*

"Go and report to John what you have seen and heard: the blind receive sight, the lame walk, the lepers are cleansed, and the deaf hear, the dead are raised up, the poor have the gospel preached to them. Blessed is he who does not take offense at Me." *verses 22b-23*

"What did you go out into the wilderness to see? A reed shaken by the wind? But what did you go out to see? A man dressed in soft clothing? Those who are splendidly clothed and live in luxury are found in royal palaces! But what did you go out to see? A prophet? Yes, I say to you, and one who is more than a prophet. This is the one about whom it is written, 'Behold, I send My messenger ahead of You, Who will prepare Your way before You.' I say to you, among those born of women there is no one greater than John; yet he who is least in the kingdom of God is greater than he." *verses 24b-28*

"To what then shall I compare the men of this generation, and what are they like? They are like children who sit in the market place and call to one another, and they say, 'We played the flute for you, and you did not dance; we sang a dirge, and you did not weep.' For John the Baptist has come eating no bread and drinking no wine, and you say, 'He has a demon!' The Son of Man has come eating and drinking, and you say, 'Behold, a gluttonous man and a drunkard, a friend of tax collectors and sinners!' Yet wisdom is vindicated by all her children." *verses 31-35*

"Simon, I have something to say to you." *verse 40b*

"A moneylender had two debtors: one owed five hundred denarii, and the other fifty. When they were unable to repay, he graciously forgave them both. So which of them will love him more?" *verses 41-42*

"You have judged correctly." *verse 43c*

"Do you see this woman? I entered your house; you gave Me no water for My feet, but she has wet My feet with her tears and wiped them with her hair. You gave Me no kiss; but she, since the time I came in, has not ceased to kiss My feet. You did not anoint My head with oil, but she anointed My feet with perfume. For this reason I say to you, her sins, which are many, have been forgiven, for she loved much; but he who is forgiven little, loves little." *verses 44b-47*

"Your sins have been forgiven." *verse 48b*

"Your faith has saved you; go in peace." *verse 50b*

CHAPTER 8

"The sower went out to sow his seed; and as he sowed, some fell beside the road, and it was trampled under foot and the birds of the air ate it up. Other seed fell on rocky soil, and as soon as it grew up, it withered away, because it had no moisture. Other seed fell among the thorns; and the thorns grew up with it and choked it out. Other seed fell into the good soil, and grew up, and produced a crop a hundred times as great. He who has ears to hear, let him hear." *verses 5-8a, and 8c*

"To you it has been granted to know the mysteries of the kingdom of God, but to the rest it is in parables, so that seeing they may not see, and hearing they may not understand. Now the parable is this: the seed is the word of God. Those beside the road are those who have heard; then the devil comes and takes away the word from their heart, so that they will not believe and be saved. Those on the rocky soil are those who, when they hear, receive the word with joy; and these have no firm root; they believe for a while, and in time of temptation fall away. The seed which fell among the thorns, these are the ones who have heard, and as they go on their way they are choked with worries and riches and pleasures of this life, and bring no fruit to maturity. But the seed in the good soil, these are the ones who have heard the word in an honest and good heart, and hold it fast, and bear fruit with perseverance.

"Now no one after lighting a lamp covers it over with a container, or puts it under a bed; but he puts it on a lampstand, so that those who come in may see the light. For nothing is hidden that will not become evident, nor anything secret that will not be known and come to light. So take care how you listen; for whoever has, to him more shall be given; and whoever does not have, even what he thinks he has shall be taken away from him." *verses 10b-18*

"My mother and My brothers are these who hear the word of God and do it." *verse 21b*

"Let us go over to the other side of the lake." *verse 22c*

"Where is your faith?" *verse 25b*

"What is your name?" *verse 30b*

"Return to your house and describe what great things God has done for you." *verse 39a*

"Who is the one who touched Me? Someone did touch Me, for I was aware that power had gone out of Me. Daughter, your faith has made you well; go in peace." *verses 45b, 46b, and 48b*

"Do not be afraid any longer; only believe, and she will be made well." *verse 50b*

"Stop weeping, for she has not died, but is asleep." *verse 52b*

"Child, arise!" *verse 54b*

CHAPTER 9

"Take nothing for your journey, neither a staff, nor a bag, nor bread, nor money; and do not even have two tunics apiece. Whatever house you enter, stay there until you leave that city. And as for those who do not receive you, as you go out from that city, shake the dust off your feet as a testimony against them." *verses 3b-5*

"You give them something to eat!" *verse 13b*

"Have them sit down to eat in groups of about fifty each." *verse 14c*

"Who do the people say that I am?" *verse 18c*

"But who do you say that I am?" *verse 20b*

"The Son of Man must suffer many things and be rejected by the elders and chief priests and scribes, and be killed and be raised up on the third day." *verse 22b*

"If anyone wishes to come after Me, he must deny himself, and take up his cross daily and follow Me. For whoever wishes to save his life will lose it, but whoever loses his life for My sake, he is the one who will save it. For what is a man profited if he gains the whole world, and loses or forfeits himself? For whoever is ashamed of Me and My words, the Son of Man will be ashamed of him when He comes in His glory, and the glory of the Father and of the holy angels. But I say to you truthfully, there are some of those standing here who will not taste death until they see the kingdom of God." *verses 23b-27*

"You unbelieving and perverted generation, how long shall I be with you and put up with you? Bring your son here." *verse 41b*

"Let these words sink into your ears; for the Son of Man is going to be delivered into the hands of men." *verse 44*

"Whoever receives this child in My name receives Me, and whoever receives Me receives Him who sent Me; for the one who is least among all of you, this is the one who is great." *verse 48b*

"Do not hinder him; for he who is not against you is for you." *verse 50b*

"The foxes have holes and the birds of the air have nests, but the Son of Man has nowhere to lay His head." *verse 58b*

"Follow Me." *verse 59b*

"Allow the dead to bury their own dead; but as for you, go and proclaim everywhere the kingdom of God." *verse 60b*

"No one, after putting his hand to the plow and looking back, is fit for the kingdom of God." *verse 62b*

CHAPTER 10

"The harvest is plentiful, but the laborers are few; therefore beseech the Lord of the harvest to send out laborers into His harvest. Go; behold, I send you out as lambs in the midst of wolves. Carry no money belt, no bag, no shoes; and greet no one on the way. Whatever house you enter, first say, 'Peace be to this house.' If a man of peace is there, your peace will rest on him; but if not, it will return to you. Stay in that house, eating and drinking what they give you; for the laborer is worthy of his wages. Do not keep moving from house to house. Whatever city you enter and they receive you, eat what is set before you; and heal those in it who are sick, and say to them, 'The kingdom of God has come near to you.' But whatever city you enter and they do not receive you, go out into its streets and say, 'Even the dust of your city which clings to our feet we wipe off in protest against you; yet be sure of this, that the kingdom of God has come near.' I say to you, it will be more tolerable in that day for Sodom than for that city. "Woe to you, Chorazin! Woe to you, Bethsaida! For if the miracles had been performed in Tyre and Sidon which occurred in you, they would have repented long ago, sitting in sackcloth and ashes. But it will be more tolerable for Tyre and Sidon in the judgment than for you. And you, Capernaum, will not be exalted to heaven, will you? You will be brought down to Hades! The one who listens to you listens to Me, and the one who rejects you rejects Me; and he who rejects Me rejects the One who sent Me." *verses 2b-16*

"I was watching Satan fall from heaven like lightning. Behold, I have given you authority to tread on serpents and scorpions, and over all the power of the enemy, and nothing will injure you. Nevertheless do not rejoice in this, that the spirits are subject to you, but rejoice that your names are recorded in heaven." *verses 18b-20*

"I praise You, O Father, Lord of heaven and earth, that You have hidden these things from the wise and intelligent and have revealed them to infants. Yes, Father, for this way was well-pleasing in Your sight. All things have been handed over to Me by My Father, and no one knows who the Son is except the Father, and who the Father is except the Son, and anyone to whom the Son wills to reveal Him." *verses 21c-22*

"Blessed are the eyes which see the things you see, for I say to you, that many prophets and kings wished to see the things which you see, and did not see them, and to hear the things which you hear, and did not hear them." *verses 23b-24*

"What is written in the Law? How does it read to you?" *verse 26b*

"You have answered correctly; do this and you will live." *verse 28b*

"A man was going down from Jerusalem to Jericho, and fell among robbers, and they stripped him and beat him, and went away leaving him half dead. And by chance a priest was going down on that road, and when he saw him, he passed by on the other side. Likewise a Levite also, when he came to the place and saw him, passed by on the other side. But a Samaritan, who was on a journey, came upon him; and when he saw him, he felt compassion, and came to him and bandaged up his wounds, pouring oil and wine on them; and he put him on his own beast, and brought him to an inn and took care of him. On the next day he took out two denarii and gave them to the innkeeper and said, 'Take care of him; and whatever more you spend, when I return I will repay you.' Which of these three do you think proved to be a neighbor to the man who fell into the robbers' hands?" *verses 30b-36*

"Go and do the same." *verse 37c*

"Martha, Martha, you are worried and bothered about so many things; but only one thing is necessary, for Mary has chosen the good part, which shall not be taken away from her." *verses 41b-42*

CHAPTER 11

"When you pray, say: Father, hallowed be Your name. Your kingdom come. Give us each day our daily bread. And forgive us our sins, for we ourselves also forgive everyone who is indebted to us. And lead us not into temptation." *verses 2b-4*

"Suppose one of you has a friend, and goes to him at midnight and says to him, 'Friend, lend me three loaves; for a friend of mine has come to me from a journey, and I have nothing to set before him'; and from inside he answers and says, 'Do not bother me; the door has already been shut and my children and I are in bed; I cannot get up and give you anything.' I tell you, even though he will not get up and give him anything because he is his friend, yet because of his persistence he will get up and give him as much as he needs.

"So I say to you, ask, and it will be given to you; seek, and you will find; knock, and it will be opened to you. For everyone who asks, receives; and he who seeks, finds; and to him who knocks, it will be opened.

"Now suppose one of you fathers is asked by his son for a loaf, he will not give him a stone, will he, or for a fish; he will not give him a snake instead of a fish, will he? Or if he is asked for an egg, he will not give him a scorpion, will he? If you then, being evil, know how to give good gifts to your children, how much more will your heavenly Father give the Holy Spirit to those who ask Him?" *verses 5b-13*

"Any kingdom divided against itself is laid waste; and a house divided against itself falls. If Satan also is divided against himself, how will his kingdom stand? For you say that I cast out demons by Beelzebul. And if I by Beelzebul cast out demons, by whom do your sons cast them out? So they will be your judges. But if I cast out demons by the finger of God, then the kingdom of God has come upon you. When a strong man, fully armed, guards his own house, his possessions are undisturbed. But when someone stronger than he attacks him and overpowers him, he takes away from him all his armor on which he had relied and distributes his plunder.

"He who is not with Me is against Me; and he who does not gather with Me, scatters.

"When the unclean spirit goes out of a man, it passes through waterless places seeking rest, and not finding any, it says, 'I will return to my house from which I came.' And when it comes, it finds it swept and put in order. Then it goes and takes along seven other spirits more evil than itself, and they go in and live there; and the last state of that man becomes worse than the first." *verses 17b-26*

"On the contrary, blessed are those who hear the word of God and observe it." *verse 28b*

"This generation is a wicked generation; it seeks for a sign, and yet no sign will be given to it but the sign of Jonah. For just as Jonah became a sign to the Ninevites, so will the Son of Man be to this generation. The Queen of the South will rise up with the men of this generation at the judgment and condemn them, because she came from the ends of the earth to hear the wisdom of Solomon; and behold, something greater than Solomon is here. The men of Nineveh will stand up with this generation at the judgment and condemn it, because they repented at the preaching of Jonah; and behold, something greater than Jonah is here.

"No one, after lighting a lamp, puts it away in a cellar nor under a basket, but on the lampstand, so that those who enter may see the light. The eye is the lamp of your body; when your eye is clear, your whole body also is full of light; but when it is bad, your body also is full of darkness. Then watch out that the light in you is not darkness. If therefore your whole body is full of light, with no dark part in it, it will be wholly illumined, as when the lamp illumines you with its rays." *verses 29b-36*

"Now you Pharisees clean the outside of the cup and of the platter; but inside of you, you are full of robbery and wickedness. You foolish ones, did not He who made the outside make the inside also? But give that which is within as charity, and then all things are clean for you.

"But woe to you Pharisees! For you pay tithe of mint and rue and every kind of garden herb, and yet disregard justice and the love of God; but these are the things you should have done without neglecting the others. Woe to you Pharisees! For you love the chief seats in the synagogues and the respectful greetings in the market places. Woe to you! For you are like concealed tombs, and the people who walk over them are unaware of it." *verses 39b-44*

"Woe to you lawyers as well! For you weigh men down with burdens hard to bear, while you yourselves will not even touch the burdens with one of your fingers. Woe to you! For you build the tombs of the prophets, and it was your fathers who killed them. So you are witnesses and approve the deeds of your fathers; because it was they who killed them, and you build their tombs. For this reason also the wisdom of God said, 'I will send to them prophets and apostles, and some of them they will kill and some they will persecute, so that the blood of all the prophets, shed since the foundation of the world, may be charged against this generation, from the blood of Abel to the blood of Zechariah, who was killed between the altar and the house of God; yes, I tell you, it shall be charged against this generation.' Woe to you lawyers! For you have taken away the key of knowledge; you yourselves did not enter, and you hindered those who were entering." *verses 46b-52*

CHAPTER 12

"Beware of the leaven of the Pharisees, which is hypocrisy. But there is nothing covered up that will not be revealed, and hidden that will not be known. Accordingly, whatever you have said in the dark will be heard in the light, and what you have whispered in the inner rooms will be proclaimed upon the housetops.

"I say to you, My friends, do not be afraid of those who kill the body and after that have no more that they can do. But I will warn you whom to fear: fear the One who, after He has killed, has authority to cast into hell; yes, I tell you, fear Him! Are not five sparrows sold for two cents? Yet not one of them is forgotten before God. Indeed, the very hairs of your head are all numbered. Do not fear; you are more valuable than many sparrows.

"And I say to you, everyone who confesses Me before men, the Son of Man will confess him also before the angels of God; but he who denies Me before men will be denied before the angels of God. And everyone who speaks a word against the Son of Man, it will be forgiven him; but he who blasphemes against the Holy Spirit, it will not be forgiven him.

"When they bring you before the synagogues and the rulers and the authorities, do not worry about how or what you are to speak in your defense, or what you are to say; for the Holy Spirit will teach you in that very hour what you ought to say." *verses 1c-12*

"Man, who appointed Me a judge or arbitrator over you?" *verse 14b*

"Beware, and be on your guard against every form of greed; for not even when one has an abundance does his life consist of his possessions. The land of a rich man was very productive. And he began reasoning to himself, saying, 'What shall I do, since I have no place to store my crops?' Then he said, 'This is what I will do: I will tear down my barns and build larger ones, and there I will store all my grain and my goods. And I will say to my soul, "Soul, you have many goods laid up for many years to come; take your ease, eat, drink and be merry."' But God said to him, 'You fool! This very night your soul is required of you; and now who will own what you have prepared?' So is the man who stores up treasure for himself, and is not rich toward God." *verses 15b and 16b-21*

"For this reason I say to you, do not worry about your life, as to what you will eat; nor for your body, as to what you will put on.

For life is more than food, and the body more than clothing. Consider the ravens, for they neither sow nor reap; they have no storeroom nor barn, and yet God feeds them; how much more valuable you are than the birds! And which of you by worrying can add a single hour to his life's span? If then you cannot do even a very little thing, why do you worry about other matters? Consider the lilies, how they grow: they neither toil nor spin; but I tell you, not even Solomon in all his glory clothed himself like one of these. But if God so clothes the grass in the field, which is alive today and tomorrow is thrown into the furnace, how much more will He clothe you? You men of little faith! And do not seek what you will eat and what you will drink, and do not keep worrying. For all these things the nations of the world eagerly seek; but your Father knows that you need these things. But seek His kingdom, and these things will be added to you. Do not be afraid, little flock, for your Father has chosen gladly to give you the kingdom.

"Sell your possessions and give to charity; make yourselves money belts which do not wear out, an unfailing treasure in heaven, where no thief comes near nor moth destroys. For where your treasure is, there your heart will be also." *verses 22b-34*

"Be dressed in readiness, and keep your lamps lit. Be like men who are waiting for their master when he returns from the wedding feast, so that they may immediately open the door to him when he comes and knocks. Blessed are those slaves whom the master will find on the alert when he comes; truly I say to you, that he will gird himself to serve, and have them recline at the table, and will come up and wait on them. Whether he comes in the second watch, or even in the third, and finds them so, blessed are those slaves.

"But be sure of this, that if the head of the house had known at what hour the thief was coming, he would not have allowed his house to be broken into. You too, be ready; for the Son of Man is coming at an hour that you do not expect." *verses 35-40*

"Who then is the faithful and sensible steward, whom his master will put in charge of his servants, to give them their rations at the proper time? Blessed is that slave whom his master finds so doing when he comes. Truly I say to you that he will put him in charge of all his possessions. But if that slave says in his heart, 'My master will be a long time in coming,' and begins to beat the slaves, both men and women, and to eat and drink and get drunk; the master of that slave will come on a day when he does not expect him and at an hour he does not know, and will cut him in pieces, and assign him a place with the unbelievers. And that slave who knew his master's will and did not get ready or act in accord with his will, will receive many lashes, but the one who did not know it, and committed deeds worthy of a flogging, will receive but few. From everyone who has been given much, much will be required; and to whom they entrusted much, of him they will ask all the more.

"I have come to cast fire upon the earth; and how I wish it were already kindled! But I have a baptism to undergo, and how distressed I am until it is accomplished! Do you suppose that I came to grant peace on earth? I tell you, no, but rather division; for from now on five members in one household will be divided, three against two and two against three. They will be divided, father against son and son against father, mother against daughter and daughter against mother, mother-in-law against daughter-in-law and daughter-in-law against mother-in-law." *verses 42b-53*

"When you see a cloud rising in the west, immediately you say, 'A shower is coming,' and so it turns out. And when you see a south wind blowing, you say, 'It will be a hot day,' and it turns out that way. You hypocrites! You know how to analyze the appearance of the earth and the sky, but why do you not analyze this present time?

"And why do you not even on your own initiative judge what is right? For while you are going with your opponent to appear before the magistrate, on your way there make an effort to settle with him, so that he may not drag you before the judge, and the judge turn you over to the officer, and the officer throw you into prison. I say to you, you will not get out of there until you have paid the very last cent." *verses 54b-59*

CHAPTER 13

"Do you suppose that these Galileans were greater sinners than all other Galileans because they suffered this fate? I tell you, no, but unless you repent, you will all likewise perish. Or do you suppose that those eighteen on whom the tower in Siloam fell and killed them were worse culprits than all the men who live in Jerusalem? I tell you, no, but unless you repent, you will all likewise perish." *verses 2b-5*

"A man had a fig tree which had been planted in his vineyard; and he came looking for fruit on it and did not find any. And he said to the vineyard-keeper, 'Behold, for three years I have come looking for fruit on this fig tree without finding any. Cut it down! Why does it even use up the ground?' And he answered and said to him, 'Let it alone, sir, for this year too, until I dig around it and put in fertilizer; and if it bears fruit next year, fine; but if not, cut it down.'" *verses 6b-9*

"Woman, you are freed from your sickness." *verse 12c*

"You hypocrites, does not each of you on the Sabbath untie his ox or his donkey from the stall and lead him away to water him? And this woman, a daughter of Abraham as she is, whom Satan has bound for eighteen long years, should she not have been released from this bond on the Sabbath day?" *verses 15b-16*

"What is the kingdom of God like, and to what shall I compare it? It is like a mustard seed, which a man took and threw into his own garden; and it grew and became a tree, and the birds of the air nested in its branches." *verses 18b-19*

"To what shall I compare the kingdom of God? It is like leaven, which a woman took and hid in three pecks of flour until it was all leavened." *verses 20b-21*

"Strive to enter through the narrow door; for many, I tell you, will seek to enter and will not be able. Once the head of the house gets up and shuts the door, and you begin to stand outside and knock on the door, saying, 'Lord, open up to us!' then He will answer and say to you, 'I do not know where you are from.' Then you will begin to say, 'We ate and drank in Your presence, and You taught in our streets'; and He will say, 'I tell you, I do not know where you are from; depart from Me, all you evildoers.' In that place there will be weeping and gnashing of teeth when you see Abraham and Isaac and Jacob and all the prophets in the kingdom of God, but yourselves being thrown out. And they will come from east and west and from north and south, and will recline at the table in the kingdom of God. And behold, some are last who will be first and some are first who will be last." *verses 24-30*

"Go and tell that fox, 'Behold, I cast out demons and perform cures today and tomorrow, and the third day I reach My goal.' Nevertheless I must journey on today and tomorrow and the next day; for it cannot be that a prophet would perish outside of Jerusalem. O Jerusalem, Jerusalem, the city that kills the prophets and stones those sent to her! How often I wanted to gather your children together, just as a hen gathers her brood under her wings, and you would not have it! Behold, your house is left to you desolate; and I say to you, you will not see Me until the time comes when you say, 'Blessed is He who comes in the name of the Lord!'" *verses 32b-35*

CHAPTER 14

"Is it lawful to heal on the Sabbath, or not?" *verse 3b*

"Which one of you will have a son or an ox fall into a well, and will not immediately pull him out on a Sabbath day?" *verse 5b*

"When you are invited by someone to a wedding feast, do not take the place of honor, for someone more distinguished than you may have been invited by him, and he who invited you both will come and say to you, 'Give your place to this man,' and then in disgrace you proceed to occupy the last place. But when you are invited, go and recline at the last place, so that when the one who has invited you comes, he may say to you, 'Friend, move up higher'; then you will have honor in the sight of all who are at the table with you. For everyone who exalts himself will be humbled, and he who humbles himself will be exalted." *verses 8b-11*

"When you give a luncheon or a dinner, do not invite your friends or your brothers or your relatives or rich neighbors, otherwise they may also invite you in return and that will be your repayment. But when you give a reception, invite the poor, the crippled, the lame, the blind, and you will be blessed, since they do not have the means to repay you; for you will be repaid at the resurrection of the righteous." *verses 12b-14*

"A man was giving a big dinner, and he invited many; and at the dinner hour he sent his slave to say to those who had been invited, 'Come; for everything is ready now.' But they all alike began to make excuses. The first one said to him, 'I have bought a piece of land and I need to go out and look at it; please consider me excused.' Another one said, 'I have bought five yoke of oxen, and I am going to try them out; please consider me excused.' Another one said, 'I have married a wife, and for that reason I cannot come.' And the slave came back and reported this to his master. Then the head of the household became angry and said to his slave, 'Go out at once into the streets and lanes of the city and bring in here the poor and crippled and blind and lame.' And the slave said, 'Master, what you commanded has been done, and still there is room.' And the master said to the slave, 'Go out into the highways and along the hedges, and compel them to come in, so that my house may be filled. For I tell you, none of those men who were invited shall taste of my dinner.'" *verses 16b-24*

"If anyone comes to Me, and does not hate his own father and mother and wife and children and brothers and sisters, yes, and even his own life, he cannot be My disciple. Whoever does not carry his own cross and come after Me cannot be My disciple. For which one of you, when he wants to build a tower, does not first sit down and calculate the cost to see if he has enough to complete it? Otherwise, when he has laid a foundation and is not able to finish, all who observe it begin to ridicule him, saying, 'This man began to build and was not able to finish.' Or what king, when he sets out to meet another king in battle, will not first sit down and consider whether he is strong enough with ten thousand men to encounter the one coming against him with twenty thousand? Or else, while the other is still far away, he sends a delegation and asks for terms of peace. So then, none of you can be My disciple who does not give up all his own possessions.

"Therefore, salt is good; but if even salt has become tasteless, with what will it be seasoned? It is useless either for the soil or for the manure pile; it is thrown out. He who has ears to hear, let him hear." *verses 26-35*

CHAPTER 15

"What man among you, if he has a hundred sheep and has lost one of them, does not leave the ninety-nine in the open pasture and go after the one which is lost until he finds it? When he has found it, he lays it on his shoulders, rejoicing. And when he comes home, he calls together his friends and his neighbors, saying to them, 'Rejoice with me, for I have found my sheep which was lost!' I tell you that in the same way, there will be more joy in heaven over one sinner who repents than over ninety-nine righteous persons who need no repentance.

"Or what woman, if she has ten silver coins and loses one coin, does not light a lamp and sweep the house and search carefully until she finds it? When she has found it, she calls together her friends and neighbors, saying, 'Rejoice with me, for I have found the coin which I had lost!' In the same way, I tell you, there is joy in the presence of the angels of God over one sinner who repents." *verses 4-10*

"A man had two sons. The younger of them said to his father, 'Father, give me the share of the estate that falls to me.' So he divided his wealth between them. And not many days later, the younger son gathered everything together and went on a journey into a distant country, and there he squandered his estate with loose living. Now when he had spent everything, a severe famine occurred in that country, and he began to be impoverished. So he went and hired himself out to one of the citizens of that country, and he sent him into his fields to feed swine. And he would have gladly filled his stomach with the pods that the swine were eating, and no one was giving anything to him. But when he came to his senses, he said, 'How many of my father's hired men have more than enough bread, but I am dying here with hunger! I will get up and go to my father, and will say to him, "Father, I have sinned against heaven, and in your sight; I am no longer worthy to be called your son; make me as one of your hired men."' So he got up and came to his father. But while he was still a long way off, his father saw him and felt compassion for him, and ran and embraced him and kissed him. And the son said to him, 'Father, I have sinned against heaven and in your sight; I am no longer worthy to be called your son.' But the father said to his slaves, 'Quickly bring out the best robe and put it on him, and put a ring on his hand and sandals on his feet;

and bring the fattened calf, kill it, and let us eat and celebrate; for this son of mine was dead and has come to life again; he was lost and has been found.' And they began to celebrate. Now his older son was in the field, and when he came and approached the house, he heard music and dancing. And he summoned one of the servants and began inquiring what these things could be. And he said to him, 'Your brother has come, and your father has killed the fattened calf because he has received him back safe and sound.' But he became angry and was not willing to go in; and his father came out and began pleading with him. But he answered and said to his father, 'Look! For so many years I have been serving you and I have never neglected a command of yours; and yet you have never given me a young goat, so that I might celebrate with my friends; but when this son of yours came, who has devoured your wealth with prostitutes, you killed the fattened calf for him.' And he said to him, 'Son, you have always been with me, and all that is mine is yours. But we had to celebrate and rejoice, for this brother of yours was dead and has begun to live, and was lost and has been found.'" *verses 11b-32*

CHAPTER 16

"There was a rich man who had a manager, and this manager was reported to him as squandering his possessions. And he called him and said to him, 'What is this I hear about you? Give an accounting of your management, for you can no longer be manager.' The manager said to himself, 'What shall I do, since my master is taking the management away from me? I am not strong enough to dig; I am ashamed to beg. I know what I shall do, so that when I am removed from the management people will welcome me into their homes.' And he summoned each one of his master's debtors, and he began saying to the first, 'How much do you owe my master?' And he said, 'A hundred measures of oil.' And he said to him, 'Take your bill, and sit down quickly and write fifty.' Then he said to another, 'And how much do you owe?' And he said, 'A hundred measures of wheat.' He *said to him, 'Take your bill, and write eighty.' And his master praised the unrighteous manager because he had acted shrewdly; for the sons of this age are more shrewd in relation to their own kind than the sons of light. And I say to you, make friends for yourselves by means of the wealth of unrighteousness, so that when it fails, they will receive you into the eternal dwellings.

"He who is faithful in a very little thing is faithful also in much; and he who is unrighteous in a very little thing is unrighteous also in much. Therefore if you have not been faithful in the use of unrighteous wealth, who will entrust the true riches to you? And if you have not been faithful in the use of that which is another's, who will give you that which is your own?

"No servant can serve two masters; for either he will hate the one and love the other, or else he will be devoted to one and despise the other. You cannot serve God and wealth." *verses 1b-13*

"You are those who justify yourselves in the sight of men, but God knows your hearts; for that which is highly esteemed among men is detestable in the sight of God.

"The Law and the Prophets were proclaimed until John; since that time the gospel of the kingdom of God has been preached, and everyone is forcing his way into it. But it is easier for heaven and earth to pass away than for one stroke of a letter of the Law to fail.

"Everyone who divorces his wife and marries another commits adultery, and he who marries one who is divorced from a husband commits adultery.

"Now there was a rich man, and he habitually dressed in purple and fine linen, joyously living in splendor every day. And a poor man named Lazarus was laid at his gate, covered with sores, and longing to be fed with the crumbs which were falling from the rich man's table; besides, even the dogs were coming and licking his sores. Now the poor man died and was carried away by the angels to Abraham's bosom; and the rich man also died and was buried. In Hades he lifted up his eyes, being in torment, and saw Abraham far away and Lazarus in his bosom. And he cried out and said, 'Father Abraham, have mercy on me, and send Lazarus so that he may dip the tip of his finger in water and cool off my tongue, for I am in agony in this flame.' But Abraham said, 'Child, remember that during your life you received your good things, and likewise Lazarus bad things; but now he is being comforted here, and you are in agony. And besides all this, between us and you there is a great chasm fixed, so that those who wish to come over from here to you will not be able, and that none may cross over from there to us.' And he said, 'Then I beg you, father, that you send him to my father's house— for I have five brothers—in order that he may warn them, so that they will not also come to this place of torment.' But Abraham said, 'They have Moses and the Prophets; let them hear them.' But he said, 'No, father Abraham, but if someone goes to them from the dead, they will repent!' But he said to him, 'If they do not listen to Moses and the Prophets, they will not be persuaded even if someone rises from the dead.'" *verses 15b-31*

CHAPTER 17

"It is inevitable that stumbling blocks come, but woe to him through whom they come! It would be better for him if a millstone were hung around his neck and he were thrown into the sea, than that he would cause one of these little ones to stumble. Be on your guard! If your brother sins, rebuke him; and if he repents, forgive him. And if he sins against you seven times a day, and returns to you seven times, saying, 'I repent,' forgive him." *verses 1b-4*

"If you had faith like a mustard seed, you would say to this mulberry tree, 'Be uprooted and be planted in the sea'; and it would obey you.

"Which of you, having a slave plowing or tending sheep, will say to him when he has come in from the field, 'Come immediately and sit down to eat'? But will he not say to him, 'Prepare something for me to eat, and properly clothe yourself and serve me while I eat and drink; and afterward you may eat and drink'? He does not thank the slave because he did the things which were commanded, does he? So you too, when you do all the things which are commanded you, say, 'We are unworthy slaves; we have done only that which we ought to have done.'" *verses 6b-10*

"Go and show yourselves to the priests." *verse 14b*

"Were there not ten cleansed? But the nine—where are they? Was no one found who returned to give glory to God, except this foreigner?" *verses 17b-18*

"Stand up and go; your faith has made you well." *verse 19b*

"The kingdom of God is not coming with signs to be observed; nor will they say, 'Look, here it is!' or, 'There it is!' For behold, the kingdom of God is in your midst." *verses 20c-21*

"The days will come when you will long to see one of the days of the Son of Man, and you will not see it. They will say to you, 'Look there! Look here!' Do not go away, and do not run after them. For just like the lightning, when it flashes out of one part of the sky, shines to the other part of the sky, so will the Son of Man be in His day. But first He must suffer many things and be rejected by this generation. And just as it happened in the days of Noah, so it will be also in the days of the Son of Man: they were eating, they were drinking, they were marrying, they were being given in marriage, until the day that Noah entered the ark, and the flood came and destroyed them all. It was the same as happened in the days of Lot: they were eating, they were drinking, they were buying, they were selling, they were planting, they were building; but on the day that Lot went out from Sodom it rained fire and brimstone from heaven and destroyed them all. It will be just the same on the day that the Son of Man is revealed. On that day, the one who is on the housetop and whose goods are in the house must not go down to take them out; and likewise the one who is in the field must not turn back. Remember Lot's wife. Whoever seeks to keep his life will lose it, and whoever loses his life will preserve it. I tell you, on that night there will be two in one bed; one will be taken and the other will be left. There will be two women grinding at the same place; one will be taken and the other will be left." *verses 22b-35*

"Where the body is, there also the vultures will be gathered." *verse 37c*

CHAPTER 18

"In a certain city there was a judge who did not fear God and did not respect man. There was a widow in that city, and she kept coming to him, saying, 'Give me legal protection from my opponent.' For a while he was unwilling; but afterward he said to himself, 'Even though I do not fear God nor respect man, yet because this widow bothers me, I will give her legal protection, otherwise by continually coming she will wear me out.'" And the Lord said, "Hear what the unrighteous judge said; now, will not God bring about justice for His elect who cry to Him day and night, and will He delay long over them? I tell you that He will bring about justice for them quickly. However, when the Son of Man comes, will He find faith on the earth?" *verses 2b-8*

"Two men went up into the temple to pray, one a Pharisee and the other a tax collector. The Pharisee stood and was praying this to himself: 'God, I thank You that I am not like other people: swindlers, unjust, adulterers, or even like this tax collector. I fast twice a week; I pay tithes of all that I get.' But the tax collector, standing some distance away, was even unwilling to lift up his eyes to heaven, but was beating his breast, saying, 'God, be merciful to me, the sinner!' I tell you, this man went to his house justified rather than the other; for everyone who exalts himself will be humbled, but he who humbles himself will be exalted." *verses 10-14*

"Permit the children to come to Me, and do not hinder them, for the kingdom of God belongs to such as these. Truly I say to you, whoever does not receive the kingdom of God like a child will not enter it at all." *verses 16b-17*

"Why do you call Me good? No one is good except God alone. You know the commandments, 'Do not commit adultery, Do not murder, Do not steal, Do not bear false witness, Honor your father and mother.'" *verses 19b-20*

"One thing you still lack; sell all that you possess and distribute it to the poor, and you shall have treasure in heaven; and come, follow Me." *verse 22b*

"How hard it is for those who are wealthy to enter the kingdom of God! For it is easier for a camel to go through the eye of a needle than for a rich man to enter the kingdom of God." *verses 24b-25*

"The things that are impossible with people are possible with God." *verse 27b*

"Truly I say to you, there is no one who has left house or wife or brothers or parents or children, for the sake of the kingdom of God, who will not receive many times as much at this time and in the age to come, eternal life." *verses 29b-30*

"Behold, we are going up to Jerusalem, and all things which are written through the prophets about the Son of Man will be accomplished. For He will be handed over to the Gentiles, and will be mocked and mistreated and spit upon, and after they have scourged Him, they will kill Him; and the third day He will rise again." *verses 31b-33*

"What do you want Me to do for you?" *verse 41*

"Receive your sight; your faith has made you well." *verse 42b*

CHAPTER 19

"Zaccheus, hurry and come down, for today I must stay at your house." *verse 5c*

"Today salvation has come to this house, because he, too, is a son of Abraham. For the Son of Man has come to seek and to save that which was lost." *verses 9b-10*

"A nobleman went to a distant country to receive a kingdom for himself, and then return. And he called ten of his slaves, and gave them ten minas and said to them, 'Do business with this until I come back.' But his citizens hated him and sent a delegation after him, saying, 'We do not want this man to reign over us.' When he returned, after receiving the kingdom, he ordered that these slaves, to whom he had given the money, be called to him so that he might know what business they had done. The first appeared, saying, 'Master, your mina has made ten minas more.' And he said to him, 'Well done, good slave, because you have been faithful in a very little thing, you are to be in authority over ten cities.' The second came, saying, 'Your mina, master, has made five minas.' And he said to him also, 'And you are to be over five cities.' Another came, saying, 'Master, here is your mina, which I kept put away in a handkerchief; for I was afraid of you, because you are an exacting man; you take up what you did not lay down and reap what you did not sow.' He said to him, 'By your own words I will judge you, you worthless slave. Did you know that I am an exacting man, taking up what I did not lay down and reaping what I did not sow? Then why did you not put my money in the bank, and having come, I would have collected it with interest?' Then he said to the bystanders, 'Take the mina away from him and give it to the one who has the ten minas.' And they said to him, 'Master, he has ten minas already.' I tell you that to everyone who has, more shall be given, but from the one who does not have, even what he does have shall be taken away. But these enemies of mine, who did not want me to reign over them, bring them here and slay them in my presence." *verses 12b-27*

"Go into the village ahead of you; there, as you enter, you will find a colt tied on which no one yet has ever sat; untie it and bring it here. If anyone asks you, 'Why are you untying it?' you shall say, 'The Lord has need of it.'" *verses 30b-31*

"I tell you, if these become silent, the stones will cry out!" *verse 40b*

"If you had known in this day, even you, the things which make for peace! But now they have been hidden from your eyes. For the days will come upon you when your enemies will throw up a barricade against you, and surround you and hem you in on every side, and they will level you to the ground and your children within you, and they will not leave in you one stone upon another, because you did not recognize the time of your visitation." *verses 42b-44*

"It is written, 'And My house shall be a house of prayer,' but you have made it a robbers' den." *verse 46b*

CHAPTER 20

"I will also ask you a question, and you tell Me: Was the baptism of John from heaven or from men?" *verses 3b-4*

"Nor will I tell you by what authority I do these things." *verse 8b*

"A man planted a vineyard and rented it out to vine-growers, and went on a journey for a long time. At the harvest time he sent a slave to the vine-growers, so that they would give him some of the produce of the vineyard; but the vine-growers beat him and sent him away empty-handed. And he proceeded to send another slave; and they beat him also and treated him shamefully and sent him away empty-handed. And he proceeded to send a third; and this one also they wounded and cast out. The owner of the vineyard said, 'What shall I do? I will send my beloved son; perhaps they will respect him.' But when the vine-growers saw him, they reasoned with one another, saying, 'This is the heir; let us kill him so that the inheritance will be ours.' So they threw him out of the vineyard and killed him. What, then, will the owner of the vineyard do to them? He will come and destroy these vine-growers and will give the vineyard to others." *verses 9b-16a*

"What then is this that is written: 'The stone which the builders rejected, this became the chief corner stone'? Everyone who falls on that stone will be broken to pieces; but on whomever it falls, it will scatter him like dust." *verses 17b-18*

"Show Me a denarius. Whose likeness and inscription does it have? Then render to Caesar the things that are Caesar's, and to God the things that are God's." *verses 24a and 25b*

"The sons of this age marry and are given in marriage, but those who are considered worthy to attain to that age and the resurrection from the dead, neither marry nor are given in marriage; for they cannot even die anymore, because they are like angels, and are sons of God, being sons of the resurrection. But that the dead are raised, even Moses showed, in the passage about the burning bush, where he calls the Lord the God of Abraham, and the God of Isaac, and the God of Jacob. Now He is not the God of the dead but of the living; for all live to Him." *verses 34b-38*

"How is it that they say the Christ is David's son? For David himself says in the book of Psalms, 'The Lord said to my Lord, "Sit at My right hand, until I make Your enemies a footstool for Your feet.' Therefore David calls Him 'Lord,' and how is He his son?" *verses 41b-44*

"Beware of the scribes, who like to walk around in long robes, and love respectful greetings in the market places, and chief seats in the synagogues and places of honor at banquets, who devour widows' houses, and for appearance's sake offer long prayers. These will receive greater condemnation." *verses 45c-47*

CHAPTER 21

"Truly I say to you, this poor widow put in more than all of them; for they all out of their surplus put into the offering; but she out of her poverty put in all that she had to live on." *verses 3b-4*

"As for these things which you are looking at, the days will come in which there will not be left one stone upon another which will not be torn down." *verse 6*

"See to it that you are not misled; for many will come in My name, saying, 'I am He,' and, 'The time is near.' Do not go after them. When you hear of wars and disturbances, do not be terrified; for these things must take place first, but the end does not follow immediately." *verses 8b-9*

"Nation will rise against nation and kingdom against kingdom, and there will be great earthquakes, and in various places plagues and famines; and there will be terrors and great signs from heaven. But before all these things, they will lay their hands on you and will persecute you, delivering you to the synagogues and prisons, bringing you before kings and governors for My name's sake. It will lead to an opportunity for your testimony. So make up your minds not to prepare beforehand to defend yourselves; for I will give you utterance and wisdom which none of your opponents will be able to resist or refute. But you will be betrayed even by parents and brothers and relatives and friends, and they will put some of you to death, and you will be hated by all because of My name. Yet not a hair of your head will perish. By your endurance you will gain your lives.

"But when you see Jerusalem surrounded by armies, then recognize that her desolation is near. Then those who are in Judea must flee to the mountains, and those who are in the midst of the city must leave, and those who are in the country must not enter the city; because these are days of vengeance, so that all things which are written will be fulfilled. Woe to those who are pregnant and to those who are nursing babies in those days; for there will be great distress upon the land and wrath to this people; and they will fall by the edge of the sword, and will be led captive into all the nations; and Jerusalem will be trampled under foot by the Gentiles until the times of the Gentiles are fulfilled.

"There will be signs in sun and moon and stars, and on the earth dismay among nations, in perplexity at the roaring of the sea and the waves, men fainting from fear and the expectation of the things which are coming upon the world; for the powers of the heavens will be shaken. Then they will see the Son of Man coming in a cloud with power and great glory. But when these things begin to take place, straighten up and lift up your heads, because your redemption is drawing near." *verses 10b-28*

"Behold the fig tree and all the trees; as soon as they put forth leaves, you see it and know for yourselves that summer is now near. So you also, when you see these things happening, recognize that the kingdom of God is near. Truly I say to you, this generation will not pass away until all things take place. Heaven and earth will pass away, but My words will not pass away.

"Be on guard, so that your hearts will not be weighted down with dissipation and drunkenness and the worries of life, and that day will not come on you suddenly like a trap; for it will come upon all those who dwell on the face of all the earth. But keep on the alert at all times, praying that you may have strength to escape all these things that are about to take place, and to stand before the Son of Man." *verses 29b-36*

CHAPTER 22

"Go and prepare the Passover for us, so that we may eat it." *verse 8b*

"When you have entered the city, a man will meet you carrying a pitcher of water; follow him into the house that he enters. And you shall say to the owner of the house, 'The Teacher says to you, "Where is the guest room in which I may eat the Passover with My disciples?"' And he will show you a large, furnished upper room; prepare it there." *verses 10b-12*

"I have earnestly desired to eat this Passover with you before I suffer; for I say to you, I shall never again eat it until it is fulfilled in the kingdom of God." *verses 15b-16*

"Take this and share it among yourselves; for I say to you, I will not drink of the fruit of the vine from now on until the kingdom of God comes." *verses 17c-18*

"This is My body which is given for you; do this in remembrance of Me." *verse 19c*

"This cup which is poured out for you is the new covenant in My blood. But behold, the hand of the one betraying Me is with Mine on the table. For indeed, the Son of Man is going as it has been determined; but woe to that man by whom He is betrayed!" *verses 20c-22*

"The kings of the Gentiles lord it over them; and those who have authority over them are called 'Benefactors.' But it is not this way with you, but the one who is the greatest among you must become like the youngest, and the leader like the servant. For who is greater, the one who reclines at the table or the one who serves? Is it not the one who reclines at the table? But I am among you as the one who serves.

"You are those who have stood by Me in My trials; and just as My Father has granted Me a kingdom, I grant you that you may eat and drink at My table in My kingdom, and you will sit on thrones judging the twelve tribes of Israel.

"Simon, Simon, behold, Satan has demanded permission to sift you like wheat; but I have prayed for you, that your faith may not fail; and you, when once you have turned again, strengthen your brothers." *verses 25-32*

"I say to you, Peter, the rooster will not crow today until you have denied three times that you know Me." *verse 34b*

"When I sent you out without money belt and bag and sandals, you did not lack anything, did you? But now, whoever has a money belt is to take it along, likewise also a bag, and whoever has no sword is to sell his coat and buy one. For I tell you that this which is written must be fulfilled in Me, 'And He was numbered with transgressors'; for that which refers to Me has its fulfillment." *verses 35b and 36b-37*

"It is enough." *verse 38c*

"Pray that you may not enter into temptation." *verse 40c*

"Father, if You are willing, remove this cup from Me; yet not My will, but Yours be done." *verse 42b*

"Why are you sleeping? Get up and pray that you may not enter into temptation." *verse 46b*

"Judas, are you betraying the Son of Man with a kiss?" *verse 48b*

"Stop! No more of this." *verse 51b*

"Have you come out with swords and clubs as you would against a robber? While I was with you daily in the temple, you did not lay hands on Me; but this hour and the power of darkness are yours." *verses 52b-53*

FINDING SOLID GROUND

"If I tell you, you will not believe; and if I ask a question, you will not answer. But from now on the Son of Man will be seated at the right hand of the power of God." *verses 67c-69*

"Yes, I am." *verse 70c*

CHAPTER 23

"It is as you say." *verse 3c*

"Daughters of Jerusalem, stop weeping for Me, but weep for yourselves and for your children. For behold, the days are coming when they will say, 'Blessed are the barren, and the wombs that never bore, and the breasts that never nursed.' Then they will begin to say to the mountains, 'Fall on us,' and to the hills, 'Cover us.' For if they do these things when the tree is green, what will happen when it is dry?" *verses 28b-31*

"Father, forgive them; for they do not know what they are doing." *verse 34b*

"Truly I say to you, today you shall be with Me in Paradise." *verse 43b*

"Father, into Your hands I commit My spirit." *verse 46b*

CHAPTER 24

"What are these words that you are exchanging with one another as you are walking?" *verse 17b*

"What things?" *verse 19b*

"O foolish men and slow of heart to believe in all that the prophets have spoken! Was it not necessary for the Christ to suffer these things and to enter into His glory?" *verses 25b-26*

"Peace be to you." *verse 36c*

"Why are you troubled, and why do doubts arise in your hearts? See My hands and My feet, that it is I Myself; touch Me and see, for a spirit does not have flesh and bones as you see that I have." *verses 38b-39*

"Have you anything here to eat?" *verse 41c*

"These are My words which I spoke to you while I was still with you, that all things which are written about Me in the Law of Moses and the Prophets and the Psalms must be fulfilled." *verse 44b*

"Thus it is written, that the Christ would suffer and rise again from the dead the third day, and that repentance for forgiveness of sins would be proclaimed in His name to all the nations, beginning from Jerusalem. You are witnesses of these things. And behold, I am sending forth the promise of My Father upon you; but you are to stay in the city until you are clothed with power from on high." *verses 46b-49*

John, dated 95-120 CE, author unknown. Audience: gentile Christian, fully separate from Judaism. (White, p. 310)

CHAPTER 1

"What do you seek?" *verse 38c*

"Come, and you will see." *verse 39b*

"You are Simon the son of John; you shall be called Cephas (Peter)." *verse 42c*

"Follow Me." *verse 43c*

"Behold, an Israelite indeed, in whom there is no deceit!" *verse 47c*

"Before Philip called you, when you were under the fig tree, I saw you." *verse 48d*

"Because I said to you that I saw you under the fig tree, do you believe? You will see greater things than these." *verse 50b*

"Truly, truly, I say to you, you will see the heavens opened and the angels of God ascending and descending on the Son of Man." *verse 51b*

CHAPTER 2

"Woman, what does that have to do with us? My hour has not yet come." *verse 4b*

"Fill the waterpots with water." *verse 7b*

"Draw some out now and take it to the headwaiter." *verse 8b*

"Take these things away; stop making My Father's house a place of business." *verse 16b*

"Destroy this temple, and in three days I will raise it up." *verse 19b*

CHAPTER 3

"Truly, truly, I say to you, unless one is born again he cannot see the kingdom of God." *verse 3b*

"Truly, truly, I say to you, unless one is born of water and the Spirit he cannot enter into the kingdom of God. That which is born of the flesh is flesh, and that which is born of the Spirit is spirit. Do not be amazed that I said to you, 'You must be born again.' The wind blows where it wishes and you hear the sound of it, but do not know where it comes from and where it is going; so is everyone who is born of the Spirit." *verses 5b-8*

"Are you the teacher of Israel and do not understand these things? Truly, truly, I say to you, we speak of what we know and testify of what we have seen, and you do not accept our testimony. If I told you earthly things and you do not believe, how will you believe if I tell you heavenly things? No one has ascended into heaven, but He who descended from heaven: the Son of Man. As Moses lifted up the serpent in the wilderness, even so must the Son of Man be lifted up; so that whoever believes will in Him have eternal life.

"For God so loved the world, that He gave His only begotten Son, that whoever believes in Him shall not perish, but have eternal life. For God did not send the Son into the world to judge the world, but that the world might be saved through Him. He who believes in Him is not judged; he who does not believe has been judged already, because he has not believed in the name of the only begotten Son of God. This is the judgment, that the Light has come into the world, and men loved the darkness rather than the Light, for their deeds were evil. For everyone who does evil hates the Light, and does not come to the Light for fear that his deeds will be exposed. But he who practices the truth comes to the Light, so that his deeds may be manifested as having been wrought in God." *verses 10b-21*

CHAPTER 4

"Give Me a drink." *verse 7c*

"If you knew the gift of God, and who it is who says to you, 'Give Me a drink,' you would have asked Him, and He would have given you living water." *verse 10b*

"Everyone who drinks of this water will thirst again; but whoever drinks of the water that I will give him shall never thirst; but the water that I will give him will become in him a well of water springing up to eternal life." *verses 13b-14*

FINDING SOLID GROUND

"Go, call your husband and come here. You have correctly said, 'I have no husband'; for you have had five husbands, and the one whom you now have is not your husband; this you have said truly." *verses 16b and 17d-18*

"Woman, believe Me, an hour is coming when neither in this mountain nor in Jerusalem will you worship the Father. You worship what you do not know; we worship what we know, for salvation is from the Jews. But an hour is coming, and now is, when the true worshipers will worship the Father in spirit and truth; for such people the Father seeks to be His worshipers. God is spirit, and those who worship Him must worship in spirit and truth." *verses 21b-24*

"I who speak to you am He." *verse 26b*

"I have food to eat that you do not know about." *verse 32b*

"My food is to do the will of Him who sent Me and to accomplish His work. Do you not say, 'There are yet four months, and then comes the harvest'? Behold, I say to you, lift up your eyes and look on the fields, that they are white for harvest. Already he who reaps is receiving wages and is gathering fruit for life eternal; so that he who sows and he who reaps may rejoice together. For in this case the saying is true, 'One sows and another reaps.' I sent you to reap that for which you have not labored; others have labored and you have entered into their labor." *verses 34b-38*

"Unless you people see signs and wonders, you simply will not believe." *verse 48b*

"Go; your son lives." *verse 50b*

CHAPTER 5

"Do you wish to get well?" *verse 6d*

"Get up, pick up your pallet and walk." *verse 8b*

"My Father is working until now, and I Myself am working." *verse 17b*

"Truly, truly, I say to you, the Son can do nothing of Himself, unless it is something He sees the Father doing; for whatever the Father does, these things the Son also does in like manner. For the Father loves the Son, and shows Him all things that He Himself is doing; and the Father will show Him greater works than these, so that you will marvel. For just as the Father raises the dead and gives them life, even so the Son also gives life to whom He wishes. For not even the Father judges anyone, but He has given all judgment to the Son, so that all will honor the Son even as they honor the Father. He who does not honor the Son does not honor the Father who sent Him.

"Truly, truly, I say to you, he who hears My word, and believes Him who sent Me, has eternal life, and does not come into judgment, but has passed out of death into life.

Truly, truly, I say to you, an hour is coming and now is, when the dead will hear the voice of the Son of God, and those who hear will live. For just as the Father has life in Himself, even so He gave to the Son also to have life in Himself; and He gave Him authority to execute judgment, because He is the Son of Man. Do not marvel at this; for an hour is coming, in which all who are in the tombs will hear His voice, and will come forth; those who did the good deeds to a resurrection of life, those who committed the evil deeds to a resurrection of judgment.

"I can do nothing on My own initiative. As I hear, I judge; and My judgment is just, because I do not seek My own will, but the will of Him who sent Me.

"If I alone testify about Myself, My testimony is not true. There is another who testifies of Me, and I know that the testimony which He gives about Me is true. You have sent to John, and he has testified to the truth. But the testimony which I receive is not from man, but I say these things so that you may be saved. He was the lamp that was burning and was shining and you were willing to rejoice for a while in his light.

"But the testimony which I have is greater than the testimony of John; for the works which the Father has given Me to accomplish—the very works that I do—testify about Me, that the Father has sent Me. And the Father who sent Me, He has testified of Me. You have neither heard His voice at any time nor seen His form. You do not have His word abiding in you, for you do not believe Him whom He sent. You search the Scriptures because you think that in them you have eternal life; it is these that testify about Me; and you are unwilling to come to Me so that you may have life. I do not receive glory from men; but I know you, that you do not have the love of God in yourselves. I have come in My Father's name, and you do not receive Me; if another comes in his own name, you will receive him. How can you believe, when you receive glory from one another and you do not seek the glory that is from the one and only God?

"Do not think that I will accuse you before the Father; the one who accuses you is Moses, in whom you have set your hope. For if you believed Moses, you would believe Me, for he wrote about Me. But if you do not believe his writings, how will you believe My words?" *verses 19b-47*

CHAPTER 6

"Where are we to buy bread, so that these may eat?" *verse 5d*

"Have the people sit down." *verse 10b*

"Gather up the leftover fragments so that nothing will be lost." *verse 12c*

"It is I; do not be afraid." *verse 20b*

"Truly, truly, I say to you, you seek Me, not because you saw signs, but because you ate of the loaves and were filled. Do not work for the food which perishes, but for the food which endures to eternal life, which the Son of Man will give to you, for on Him the Father, God, has set His seal." *verses 26b-27*

"This is the work of God, that you believe in Him whom He has sent." *verse 29b*

"Truly, truly, I say to you, it is not Moses who has given you the bread out of heaven, but it is My Father who gives you the true bread out of heaven. For the bread of God is that which comes down out of heaven, and gives life to the world." *verses 32b-33*

"I am the bread of life; he who comes to Me will not hunger, and he who believes in Me will never thirst. But I said to you that you have seen Me, and yet do not believe. All that the Father gives Me will come to Me, and the one who comes to Me I will certainly not cast out. For I have come down from heaven, not to do My own will, but the will of Him who sent Me. This is the will of Him who sent Me, that of all that He has given Me I lose nothing, but raise it up on the last day. For this is the will of My Father, that everyone who beholds the Son and believes in Him will have eternal life, and I Myself will raise him up on the last day." *verses 35b-40*

"Do not grumble among yourselves. No one can come to Me unless the Father who sent Me draws him; and I will raise him up on the last day. It is written in the prophets, 'And they shall all be taught of God.' Everyone who has heard and learned from the Father, comes to Me. Not that anyone has seen the Father, except the One who is from God; He has seen the Father. Truly, truly, I say to you, he who believes has eternal life. I am the bread of life. Your fathers ate the manna in the wilderness, and they died. This is the bread which comes down out of heaven, so that one may eat of it and not die. I am the living bread that came down out of heaven; if anyone eats of this bread, he will live forever; and the bread also which I will give for the life of the world is My flesh." *verses 43b-51*

"Truly, truly, I say to you, unless you eat the flesh of the Son of Man and drink His blood, you have no life in yourselves. He who eats My flesh and drinks My blood has eternal life, and I will raise him up on the last day. For My flesh is true food, and My blood is true drink. He who eats My flesh and drinks My blood abides in Me, and I in him. As the living Father sent Me, and I live because of the Father, so he who eats Me, he also will live because of Me. This is the bread which came down out of heaven; not as the fathers ate and died; he who eats this bread will live forever." *verses 53b-58*

"Does this cause you to stumble? What then if you see the Son of Man ascending to where He was before? It is the Spirit who gives life; the flesh profits nothing; the words that I have spoken to you are spirit and are life. But there are some of you who do not believe." *verses 61c-64*

"For this reason I have said to you, that no one can come to Me unless it has been granted him from the Father." *verse 65b*

"You do not want to go away also, do you?" *verse 67b*

"Did I Myself not choose you, the twelve, and yet one of you is a devil?" *verse 70b*

CHAPTER 7

"My time is not yet here, but your time is always opportune. The world cannot hate you, but it hates Me because I testify of it, that its deeds are evil. Go up to the feast yourselves; I do not go up to this feast because My time has not yet fully come." *verses 6b-8*

"My teaching is not Mine, but His who sent Me. If anyone is willing to do His will, he will know of the teaching, whether it is of God or whether I speak from Myself. He who speaks from himself seeks his own glory; but He who is seeking the glory of the One who sent Him, He is true, and there is no unrighteousness in Him.

"Did not Moses give you the Law, and yet none of you carries out the Law? Why do you seek to kill Me?" *verses 16b-19*

"I did one deed, and you all marvel. For this reason Moses has given you circumcision (not because it is from Moses, but from the fathers), and on the Sabbath you circumcise a man. If a man receives circumcision on the Sabbath so that the Law of Moses will not be broken, are you angry with Me because I made an entire man well on the Sabbath? Do not judge according to appearance, but judge with righteous judgment." *verses 21b-24*

"You both know Me and know where I am from; and I have not come of Myself, but He who sent Me is true, whom you do not know. I know Him, because I am from Him, and He sent Me." *verses 28b-29*

"For a little while longer I am with you, then I go to Him who sent Me. You will seek Me, and will not find Me; and where I am, you cannot come." *verses 33b-34*

"If anyone is thirsty, let him come to Me and drink. He who believes in Me, as the Scripture said, 'From his innermost being will flow rivers of living water.'" *verses 37c-38*

CHAPTER 8

"He who is without sin among you, let him be the first to throw a stone at her. Woman, where are they? Did no one condemn you? I do not condemn you, either. Go. From now on sin no more." *verses 7b, 10b and 11c*

"I am the Light of the world; he who follows Me will not walk in the darkness, but will have the Light of life." *verse 12b*

"Even if I testify about Myself, My testimony is true, for I know where I came from and where I am going; but you do not know where I come from or where I am going. You judge according to the flesh; I am not judging anyone. But even if I do judge, My judgment is true; for I am not alone in it, but I and the Father who sent Me. Even in your law it has been written that the testimony of two men is true. I am He who testifies about Myself, and the Father who sent Me testifies about Me." *verses 14b-18*

"You know neither Me nor My Father; if you knew Me, you would know My Father also." *verse 19c*

"I go away, and you will seek Me, and will die in your sin; where I am going, you cannot come." *verse 21b*

"You are from below, I am from above; you are of this world, I am not of this world. Therefore I said to you that you will die in your sins; for unless you believe that I am He, you will die in your sins." *verses 23b-24*

"What have I been saying to you from the beginning? I have many things to speak and to judge concerning you, but He who sent Me is true; and the things which I heard from Him, these I speak to the world." *verses 25c-26*

"When you lift up the Son of Man, then you will know that I am He, and I do nothing on My own initiative, but I speak these things as the Father taught Me. And He who sent Me is with Me; He has not left Me alone, for I always do the things that are pleasing to Him." *verses 28b-29*

"If you continue in My word, then you are truly disciples of Mine; and you will know the truth, and the truth will make you free." *verses 31b-32*

"Truly, truly, I say to you, everyone who commits sin is the slave of sin. The slave does not remain in the house forever; the son does remain forever. So if the Son makes you free, you will be free indeed. I know that you are Abraham's descendants; yet you seek to kill Me, because My word has no place in you. I speak the things which I have seen with My Father; therefore you also do the things which you heard from your father." *verses 34b-38*

"If you are Abraham's children, do the deeds of Abraham. But as it is, you are seeking to kill Me, a man who has told you the truth, which I heard from God; this Abraham did not do. You are doing the deeds of your father." *verses 39c-41a*

"If God were your Father, you would love Me, for I proceeded forth and have come from God, for I have not even come on My own initiative, but He sent Me. Why do you not understand what I am saying? It is because you cannot hear My word. You are of your father the devil, and you want to do the desires of your father. He was a murderer from the beginning, and does not stand in the truth because there is no truth in him. Whenever he speaks a lie, he speaks from his own nature, for he is a liar and the father of lies. But because I speak the truth, you do not believe Me. Which one of you convicts Me of sin? If I speak truth, why do you not believe Me? He who is of God hears the words of God; for this reason you do not hear them, because you are not of God." *verses 42b-47*

"I do not have a demon; but I honor My Father, and you dishonor Me. But I do not seek My glory; there is One who seeks and judges. Truly, truly, I say to you, if anyone keeps My word he will never see death." *verses 49b-51*

"If I glorify Myself, My glory is nothing; it is My Father who glorifies Me, of whom you say, 'He is our God'; and you have not come to know Him, but I know Him; and if I say that I do not know Him, I will be a liar like you, but I do know Him and keep His word. Your father Abraham rejoiced to see My day, and he saw it and was glad." *verses 54b-56*

"Truly, truly, I say to you, before Abraham was born, I am." *verse 58b*

CHAPTER 9

"It was neither that this man sinned, nor his parents; but it was so that the works of God might be displayed in him. We must work the works of Him who sent Me as long as it is day; night is coming when no one can work. While I am in the world, I am the Light of the world." *verses 3b-5*

"Go, wash in the pool of Siloam." *verse 7b*

"Do you believe in the Son of Man?" *verse 35b*

"You have both seen Him, and He is the one who is talking with you." *verse 37b*

"For judgment I came into this world, so that those who do not see may see, and that those who see may become blind." *verse 39b*

"If you were blind, you would have no sin; but since you say, 'We see,' your sin remains." *verse 41b*

CHAPTER 10

"Truly, truly, I say to you, he who does not enter by the door into the fold of the sheep, but climbs up some other way, he is a thief and a robber. But he who enters by the door is a shepherd of the sheep. To him the doorkeeper opens, and the sheep hear his voice, and he calls his own sheep by name and leads them out. When he puts forth all his own, he goes ahead of them, and the sheep follow him because they know his voice. A stranger they simply will not follow, but will flee from him, because they do not know the voice of strangers." *verses 1-5*

"Truly, truly, I say to you, I am the door of the sheep. All who came before Me are thieves and robbers, but the sheep did not hear them. I am the door; if anyone enters through Me, he will be saved, and will go in and out and find pasture. The thief comes only to steal and kill and destroy; I came that they may have life, and have it abundantly.

"I am the good shepherd; the good shepherd lays down His life for the sheep. He who is a hired hand, and not a shepherd, who is not the owner of the sheep, sees the wolf coming, and leaves the sheep and flees, and the wolf snatches them and scatters them. He flees because he is a hired hand and is not concerned about the sheep. I am the good shepherd, and I know My own and My own know Me, even as the Father knows Me and I know the Father; and I lay down My life for the sheep. I have other sheep, which are not of this fold; I must bring them also, and they will hear My voice; and they will become one flock with one shepherd. For this reason the Father loves Me, because I lay down My life so that I may take it again. No one has taken it away from Me, but I lay it down on My own initiative. I have authority to lay it down, and I have authority to take it up again. This commandment I received from My Father." *verses 7b-18*

"I told you, and you do not believe; the works that I do in My Father's name, these testify of Me. But you do not believe because you are not of My sheep. My sheep hear My voice, and I know them, and they follow Me; and I give eternal life to them, and they will never perish; and no one will snatch them out of My hand. My Father, who has given them to Me, is greater than all; and no one is able to snatch them out of the Father's hand. I and the Father are one." *verses 25b-30*

"I showed you many good works from the Father; for which of them are you stoning Me?" *verse 32b*

"Has it not been written in your Law, 'I said, you are gods'? If he called them gods, to whom the word of God came (and the Scripture cannot be broken), do you say of Him, whom the Father sanctified and sent into the world, 'You are blaspheming,' because I said, 'I am the Son of God'? If I do not do the works of My Father, do not believe Me; but if I do them, though you do not believe Me, believe the works, so that you may know and understand that the Father is in Me, and I in the Father." *verses 34b-38*

CHAPTER 11

"This sickness is not to end in death, but for the glory of God, so that the Son of God may be glorified by it." *verse 4b*

"Let us go to Judea again." *verse 7b*

"Are there not twelve hours in the day? If anyone walks in the day, he does not stumble, because he sees the light of this world. But if anyone walks in the night, he stumbles, because the light is not in him." *verses 9b-10*

"Our friend Lazarus has fallen asleep; but I go, so that I may awaken him out of sleep." *verse 11b*

"Lazarus is dead, and I am glad for your sakes that I was not there, so that you may believe; but let us go to him." *verses 14b-15*

"Your brother will rise again." *verse 23b*

"I am the resurrection and the life; he who believes in Me will live even if he dies, and everyone who lives and believes in Me will never die. Do you believe this?" *verses 25b-26*

"Where have you laid him?" *verse 34b*

"Remove the stone." *verse 39b*

"Did I not say to you that if you believe, you will see the glory of God?" *verse 40b*

"Father, I thank You that You have heard Me. I knew that You always hear Me; but because of the people standing around I said it, so that they may believe that You sent Me." *verses 41c-42*

"Lazarus, come forth." *verse 43b*

"Unbind him, and let him go." *verse 44c*

CHAPTER 12

"Let her alone, so that she may keep it for the day of My burial. For you always have the poor with you, but you do not always have Me." *verses 7b-8*

"The hour has come for the Son of Man to be glorified. Truly, truly, I say to you, unless a grain of wheat falls into the earth and dies, it remains alone; but if it dies, it bears much fruit. He who loves his life loses it, and he who hates his life in this world will keep it to life eternal. If anyone serves Me, he must follow Me; and where I am, there My servant will be also; if anyone serves Me, the Father will honor him.

"Now My soul has become troubled; and what shall I say, 'Father, save Me from this hour'? But for this purpose I came to this hour. Father, glorify Your name." *verses 23b-28a*

"This voice has not come for My sake, but for your sakes. Now judgment is upon this world; now the ruler of this world will be cast out. And I, if I am lifted up from the earth, will draw all men to Myself." *verses 30b-32*

"For a little while longer the Light is among you. Walk while you have the Light, so that darkness will not overtake you; he who walks in the darkness does not know where he goes. While you have the Light, believe in the Light, so that you may become sons of Light." *verses 35b-36*

"He who believes in Me, does not believe in Me but in Him who sent Me. He who sees Me sees the One who sent Me. I have come as Light into the world, so that everyone who believes in Me will not remain in darkness. If anyone hears My sayings and does not keep them, I do not judge him; for I did not come to judge the world, but to save the world. He who rejects Me and does not receive My sayings, has one who judges him; the word I spoke is what will judge him at the last day. For I did not speak on My own initiative, but the Father Himself who sent Me has given Me a commandment as to what to say and what to speak. I know that His commandment is eternal life; therefore the things I speak, I speak just as the Father has told Me." *verses 44b-50*

CHAPTER 13

"What I do you do not realize now, but you will understand hereafter." *verse 7b*

"If I do not wash you, you have no part with Me." *verse 8d*

"He who has bathed needs only to wash his feet, but is completely clean; and you are clean, but not all of you." *verse 10b*

"Do you know what I have done to you? You call Me Teacher and Lord; and you are right, for so I am. If I then, the Lord and the Teacher, washed your feet, you also ought to wash one another's feet. For I gave you an example that you also should do as I did to you. Truly, truly, I say to you, a slave is not greater than his master, nor is one who is sent greater than the one who sent him. If you know these things, you are blessed if you do them. I do not speak of all of you. I know the ones I have chosen; but it is that the Scripture may be fulfilled, 'He who eats My bread has lifted up his heel against Me.' From now on I am telling you before it comes to pass, so that when it does occur, you may believe that I am He. Truly, truly, I say to you, he who receives whomever I send receives Me; and he who receives Me receives Him who sent Me." *verses 12c-20*

"Truly, truly, I say to you, that one of you will betray Me." *verse 21b*

"That is the one for whom I shall dip the morsel and give it to him." *verse 26b*

"What you do, do quickly." *verse 27c*

"Now is the Son of Man glorified, and God is glorified in Him. *verse 31b*

"Little children, I am with you a little while longer. You will seek Me; and as I said to the Jews, now I also say to you, 'Where I am going, you cannot come.' A new commandment I give to you, that you love one another, even as I have loved you, that you also love one another. By this all men will know that you are My disciples, if you have love for one another." *verses 33-35*

"Where I go, you cannot follow Me now; but you will follow later." *verse 36d*

"Will you lay down your life for Me? Truly, truly, I say to you, a rooster will not crow until you deny Me three times." *verse 38b*

CHAPTER 14

"Do not let your heart be troubled; believe in God, believe also in Me. In My Father's house are many dwelling places; if it were not so, I would have told you; for I go to prepare a place for you. If I go and prepare a place for you, I will come again and receive you to Myself, that where I am, there you may be also. And you know the way where I am going." *verses 1-4*

"I am the way, and the truth, and the life; no one comes to the Father but through Me. If you had known Me, you would have known My Father also; from now on you know Him, and have seen Him." *verses 6b-7*

"Have I been so long with you, and yet you have not come to know Me, Philip? He who has seen Me has seen the Father; how can you say, 'Show us the Father'? Do you not believe that I am in the Father, and the Father is in Me? The words that I say to you I do not speak on My own initiative, but the Father abiding in Me does His works. Believe Me that I am in the Father and the Father is in Me; otherwise believe because of the works themselves. Truly, truly, I say to you, he who believes in Me, the works that I do, he will do also; and greater works than these he will do; because I go to the Father. Whatever you ask in My name, that will I do, so that the Father may be glorified in the Son. If you ask Me anything in My name, I will do it.

"If you love Me, you will keep My commandments.

"I will ask the Father, and He will give you another Helper, that He may be with you forever; that is the Spirit of truth, whom the world cannot receive, because it does not see Him or know Him, but you know Him because He abides with you and will be in you.

"I will not leave you as orphans; I will come to you. After a little while the world will no longer see Me, but you will see Me; because I live, you will live also. In that day you will know that I am in My Father, and you in Me, and I in you. He who has My commandments and keeps them is the one who loves Me; and he who loves Me will be loved by My Father, and I will love him and will disclose Myself to him." *verses 9b-21*

"If anyone loves Me, he will keep My word; and My Father will love him, and We will come to him and make Our abode with him. He who does not love Me does not keep My words; and the word which you hear is not Mine, but the Father's who sent Me.

"These things I have spoken to you while abiding with you. But the Helper, the Holy Spirit, whom the Father will send in My name, He will teach you all things, and bring to your remembrance all that I said to you. Peace I leave with you; My peace I give to you; not as the world gives do I give to you. Do not let your heart be troubled, nor let it be fearful. You heard that I said to you, 'I go away, and I will come to you.' If you loved Me, you would have rejoiced because I go to the Father, for the Father is greater than I. Now I have told you before it happens, so that when it happens, you may believe. I will not speak much more with you, for the ruler of the world is coming, and he has nothing in Me; but so that the world may know that I love the Father, I do exactly as the Father commanded Me. Get up, let us go from here." *verses 23b-30*

CHAPTER 15

"I am the true vine, and My Father is the vinedresser. Every branch in Me that does not bear fruit, He takes away; and every branch that bears fruit, He prunes it so that it may bear more fruit. You are already clean because of the word which I have spoken to you. Abide in Me, and I in you. As the branch cannot bear fruit of itself unless it abides in the vine, so neither can you unless you abide in Me. I am the vine, you are the branches; he who abides in Me and I in him, he bears much fruit, for apart from Me you can do nothing. If anyone does not abide in Me, he is thrown away as a branch and dries up; and they gather them, and cast them into the fire and they are burned. If you abide in Me, and My words abide in you, ask whatever you wish, and it will be done for you. My Father is glorified by this, that you bear much fruit, and so prove to be My disciples. Just as the Father has loved Me, I have also loved you; abide in My love.

"If you keep My commandments, you will abide in My love; just as I have kept My Father's commandments and abide in His love. These things I have spoken to you so that My joy may be in you, and that your joy may be made full.

"This is My commandment, that you love one another, just as I have loved you.

"Greater love has no one than this, that one lay down his life for his friends. You are My friends if you do what I command you. No longer do I call you slaves, for the slave does not know what his master is doing; but I have called you friends, for all things that I have heard from My Father I have made known to you. You did not choose Me but I chose you, and appointed you that you would go and bear fruit, and that your fruit would remain, so that whatever you ask of the Father in My name He may give to you.

"This I command you, that you love one another.

"If the world hates you, you know that it has hated Me before it hated you. If you were of the world, the world would love its own; but because you are not of the world, but I chose you out of the world, because of this the world hates you. Remember the word that I said to you, 'A slave is not greater than his master.' If they persecuted Me, they will also persecute you; if they kept My word, they will keep yours also. But all these things they will do to you for My name's sake, because they do not know the One who sent Me. If I had not come and spoken to them, they would not have sin, but now they have no excuse for their sin. He who hates Me hates My Father also. If I had not done among them the works which no one else did, they would not have sin; but now they have both seen and hated Me and My Father as well. But they have done this to fulfill the word that is written in their Law, 'They hated Me without a cause.'

"When the Helper comes, whom I will send to you from the Father, that is the Spirit of truth who proceeds from the Father, He will testify about Me, and you will testify also, because you have been with Me from the beginning." *verses 1-27*

CHAPTER 16

"These things I have spoken to you so that you may be kept from stumbling. They will make you outcasts from the synagogue, but an hour is coming for everyone who kills you to think that he is offering service to God. These things they will do because they have not known the Father or Me. But these things I have spoken to you, so that when their hour comes, you may remember that I told you of them. These things I did not say to you at the beginning, because I was with you.

"But now I am going to Him who sent Me; and none of you asks Me, 'Where are You going?' But because I have said these things to you, sorrow has filled your heart. But I tell you the truth, it is to your advantage that I go away; for if I do not go away, the Helper will not come to you; but if I go, I will send Him to you. And He, when He comes, will convict the world concerning sin and righteousness and judgment; concerning sin, because they do not believe in Me; and concerning righteousness, because I go to the Father and you no longer see Me; and concerning judgment, because the ruler of this world has been judged.

"I have many more things to say to you, but you cannot bear them now. But when He, the Spirit of truth, comes, He will guide you into all the truth; for He will not speak on His own initiative, but whatever He hears, He will speak; and He will disclose to you what is to come. He will glorify Me, for He will take of Mine and will disclose it to you. All things that the Father has are Mine; therefore I said that He takes of Mine and will disclose it to you.

"A little while, and you will no longer see Me; and again a little while, and you will see Me." *verses 1-16*

"Are you deliberating together about this, that I said, 'A little while, and you will not see Me, and again a little while, and you will see Me'? Truly, truly, I say to you, that you will weep and lament, but the world will rejoice; you will grieve, but your grief will be turned into joy. Whenever a woman is in labor she has pain, because her hour has come; but when she gives birth to the child, she no longer remembers the anguish because of the joy that a child has been born into the world. Therefore you too have grief now; but I will see you again, and your heart will rejoice, and no one will take your joy away from you. In that day you will not question Me about anything. Truly, truly, I say to you, if you ask the Father for anything in My name, He will give it to you. Until now you have asked for nothing in My name; ask and you will receive, so that your joy may be made full.

"These things I have spoken to you in figurative language; an hour is coming when I will no longer speak to you in figurative language, but will tell you plainly of the Father. In that day you will ask in My name, and I do not say to you that I will request of the Father on your behalf; for the Father Himself loves you, because you have loved Me and have believed that I came forth from the Father. I came forth from the Father and have come into the world; I am leaving the world again and going to the Father." *verses 19b-28*

"Do you now believe? Behold, an hour is coming, and has already come, for you to be scattered, each to his own home, and to leave Me alone; and yet I am not alone, because the Father is with Me. These things I have spoken to you, so that in Me you may have peace. In the world you have tribulation, but take courage; I have overcome the world." *verses 31b-33*

CHAPTER 17

"Father, the hour has come; glorify Your Son, that the Son may glorify You, even as You gave Him authority over all flesh, that to all whom You have given Him, He may give eternal life. This is eternal life, that they may know You, the only true God, and Jesus Christ whom You have sent. I glorified You on the earth, having accomplished the work which You have given Me to do. Now, Father, glorify Me together with Yourself, with the glory which I had with You before the world was.

"I have manifested Your name to the men whom You gave Me

out of the world; they were Yours and You gave them to Me, and they have kept Your word. Now they have come to know that everything You have given Me is from You; for the words which You gave Me I have given to them; and they received them and truly understood that I came forth from You, and they believed that You sent Me. I ask on their behalf; I do not ask on behalf of the world, but of those whom You have given Me; for they are Yours; and all things that are Mine are Yours, and Yours are Mine; and I have been glorified in them. I am no longer in the world; and yet they themselves are in the world, and I come to You. Holy Father, keep them in Your name, the name which You have given Me, that they may be one even as We are. While I was with them, I was keeping them in Your name which You have given Me; and I guarded them and not one of them perished but the son of perdition, so that the Scripture would be fulfilled. But now I come to You; and these things I speak in the world so that they may have My joy made full in themselves. I have given them Your word; and the world has hated them, because they are not of the world, even as I am not of the world. I do not ask You to take them out of the world, but to keep them from the evil one. They are not of the world, even as I am not of the world. Sanctify them in the truth; Your word is truth. As You sent Me into the world, I also have sent them into the world. For their sakes I sanctify Myself, that they themselves also may be sanctified in truth.

"I do not ask on behalf of these alone, but for those also who believe in Me through their word; that they may all be one; even as You, Father, are in Me and I in You, that they also may be in Us, so that the world may believe that You sent Me. The glory which You have given Me I have given to them, that they may be one, just as We are one; I in them and You in Me, that they may be perfected in unity, so that the world may know that You sent Me, and loved them, even as You have loved Me. Father, I desire that they also, whom You have given Me, be with Me where I am, so that they may see My glory which You have given Me, for You loved Me before the foundation of the world.

"O righteous Father, although the world has not known You, yet I have known You; and these have known that You sent Me; and I have made Your name known to them, and will make it known, so that the love with which You loved Me may be in them, and I in them." *verses 1c-26*

CHAPTER 18

"Whom do you seek?" *verse 4c*

"I am He." *verse 5c*

"Whom do you seek?" *verse 7b*

"I told you that I am He; so if you seek Me, let these go their way" *verse 8b*

"Put the sword into the sheath; the cup which the Father has given Me, shall I not drink it?" *verse 11b*

"I have spoken openly to the world; I always taught in synagogues and in the temple, where all the Jews come together; and I spoke nothing in secret. Why do you question Me? Question those who have heard what I spoke to them; they know what I said." *verses 20b-21*

"If I have spoken wrongly, testify of the wrong; but if rightly, why do you strike Me?" *verse 23b*

"Are you saying this on your own initiative, or did others tell you about Me?" *verse 34b*

"My kingdom is not of this world. If My kingdom were of this world, then My servants would be fighting so that I would not be handed over to the Jews; but as it is, My kingdom is not of this realm." *verse 36b*

"You say correctly that I am a king. For this I have been born, and for this I have come into the world, to testify to the truth. Everyone who is of the truth hears My voice." *verse 37c*

CHAPTER 19

"You would have no authority over Me, unless it had been given you from above; for this reason he who delivered Me to you has the greater sin." *verse 11b*

"I am thirsty." *verse 28c*

"It is finished!" *verse 30c*

CHAPTER 20

"Woman, why are you weeping? Whom are you seeking?" *verse 15b*

"Mary!" *verse 16b*

"Stop clinging to Me, for I have not yet ascended to the Father; but go to My brethren and say to them, 'I ascend to My Father and your Father, and My God and your God.'" *verse 17b*

"Peace be with you." *verse 19d*

"Peace be with you; as the Father has sent Me, I also send you." *verse 21b*

"Receive the Holy Spirit. If you forgive the sins of any, their sins have been forgiven them; if you retain the sins of any, they have been retained." *verses 22b-23*

"Peace be with you." *verse 26c*

"Reach here with your finger, and see My hands; and reach here your hand and put it into My side; and do not be unbelieving, but believing." *verse 27b*

"Because you have seen Me, have you believed? Blessed are they who did not see, and yet believed." *verse 29b*

CHAPTER 21

"Children, you do not have any fish, do you?" *verse 5b*

"Cast the net on the right-hand side of the boat and you will find a catch." *verse 6b*

"Bring some of the fish which you have now caught." *verse 10b*

"Come and have breakfast." *verse 12b*

"Simon, son of John, do you love Me more than these?" *verse 15b*

"Tend My lambs." *verse 15e*

"Simon, son of John, do you love Me?" *verse 16b*

"Shepherd My sheep." *verse 16e*

"Simon, son of John, do you love Me?" *verse 17b*

"Tend My sheep. Truly, truly, I say to you, when you were younger, you used to gird yourself and walk wherever you wished; but when you grow old, you will stretch out your hands and someone else will gird you, and bring you where you do not wish to go." *verses 17e-18*

"Follow Me!" *verse 19c*

"If I want him to remain until I come, what is that to you? You follow Me!" *verse 22b*

RESOURCES

PART ONE RESOURCES

Each of the resources will lead you to many others.

Cited Resources

Acemoglu, Daron, and James A. Robinson. *Why Nations Fail: The Origins of Power, Prosperity, and Poverty.* NY: Crown Business/Random House, 2012.

Adler, Mortimer J., and William Gorman. *The American Testament.* NY: Praeger Publishers, 1975.

PIDI: Ball, Terence, and Richard Dagger. *Political Ideologies and The Democratic Ideal.* NY: HarperCollins Publishers Inc., 1991.

IIR: Ball, Terence, and Richard Dagger. *Ideals and Ideologies: A Reader.* NY: HarperCollins Publishers Inc., 1991.

Barth, Karl. *From Rousseau to Ritschl.* London: SCM Press, LTD., 1959.

Canterbery, E. Ray. *A Brief History of Economics*, 2nd Edition. Hackensack, NJ: World Scientific Publishing Co., 2011.

Darwin, Charles. *The Descent of Man.* NY: Penguin Putnam, Inc., 2004. First published in 1871.

Emerick, Robert W. *Soul Affirmation: Introduction to a Philosophy of Life.* Pittsburgh: Dorrance Publishing Co., Inc., 2010.

Erdal, David, and Andrew Whiten. "Egalitarianism and Machiavellian Intelligence in Human Evolution." *Modelling The Early Human Mind.* Paul Mellars and Kathleen Gibson, eds., Cambridge: McDonald Institute for Archaelogical Research, McDonald Institute Monographs, University of Cambridge, 1996.

Frank, Robert H. *The Darwin Economy: Liberty, Competition, and the Common Good.* Princeton: Princeton University Press, 2011.

GT: Gomory, Ralph, and William J. Baumol. *Global Trade and Conflicting National Interests.* Cambridge, MA: The Massachusetts Institute of Technology Press, 2000.

Gomory, Ralph, and Richard Sylla. "The American Corporation." *Daedalus, Journal of the American Academy of Arts & Sciences,* 142(2), Spring, 2013, pp. 102-118.

TWP: Heilbroner, Robert. *Teachings From The Worldly Philosophy.* NY: W. W. Norton & Company, 1996.

WP: Heilbroner, Robert. *The Worldly Philosophers.* Updated 7th Edition. NY: Simon & Schuster, 1999.

Hofstadter, Richard. *Social Darwinism in American Thought.* Boston: Beacon Press, 1983.

Kelly, Hugh F. *24 Hour Cities.* NY: Routledge, 2016.

Kleveman, Lutz. *The New Great Game.* NY: Grove Press, 2003.

Larson, John Lauritz. *The Market Revolution in America.* NY: Cambridge University Press, 2010.

Lind, Michael. *Land Of Promise: An Economic History of the United States.* NY: HarperCollins Publishers, 2012.

McNeill, William H. *History of Western Civilization.* Chicago: University of Chicago Press, 1969.

Mettler, Suzanne. *Soldiers to Citizens: The G.I. Bill and the Making of the Greatest Generation.* NY: Oxford University Press, 2005.

Minsky, Hyman. *Stabilizing an Unstable Economy.* New York: McGraw Hill, 2008. First published in 1986 by Yale University Press.

Morris, Colin. *The Discovery Of The Individual, 1050-1200.* Toronto: University of Toronto Press, 1972.

Mott, Tracy. *Kalecki's Principle of Increasing Risk and Keynesian Economics.* NY: Routledge, Routledge Studies in the History of Economics, 2010.

Mowbray, Joel. *Dangerous Diplomacy.* Washington, DC: Regnery Publishing, Inc., 2003.

Moyo, Dambisa. *Dead Aid.* Vancouver, BC, Canada: Douglas & McIntyre, 2009.

New American Standard Bible, Updated Edition. La Habra, CA: The Lockman Foundation, 2001.

Painter, Sidney. *Feudalism and Liberty.* Baltimore: The Johns Hopkins Press, 1961.

Reese, William L. *Dictionary of Philosophy and Religion*, Expanded Edition. NY: Humanity Books, Amherst, 1996.

Roberts, J. M. *A Short History Of The World.* NY: Oxford University Press, 1993.

Rudolph, Frederick. "The American Liberty League, 1934-1940." *The American Historical Review,* The American Historical Association, Vol. 56, No. 1, October, 1950, pp. 19-33.

Russell, Bertrand. *Authority and the Individual.* London: Routledge, 1949.

Smith, Adam. *An Inquiry Into The Nature And Causes Of The Wealth Of Nations.* NY: Random House, Inc., 1994. First published in 1776.

Stiglitz, Joseph. *The Price of Inequality.* NY: W. W. Norton & Company, 2012.

Ullmann, Walter. *The Individual And Society In The Middle Ages.* Baltimore: The Johns Hopkins Press, 1966.

Whalen, Charles J., editor. *Political Economy for the 21st Century: Contemporary Views on the Trend of Economics.* Armonk, N.Y.: M. E. Sharpe, 1996.

<u>Consulted Resources</u>
Government's Role in Research and Economic Development:

Eisinger, Peter K. *The Rise of the Entrepreneurial State: State And Local Economic Development Policy in the United States.* Madison: The University of Wisconsin Press, 1988.

Mazzucato, Mariana. *The Entrepreneurial State: Debunking Public vs. Private Sector Myths.* NY: Anthem Press, 2013.

Mixed Economy:
Hacker, Jacob S., and Paul Pierson. *American Amnesia: How The War On Government Led Us To Forget What Made America Prosper.* NY: Simon & Schuster, 2016.

Kleinbard, Edward D. *We Are Better Than This: How Government Should Spend Our Money.* NY: Oxford University Press, 2015.

Sidgwick, Henry. *Principles of Political Economy*, Second Edition. London: MACMILLAN AND CO., 1887. Available through Scholar Select. It is now in the public domain.

In my opinion, Sidgwick makes the case for Mixed Economy on pp. 395-595.

History, Theory, and Current Circumstances:

Caporaso, James A., and David P. Levine. *Theories of Political Economy*. NY: Cambridge University Press, 1992.

Collins, Randall, and Michael Makowsky. *The Discovery of Society*. 5th Edition. New York: McGraw-Hill, Inc., 1972.

Deaton, Angus. *The Great Escape: Health, Wealth, and the Origins of Inequality*. Princeton: Princeton University Press, 2013.

Frank, Robert H., and Philip J. Cook. *The Winner-Take-All Society*. NY: Penguin Books, 1995.

Grimes, Alan Pendleton. *American Political Thought*, Revised Edition. NY: University Press of America, Inc., 1983.

Hacker, Jacob S., and Paul Pierson. *Winner-Take-All Politics*. NY: Simon & Schuster, 2010.

Hiltzik, Michael. *The New Deal: A Modern History*. NY: Free Press, 2011.

Kuznets, Simon. *Toward a Theory of Economic Growth*. NY: W.W. Norton & Company, Inc., 1968.

Maryanski, Alexandra, and Jonathan H. Turner. *The Social Cage: Human Nature and the Evolution of Society*. Stanford, CA: Stanford University Press, 1992.

Niehans, Jürg. *A History of Economic Theory*. Baltimore: The Johns Hopkins University Press, 1990.

Painter, Sidney. *Medieval Society*. Ithaca: Cornell University Press, 1951.

Sherman, Zoe, Alejandro Reuss, and Chris Sturr, eds. *Our Economic Well-Being*. Boston: Dollars & Sense, 2017.

Somerville, John, and Ronald E. Santoni. *Social and Political Philosophy*. NY: Anchor Books, Doubleday, 1963.

Strauss, Leo, and Joseph Cropsey. *History of Political Philosophy*, Third Edition. Chicago: University of Chicago Press, 1987.

Ullmann, Walter. *Medieval Political Thought*. Baltimore: Penguin Books, Inc., 1965.

Ullmann, Walter. *Principles of Government and Politics in the Middle Ages*. London: Methuen & Co. LTD, 1966.

Vatter, Harold G., and John F. Walker, eds. *History of the U.S. Economy Since World War II*. Armonk, NY: M.E. Sharpe, Inc., 1996.

PART TWO RESOURCES

Cited Resources

Coverly, Merlin. *Utopia*. Harpenden: Pocket Essentials, 2010.

Unless otherwise specified, Bible quotations are from *The New American Standard Bible,* Updated Edition. La Habra, CA: The Lockman Foundation, 2001.

Rebhorn, Wayne A. (Introduction and Notes), and Ralph Robinson (Translator). *Utopia* by Sir Thomas More. NY: Barnes & Noble Classics, 2005. First published in Latin In 1516.

The United Methodist Hymnal. Nashville: The United Methodist Publishing House, 1989.

Consulted Resources

Bass, Diana Butler. *A People's History of Christianity: The Other Side of the Story.* NY: Harper One, 2009.

Bettenson, Henry. *Documents Of The Christian Church*, Second Edition. London: Oxford University Press, 1963.

Dwyer, John C. *Church History: Twenty Centuries of Catholic Christianity.* NY: Paulist Press, 1985.

Ehrman, Bart D. *Misquoting Jesus.* NY: HarperSanFrancisco, 2005.

Forell, George Wolfgang. *History Of Christian Ethics, Volume I, From the New Testament to Augustine.* Minneapolis: Augsburg Publishing House, 1979.

Hatch, Edwin. *The Influence of Greek Ideas and Usages Upon The Christian Church*, 2nd Edition. Oxford: The Hibbert Lectures, 1888. Forgotten Books, 2012: www.forgottenbooks.org

Lohse, Bernhard. Translated by F. Ernest Stoeffler. *A Short History of Christian Doctrine.* Philadelphia: Fortress Press, 1966.

Richardson, Alan. *Creeds in the Making.* Philadelphia: Fortress Press, 1981.

Shelley, Bruce L. *Church History In Plain Language.* Waco: Word, Inc., 1982.

White, L. Michael. *From Jesus To Christianity.* NY: HarperSanFrancisco, 2004.

FINDING SOLID GROUND

"In 2011, Emerick, an ordained minister in the United Methodist Church and a licensed clinical social worker, embarked on a self-directed study to educate himself about the nation's principal political disputes. He discovered that America's dominant political and economic theories...are...pitting the demands of the individual against the needs of the community. But in the Constitution's preamble...the concerns of individual liberty and the general welfare are given equal weight, and a more equitable national philosophy will...combine the two. [He] also... discovers, contrary to the opinions of many, that the federal government's active role in fiscal affairs can have a stimulating effect...and trickle-down economics has largely been a failure... [Emerick] makes an...attempt to reconcile political polarities, offering a way to structure an economy that...he calls a 'Preamble Economy.'

"In the second part of the book, the author argues that Christianity has drifted away from the true ministry of Jesus, replacing his core message of love with errant institutional doctrine. [Emerick] singularly focuses on the sayings of Jesus...the book includes a collection of all of them—in order to excavate that teaching.

"Emerick writes in unfailingly lucid prose, and his command of the issues is notable..." *Kirkus Reviews*

Robert Emerick holds degrees from Albright College (Reading, PA), Union Theological Seminary (NYC), and Yeshiva University's Wurzweiler School of Social Work (NYC). In his 42 year career he has served as a pastor, psychotherapist, adjunct professor of psychology, hospice social worker, and military chaplain. He resides in Brooklyn, NY, where he is pastor of Bay Ridge United Methodist Church.

CPSIA information can be obtained
at www.ICGtesting.com
Printed in the USA
BVHW01s2129150118
505300BV00011BA/79/P